Fabric for Fashion

A comprehensive guide
to natural fibres

Clive Hallett and
Amanda Johnston

Laurence King Publishing

Introduction

Section 1:
Animal fibres

Section 2:
Plant fibres

Useful information

Introduction

Fashion design and textile knowledge are often taught as separate disciplines, and knowledge of the raw materials and processes that make up a fabric are not usually integrated into fashion studies.

A confident understanding of fabrics, and the fibres they are composed of, is fundamental to the design process, allowing one to make informed choices rather than arbitrary decisions based upon surface appeal.

This book is intended as an easily navigable fabric lexicon that explores the relationship between fashion and textiles and encourages an awareness of fibres and fabrics in a broader fashion context. It is designed to inform the reader of the endless possibilities that fabrics offer to the design process. It is not intended as an exhaustive technical manual, but rather as a tool to inform, inspire and encourage the creative use of fabrics. The content of the book is intended to support an essential knowledge base, which is fundamental to developing a range of fashion products.

Focusing on the natural, and naturally-derived fibre sources, each section considers the origins of a specific natural fibre, its history, provenance and the processing journey to finished fabric. Additionally, it explores the socio-economic factors that may have influenced the importance of a specific fibre, in order to create an awareness of how one's choice of material may impact upon ecological, sustainable and ethical issues.

Each section provides an extensive database of terminology, to encourage informed and effective communication with industry professionals. This is underpinned with information about processes generic to all fibres regardless of origin. The importance of colour is explored within a separate section and the final chapter contextualizes the interrelationship of all the components that make up the fashion industry.

'The bond between fashion and textiles is one of mutual dependency and reciprocal influence; a shared destiny based upon our need for clothing.'
Fashion and Textiles: An Overview
Colin Gale and Jasbir Kaur (Berg Publishers, 2004)

Our relationship with fibres and fabrics is intimate and all-encompassing; we are surrounded by, sleep in and are clothed by them. Historically textiles have been valued not only for their practical and aesthetic properties, but also as incredibly powerful cultural indicators. Textiles display the artistry and ingenuity of a civilization, the most precious examples of which even help to denote status within society. In contemporary life an ever-more sophisticated and growing range of fabrics expresses the complex language of fashion.

The textile industry may be simplistically viewed as the supplier of the raw materials for the fashion industry, whereas in reality the two industries are inextricably linked. Developments in the textile industry invariably impact upon the fashion industry, and vice versa. Fabrics are also incredibly powerful as a strong visual indicator of a brand, often defining aspects of a brand identity.

The fashion designer's relationship with fabric is at the heart of the creative process. The right choice of fabric is fundamental to good design and is instrumental to its success. The better the understanding of the material, the more effective is the symbiosis between the design and fabric.

'The future of fashion lies in fabrics. Everything comes from fabrics.'
Donna Karan

(opposite page) The Op-art inspired man-made fabrics and Space-age aesthetic, captured in this advertising image for KaneKalon from the mid 1960s, conveys the interest in futurism that defined part of this decade.

Fabrics: the raw material of fashion

Throughout history people have clothed themselves with natural fabrics made from animal or plant fibres. Man's ingenuity in developing and processing these raw materials has become more sophisticated over time.

The twentieth century heralded the invention of synthetic fabrics, originally developed to mimic the attributes of natural fibres, and provide inexpensive alternatives with a low-maintenance appeal. Brand names such as Dacron, Terylene, Orlon, Acrylan and Crimplene are examples of materials that were made from the main generic synthetics group that includes polyamide, nylon, polyester, acetate and acrylic. These fibres and filaments are primarily derived from coal and oil-based raw materials. The cotton and wool trade organizations have invested in fibre development technology and proactive marketing campaigns to regain the market share initially lost to the man-made materials.

Recent decades have seen a growing appreciation of natural fibres at accessible price points. Today, exciting potential is offered by leaps in technology with natural fibres, man-made artificial regenerates and refined synthetics. They offer exciting options for an increasingly complex range of consumer demands. Sophisticated developments in man-made textiles offer a look quite different to traditional, natural materials, and do not work against them but alongside them instead. Combinations of microfibres (the new generation of ultra-fine synthetics), with regenerated yarns, silks, cottons and linens provide new looks and performance potential. The emphasis placed on recycling in our everyday life has influenced current research into the development of biodegradable synthetics.

'Fashion designers are alert to the recent developments in fibres and fabrics and the importance of the right choice for their collections.'
Sarah E. Braddock Clark and Marie Mahoney,
Techno Textiles 2

The future of fabrics

As well as aesthetic considerations, there are many issues to take into account when working with fabrics. This showpiece from the exhibition 'Wonderland' (opposite page) explores alternative approaches informed by factors such as biodegradability and the lifespan of a product.

'Wonderland' is the result of a dynamic collaborative project between Professor Tony Ryan from Sheffield University and designer Helen Storey, incorporating the work of textile designer Trish Belford. The project brings together the worlds of art, fashion and science in an engaging installation first opened as an exhibition at the London College of Fashion in January 2008.

'Wonderland' was conceived as a series of disappearing dresses made from textiles that slowly dissolve in water to create a visually arresting metaphor for the central themes of the project. Each dress behaves differently as it enters the water, resulting in vibrant underwater fireworks that express the beauty of biodegradability.

The disappearing dresses provoke inquiry into the environmental sustainability of our current fashion industry and how we deal with waste. The original focus of the collaboration was the problem of plastic bottle waste and the concept of 'intelligent' packaging. This has resulted in the development of a material that dissolves in hot water to form a gel in which seeds can be sown, with the potential to revolutionize the packaging industry.

Fibres to fabrics

As an introduction to the world of natural fabrics, this chapter examines the processes involved in the manufacturing of textiles, from the raw fibre through to the finished material, ready to use. It is a generic account irrespective of fibre category, whether derived from animal or vegetable sources. Each fibre type will be examined in detail in its respective chapter.

Fibre to yarn

All natural fabrics begin life as **fibres**. These natural fibres, whether animal or plant in origin, are spun into **yarn**, which in turn is constructed into fabric.

Fibre

The term fibre can be applied to animal, vegetable or mineral substances, and describes a long, thin, flexible structure. Fibres exist in a natural or **synthetic** form and can be processed into yarns.

Yarn

Yarns, or threads, are fibres that have been spun together to create a continuous length of interlocked fibres. They are usually knitted or woven together to make fabric, and may be dyed before or after this process.

Carding

Carding is the process of brushing raw or washed fibres to prepare them for spinning. A large variety of fibres can be carded, including all animal hairs, wool and cotton. **Flax** is not carded, but is threshed, a process of beating cereal plants in order to separate the grain from the straw. Carding can also be used to create mixes of different fibres or of different colours.

Hand carding uses two brushes that look a little like dog brushes. The fibres are brushed between them until they all align, more or less, in the same direction. The fibres are then rolled off the brushes and evenly distributed into a **rolag**, a loose roll of fibres, ready for spinning.

The machine-carding device is called a drum carder and can vary in size from tabletop to room size. The fibres are fed into a series of rollers that straighten and align them. When the fibres are removed from the roller drums they form a flat orderly mass known as a **bat**.

Combing

Combing is usually an additional operation after carding, and gives a better, smoother finish to the fibres and to the eventual fabric. Combs are used to remove the short fibres, known as **noils**, and arrange the remaining fibres in a flat bundle, all facing in the same direction.

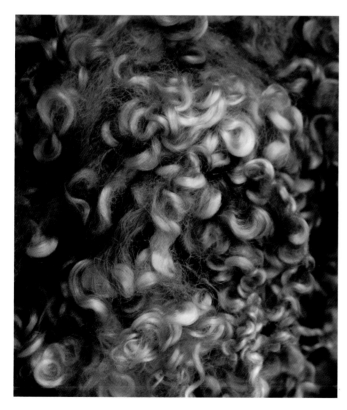

Wool fibre dyed in a range of glowing autumnal shades in preparation for the spinning process. This image captures the characteristic springy ringlets of wool fibre.

(opposite page) Tangle of chunky and fine wool yarns.

Hand carding and blending fibres. Association of Weavers, Spinners and Dyers.

Blending fibres of different characteristics together creates innovative new yarns that can embody the best aspects of each fibre. The mixture of alpaca and silk in this example creates a mélange of both texture and colour; the alpaca lends warmth and softness while the silk sharpens the texture by lending it lustre.

(above) Hand spinning – in this case llama wool in Peru – is a labour-intensive process that is today only practised for specialist craft purposes. The yarn is spun by means of a hand-held wooden spindle, using methods that remain fundamentally unchanged since early spinning techniques that predate the spinning wheel.

Useful terminology

Blend A yarn containing two or more different fibres.

Bouclé yarns Curled or looped yarns.

Cellulose fibres Natural and man-made fibres regenerated from plants.

Chenille yarn Woven fabric is cut into warp strips and used as yarn, which has a velvet-like, 'caterpillar' appearance.

Cotton system Spinning system for cotton and similar fibres.

Crêpe yarn Highly twisted yarn with a granular texture.

Crimp Natural or artificial wave to the fibre or yarn.

Elastane Generic name for stretch yarn.

Filament A single, continuous strand of fibre. Any man-made yarn of one or more strands running the entire length of the yarn.

Hank Unsupported coil of yarn. The two ends are tied together to maintain the shape. Also called a skein.

Marl yarns Two different-coloured yarns twisted together.

Metallic yarns Yarns containing metal threads or metallic elements.

Roving A long narrow bundle of fibre with a slight twist to hold it together.

Scouring Removal of natural fats, oils and dirt from a yarn.

Skein Coiled yarn with tied ends to keep the shape.

Tow Mass of man-made filaments without twist.

Yarn count Numerical expression for size of yarn, denoting a certain length of yarn for a fixed weight. The higher the count, the finer the yarn.

Spinning

Twisting fibres together by **spinning** binds them into a stronger, longer yarn. Originally fibres were twisted by hand, then a hand-held 'stick', or spindle, made the process a little more comfortable. The invention of the spinning wheel allowed continuous, faster spinning. Used in a domestic environment, spinning wheels were hand or foot operated. Water-driven spinning machines were followed by steam-driven machinery, which took domestic spinning out of the home and into the factory. The invention of electricity made the spinning process much more sophisticated and, with the exception of handicraft spinning, made it a full-time commercial enterprise.

Twist and ply

The direction in which the yarn is spun is called **twist**. A 'Z' twist shows a right-hand angle, while an 'S' twist has a left-hand angle. The tightness of the twist is measured in TPI (twists per inch).

Two or more spun yarns may be twisted together to make a **ply**, a thicker yarn, or as a way of introducing an alternative yarn to create a **mélange** effect.

(left) Sophisticated modern spinning in a pristine industrial environment.

(above and right) Spinning frames processing single-ply and two-ply yarn at Lightfoot Farm in Maine, USA.

Marl jersey is a sportswear perennial, due to its comfort and practicality. The marl effect is achieved by twisting together two yarns of differing colours, and, often, different fibre types (usually polyester and cotton). Ioannis Dimitrousis twists the perception of this generic fabrication in a reinterpretation of the classic sweatshirt.

(above) Direction of yarn twist. 'Z' twist and 'S' twist

(right) Plying yarn. Simple 'S' twist with two single yarns, 'S' twist with three single yarns and 'Z' twist with two two-ply yarns

Warp and weft threads. Warp threads run along the length of the fabric. Weft threads run across the width of the fabric from selvedge to selvedge. Weaving can be described as the incorporation of the weft threads, which are sometimes referred to as picks or filling yarns.

Fabric construction

Fabric is a flexible material comprised of natural or artificial fibres that have been spun into threads or yarns. Textile fabric can be manufactured in several ways. The primary techniques are **weaving** or **knitting**, although yarns can also be knotted or interlaced, for example by **crocheting**, **lace** making or **macramé**. **Felting**, the process of pressing together and matting fibres so that they interlock, is another alternative.

Weaving

Weaving is the process of interweaving two sets of threads, the **warps** (vertical) and the **wefts** (horizontal), on a weaving loom. Three basic weave types, **plain**, **twill** and **satin**, form the majority of woven fabrics. There are also several alternative weaving techniques that create more complex fabrics.

Plain weave

Plain weave is the most basic and possibly the oldest type of weave construction. The warps and wefts criss-cross each other at right angles, with each weft thread passing over one warp thread then under the next warp thread. Plain weaves are sometimes referred to as **taffeta** weaves.

A plain weave can be coarse or smooth in texture, dependant on the fineness or coarseness of the **thread count** used to weave the fabric.

Basket weave is a variation on plain weave, where two or more threads are bundled together and woven as one in the warp and weft directions, resulting in a more pronounced 'basket' construction.

Types of plain-woven fabrics include chiffon, organza, taffeta and canvas.

Twill weave

Twill weave has a visual diagonal line or rib effect, caused when the weft yarn crosses over and under two or more warp yarns. The diagonal line may also be referred to as a **wale**. The visual effect is most obvious on a heavyweight cotton fabric. By contrast, on a lightweight shirting cotton the diagonal rib will be hardly visible.

Unlike plain weaves, twill-weave fabrics have a different appearance from the **face** (right side) to the reverse or back, the face side having the more pronounced wale. Twill weaves are harder wearing than plain weaves of the same yarn and count, and are therefore particularly suited to utility wear. **Denim** is possibly the most famous of all the workwear fabrics, and true denim is of twill-weave construction.

Any fibre type can be woven in this way, however the term is generically used to describe cotton fabrics.

Twill fabrics are more pliable and have a better **drape** than similar plain-weave fabrics, and they also tend to recover better from wrinkles. Higher/finer yarn counts can be used for twill weaving and can be packed much closer together, therefore producing higher-count fabrics that are more durable and **water-resistant**. An example is the traditional Burberry trench coat, which was designed and made for army officers and worn in the trenches of World War I.

Types of twill-woven fabrics include serge, flannel, denim, gabardine, cavalry twill and chino. Traditional iconic herringbone and hound's-tooth design fabrics, as well as Scottish tartans, are all of twill-weave construction.

(above) Weaving frame.

(right and far right) Twill weaves. Weft threads pass over and then under two warp threads (2x2 twill) and are staggered by one thread per row creating the visible diagonal construction. If the wefts pass over three and under one (warps) it would be referred to as 1x3 twill.

(above and right) Plain weaves. Weft threads pass under and over alternative warp threads forming a criss-cross construction.

This striking rescaled hound's-tooth abandons its tailoring connotations when expressed in oversized sequins. This A-line shift with cut-out shoulders references 1960s op art aesthetics. Autumn/Winter 2008 collection by Ashish.

An updated classic hound's-tooth fabric from Linton Tweeds.

Designer Derek Lam sculpts and feminizes the appeal of this traditional wool herringbone, a fabric that is usually associated with men's outerwear.

The alternating diagonal ribs of this traditional woollen tweed fabric, with a twill-weave construction, are executed in two colours, creating a classic herringbone design. The scale of design and the contrasting colours have almost limitless possibilities.

Up-cycling

This term describes the reappropriation of fabric that has already had one life for one purpose, and reworking, reassigning or reinventing it to give it a new life serving a different purpose or aesthetic. Here, cotton twill is glamorized through this process. This conceptual evening dress from Gary Harvey Creative was constructed to showcase the concept of up-cycling. Vintage Burberry trench coats are used to model the skirt. Raincoats were originally made from a tightly-woven fine yarn-count twill weave to provide a drapable and water-resistant fabric.

Satin and sateen weaves

The most visible aspect of a satin weave is its smooth surface sheen. A typical satin-weave construction has four or more weft threads floating over one warp thread, or vice versa.

If there is a predominance of warp threads to the face or right side of the fabric then the fabric is referred to as satin. The **floats** will be in the warp or vertical direction. Conversely, if the fabric has a predominance of weft threads to the face or right side it is called **sateen**. The floats will be horizontal or in the weft direction.

Satin weave could refer to many different types of fabric, of any fibre type. It should not to be confused with satin, which is a specific fabric in its own right, originally made from silk and now predominantly made from synthetic yarn.

Pile weaving

When **pile weaving**, the warps that will eventually create the pile are woven over rods or wires that have been inserted into the gaps or 'loops' of the raised alternative yarns. These then lie in loops over the rods. When the rods are removed the loops can be cut to create a **pile fabric**, or left intact to create a **loop-back fabric**. Velvet and corduroy are examples of pile woven fabric.

Corduroy

Corduroy is described using the term wales; these refer to the raised ridges or ribs that run vertically down the fabric parallel to the **selvedge**. The wider the wales, the lower the numerical expression, and vice versa. The number of wales that fit into one inch (2.5 cm) is the wale count. 21-wale corduroy implies there are 21 wales per inch. Counts range from 1.5 to 21. 16 and above can be referred to as pin cord, while 3 and under is sometimes referred to as elephant or jumbo cord. Corduroy was originally made from cotton. Bedford cord has a flatter surface with a minimal raised wale, originally made from cotton or wool.

21 wale

16 wale

10 wale

(above and right) Satin weaves are characterized by a shiny surface and are of a tight weave construction. Weft threads pass over four or more warps and then under one warp. A sateen weave is the reverse construction.

18

Double-cloth weaving

Double-cloth weaving creates a fabric that has two face or right sides (**double face**) and no wrong or reverse side. The fabric is constructed by using several sets of warps and wefts, interconnected to form a cloth of two layers held together by additional binding wefts.

Examples of double-cloth weaving date back to pre-Columbian Peru, where cotton and **alpaca** yarns were woven to create a warm alpaca outer layer and a comfortable cotton under layer, all as a single fabric.

Double-cloth weaves make up well into self-lined or double-faced coats and jackets, closed off with quasi-invisible hand stitching that eliminates the need for facings or bindings to finish off the raw edges.

Examples of double-cloth weave include **brocade** fabric, blankets and satin ribbons.

Men's silk velvet quilted baseball-influenced jacket and multi-coloured straight weave trousers by Ioannis Dimitrousis. The sporty styling lends this traditionally luxe woven pile fabric a casual appeal.

Gloverall double-faced check-back cloth. The cloth is woven and held together with draw threads. After being woven the cloth is teasled up to create a face pile, then it is cropped/brushed and finally finished off. The little torn threads on the edge of the solid red face side of the fabric are the draw threads that hold the two sides together.

Jacquard weaving

The **jacquard loom** enables the automatic production of an unlimited variety of designs. Prior to the jacquard process the warp ends had to be manually selected and lifted by a second operator apart from the weaver. This was a slow and labour-intensive process that limited the complexity of the design. With the jacquard loom selected warps are programmed to lift independently of each other, thus creating far greater versatility of design.

This form of weaving was developed and perfected by French inventor Joseph Jacquard (1752–1834), at the advent of the nineteenth century. The mechanism allowed for the production of sophisticated patterns without lengthy, repetitive manual processing. The original machines were mechanical, with the fabric design punched onto cards that were joined to form a chain that would direct the machine. In the early 1980s, Italian manufacturers introduced the first electronic jacquard machines.

The term **jacquard** is not specific to any loom, but indicative of the added control mechanism that automates the design. It refers to a type of weaving process and is also descriptive of a type of fabric. The term can be applied to both woven and knitted fabrics, as well as some **fully-fashioned** knitwear.

Tapestry weaving

Considered an art form, **tapestry weaving** is done on a vertical loom. It is sometimes called weft-faced weaving because all the warps are hidden, unlike fabric weaving where both the warps and the wefts may be visible. By only having the wefts visible it is possible to create more precise designs. Historically the imagery was usually pictorial and very often allegorical.

Kilims and Navajo blankets and rugs are all forms of tapestry weaving.

(left) A traditional Indo-Pakistani brocade-type fabric of jacquard construction. These sometimes contained real gold and silver threads, today they more commonly use coloured metallic threads.

(above) The floral pattern created by a jacquard loom is apparent in the light-reflective satin weave and contrasting plain weave in this Alexander McQueen oyster silk jacquard dress with tulle underskirt.

Ikat weaving

Before weaving, the warps or wefts are dyed different colours at predetermined intervals along their length, using a form of **resist** or **tie-dyeing** process. Double **ikat** implies that both wefts and warps have been dyed.

If the dyed threads are warps the pattern is visible to the weaver, who can adjust them to line up to each other. In some cultures the patterns will be aligned to perfection, while in others misalignment is preferred. Weaving with dyed wefts makes it much harder to control the design, therefore this technique is used when precision is not the objective. Double ikats are the most difficult to produce. The most precise forms of ikat weaving are the Japanese **oshima** and **kasuri**.

There is evidence of ikat weaving in pre-Columbian Central and South America as well as many regions of South and East Asia. However, the name ikat has its origins in the Malay language. Today, through extensive common use, the word describes both the weaving technique and the fabric itself.

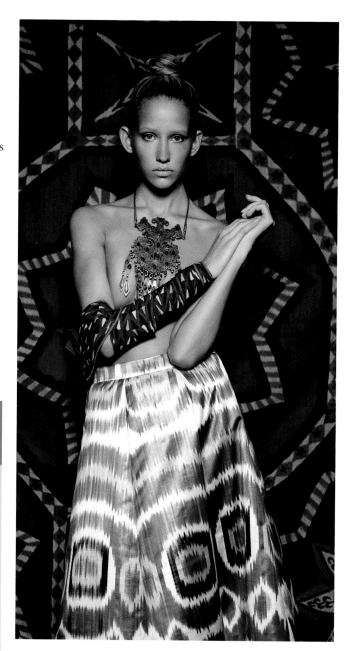

Ikat weave silk skirt featuring the characteristic 'blurred' edge of the woven motif by Tamerlane's Daughters, launched in 2004 by Karina Deubner. The designer's own European and Asian background influences the signature aesthetic of cultural fusion that her unique pieces embody. The label pays homage to traditional crafts and vanishing cultures by creating one-off pieces incorporating nineteenth-century textiles from Central Asia and Europe.

Useful terminology

Bias Fabric cut at 45 degrees to warp and weft. This cut exploits the natural stretch of the fabric so that it drapes well over the curves of the body.

Cut pile Cut loops of yarn that form a pile, as with velvet and corduroy.

Drape The behaviour of the fabric, how it falls and hangs, affected by the yarn, weave construction, weight and finishing processes.

Grain The straight of the fabric or warp.

Handle The touch of the fabric, warm, cool, smooth, granular, fluffy, etc.

Left-hand twill Diagonal ribs run up from bottom right to top left on face.

Loop pile Uncut pile fabric, such as towelling.

Nap Raised surface of fabric.

Piece A complete length of fabric as purchased from a mill or wholesaler.

Reversible Fabric that can be used either side up.

Right-hand twill Diagonal ribs run up from bottom left to top right on face.

Selvedge The firm side edges of the fabric running parallel to the warp.

Union fabric Fabric with wefts and warps of different fibres, for example a cotton warp and wool weft.

Knitting

Knitting can refer to two areas of clothing. Sweater-knits are garments that are partially or totally constructed on a knitting machine or by hand knitting. **Jerseywear** is a range of various garments, including T-shirts and polo shirts, that are cut and made from fabric that has been knitted. Integral knitting using advanced technology is also known as jerseywear, and is used for seamless men's underwear and women's brassieres.

The term knitwear refers to any fabric that has been knitted, regardless of how fine it is.

Knitted fabrics

Knitted fabric is constructed from yarn by means of a series of interlinked loops. This can be achieved by hand using individual needles, by using hand-operated machines, known as hand-frame knitting, or by power machine, simply called machine knitting. The introduction of machine knitting turned hand knitting into a craft that has gone into and out of fashion depending on social moods of the time.

The size of the **stitch**, whether hand or machine knitted, dictates the fineness or chunkiness of the fabric, and is dependent on the size of the needles and the thickness of the yarn. In hand knitting the needles are described by a number, while in machine knitting the term **gauge** is used, but is also reflective of the needle size. In both cases the higher the numerical expression the finer the knitting. Standard gauges in commercial knitting are: 2.5 for chunky outdoor sweaters; 7 and 15 gauges are mid-weights; 18 and 21 gauges for fine knitwear; 28 gauge is interlock, used for rugby shirts and heavier-weight loop-back fabrics; 30 is classified as superfine; 32 gauge is jerseywear.

Fully fashioned knitwear

All hand knitting is fully fashioned. This means that the garment is made by increasing and decreasing the number of stitches in a row to create the desired shape.

Machine knitting, irrespective of gauge, is further divided into fully fashioned or cut and sewn. With fully-fashioned machine knitting, as with hand knitting, the garment is shaped by the increment and decrement of stitches. The amount of fashioning used depends on the quality of the product and machinery. Fully fashioned is more viable with expensive yarns such as **cashmere**, and yarn usage and labour is decreased when garments are fully fashioned. A really good piece of knitwear will be totally fully fashioned, while a mass-market product may be only fashioned at the armhole, to eliminate wastage.

(above and right) The face side of jersey knitting is referred to as plain stitch.

(above and right) The reverse side of jersey knitting is referred to as purl stitch.

This pale grey sweater by SANS explores the differing needle sizes or gauges possible in knitwear, and alternates plain and purl knits to create the three-dimensional 'striping'. The armhole is fully fashioned.

Iconic knitting styles

Traditional Fair Isle intarsia knit designs inspired this hooded sweater in neutral tones by Hildigunnur Sigurdardottirs.

Fair Isle

This traditional technique originates from **Fair Isle**, a small island between the Orkney and Shetland Islands in the very north of Scotland. Originally, these sweaters were knitted using Shetland wool by fishermen's wives, and were worn at sea. They traditionally use five to seven colours to create complex horizontal patterns, with each sweater featuring a different pattern and **colour-way**. Fair-Isle knitting is notorious for its many floats of yarn, meaning that on the reverse of the fabric the yarn 'floats' across several needles. The floats need to remain short to avoid snagging. Fair-Isle patterns can now be replicated on a jacquard system without the floats, however these are intrinsic to the authenticity of the product.

An installation artwork by Alfreda McHale showing extremely large-scale knitting, exhibited at the Stitching and Knitting Fair, Alexandra Palace, London, 2008.

Ashish glamorizes the traditional Argyle pattern by rescaling the motif and playing with texture.

Argyle (also Argyll)

The **Argyle** pattern, believed to derive from the tartan of the Campbell clan in western Scotland, is made up of diamond blocks of colour laid out as a diagonal chequerboard, overlaid with a further 'diamond' line called a **raker**. This particular design uses the **intarsia** technique, a single flat knit with several colours in one row of knitting. The pattern is formed by stopping one colour and twisting in a new colour over the needles each time there is a colour change. This was traditionally done by hand-frame machine or by hand knitting, but now can be done by computerized flatbed machines.

Argyle knitwear has seen a renaissance in popularity, thanks to its use by Pringle of Scotland.

Aran

Aran is a style of Gaelic knitwear originating from the Aran Islands off the west coast of Ireland. This style of knitting is believed to originate from the early 1900s, although the three-dimensional motifs used for the stitch formation have ancient megalith origins. The knitwear was first shown in British *Vogue* in the 1940s, and became an instant success in the United States.

Traditionally, authentic Aran is hand knitted with undyed cream wool, and occasionally natural black wool, both of which still contain natural sheep **lanolin**, which provides an intrinsic water-resistance.

Cream giant trellis knit oversized jumper in 100% merino wool. From the menswear collection 'Modern Medieval Soldiers' by James Long.

Cut and sew

Cut-and-sew knitwear is fabric that has been knitted and is then cut and sewn in a similar way to woven fabric styles. Cut-and-sew knitwear is mainly used for styling inexpensive yarns due to the wastage incurred.

Generally shirt and sweatshirt styles are cut and sew. To fully fashion very fine 30-gauge garments would require the use of very expensive yarn, and the process would be time consuming, therefore manufacturing production runs would have to be very long.

The majority of T-shirts are either of **single jersey** or interlock fabric construction. Rib fabrics can be used for close body-fitting styles.

Alexander McQueen knitted wool jacquard style poncho with horizontal-banded design referencing traditional ethnic motifs and weave techniques.

Useful knitting terminology

Cable knitting Three-dimensional twisting effects that mimic ropes, braids and plaits, made by crossing over stitches.

Circular knitting Mainly for T-shirt fabrics, knitted on a circular machine resulting in tubular fabric. Garments tend to **spiral** after washing unless opened up and stented – the process of passing the fabric through a hot-air cabinet, which stabilizes it.

Course The row of loops that runs along the width of the fabric, equivalent to the weft in a woven fabric.

Double jersey All needle rib knitted fabric where both the face and reverse side are the same.

Jacquard Intricate design where every colour of yarn used is knitted into the back of the fabric when not in use.

Jersey Generically used to describe many types of knitted fabric. Single jersey is plain knit on one side and purl on the reverse and is used for tops. Double jersey is plain on both sides and can be double in weight. It does not unravel when cut so is fine for cutting and sewing more complicated styles.

Inlaid yarn Yarn that is held in place by the loops of the knitting rather than being knitted in, making a rigid fabric with no stretch.

Plain knit The face side of basic jersey knitting, the reverse side is known as purl.

Plated A double face knitted fabric. This technique uses two different types or colours of yarn. One is thrown to the face side and the other to the reverse side .The fabric is knitted using a plating device fixed to the bed of the machine.

Purl The reverse side of basic jersey knitting, the face side is known as plain knit.

Single jersey Another term for plain knit.

Tuck stitch In knitwear, a held stitch giving a raised effect.

Welt A form of edge finishing on knitwear, usually knitted as a separate piece e.g. pocket.

Felting

Felt is a non-woven cloth produced by matting, condensing and pressing fibres together to form the structure of the fabric. **Felted** fabrics are the oldest known to mankind and today may be soft and supple or tough enough for industry use. The technique of felting is still practised by nomadic tribes of Central Asia, while in the Western world felting is seen as an expression of art in textiles with strong eco-credentials.

Wet felting is the traditional process, whereby the natural fibres are stimulated by friction and lubricated with water and alkaline, usually soap. This causes the fibres to interlock and matt together.

In industry, felting is done by a chemical process or by using felting needles. A felting effect can be achieved using a hot cycle on a domestic washing machine. Felting should not be confused with **fulling**, which is a felting-like process, carried out after the fabric has been constructed, similar to washing a sweater in a washing machine at a high temperature.

Inexpensive felt is usually made with artificial fibres, although a minimum of 30 per cent wool is necessary for the fabric to hold together adequately.

Loden fabric, from the Alpine regions, was originally a felted fabric, however today lodens are usually woven, the name referring to the feeling of the fabric rather than its true definition.

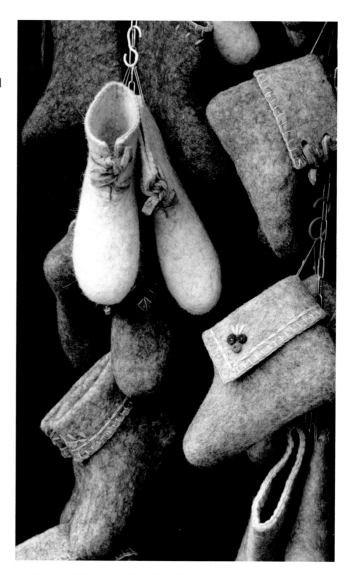

(above) Traditional felted wool boots from Russia are known as valenki. These boots express a pure aesthetic due to the practical and comforting moulding of the felt around the foot to achieve effective and seamless insulation. The result is a perfect meeting of form and function that transcends fashion.

(above) Wet felting. The merino wool fibres are layered at 90 degrees and hot soapy water and friction cause the wool's natural scales to interlock and felt.

(right) Hand-operated needle felting. Needle felting is the alternative to wet or chemical felting. Industrial needle felting involves machines with hundreds of tiny barbed needles, which push up and down punching and entangling the fibres together. Many non-woven fabrics are made by needle felting or needle punching.

(left and below) Dress and waistcoat from Ravensbourne graduate Sue Pei Ho's collection. The pieces feature wisps of wool fibres fused onto silk – a technique originally developed by textile artists Polly Blakney Sirling and Sachiko Kotaka.

(left) Anne Kyyrö Quinn expresses the exceptional sculptural qualities of felt in this cut-edge three-dimensional application on felt cushion.

Crocheting

Crocheting is the process of creating fabric from yarn or thread using a hooked needle to pull loops of yarn through other loops.

Although scholars theorize that crochet has Arabic origins, there is no real evidence of it being practised before the eighteenth century in Europe. Ireland and northern France were centres of crochet making, much of it done to support poor communities whose livelihoods had been compromised, and hence it was often considered a domestic craft. However, crocheted items sold well to the new emerging middle classes. Crochet experienced a revival of interest in the mid-1960s with the new-wave hippy movements and their embracing of rural cultures.

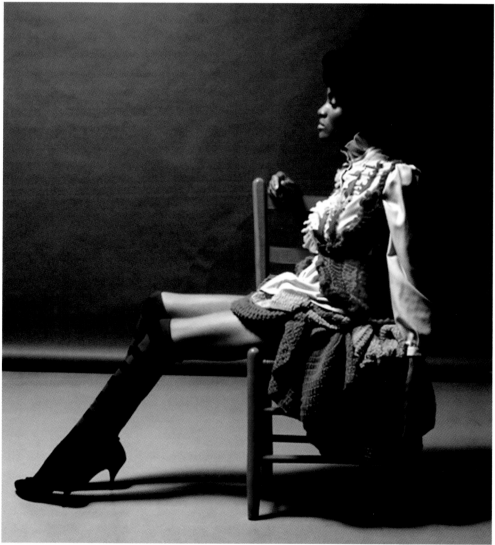

(above) Unique crocheted wearable sculptures by Polish artist Agata Olek highlight the surreal aspect of creating 'moulded' clothing (such as crochet or knit). Amateur knitters often find that their work 'grows' and takes on a life of its own. Premiered in New York at the Williamsburg Arts and Historical Society Surrealist Fashion Show in 2003.

(left) Designer Ladene Clark reinterprets the homely craft of crochet and playfully creates whimsical silhouettes that reference historical costume. The fitted corset waistcoat and layered panniers of the skirt highlight the three-dimensional texture of crochet, lending it a modernized appeal.

Lace making

Lace is a lightweight fabric patterned with open holes and can be hand or machine made. The holes may be created by removing threads of previously woven cloth, however more often the holes are created as part of the lace-making process, where thread is looped, twisted or braided to other threads independently from any backing fabric. Lace was first used by priests for religious rituals, then popularized in the sixteenth century when it was highly valued as a symbol of wealth and status.

Originally linen, silk, gold or silver threads were preferred, however today cotton is also used, as are synthetic yarns for machine-made lace.

Vintage inspired slip dress in linen by designer Marina Shlosberg. Linen is the ideal fabric to showcase the Venetian-style drawn thread openwork embroidery shown on the front of the dress.

(above) Up-cycled dress featuring a bodice that incorporates different types of reclaimed and vintage cotton lace with a silk dupion skirt designed by London College of Fashion graduate Rachael Cassar. Her designs aim to use 90% recycled materials in their composition, and to challenge preconceptions of the term 'recycling'.

(left) Hand-worked lace border showing a section in process. Dozens of colour-coded bobbins show the complexity of this craft technique. Myriad overlapped and twisted threads form the intricate patterns that are indicated by the designs marked out on the card underneath. Pins are used to hold the threads in place while the patterns are formed.

Modernizing lace, Rae III, 2002, features cotton lace and elastane and is from a photographic series by Georgina McNamara that explores the relationship between the body and the imagination. The traditional associations of lace, clothing and how they work with the human form are inverted in this super-structured realization.

Types of lace

Some of the popular types of lace include:

Needle lace Made using a needle and thread, and the most flexible of the lace-making techniques. It can be very time consuming and is regarded as the purist form of lace art. Today it is impossible to reproduce some of the fine antique lace. Types of needle lace include punto in Aria, point de Venise, point de France, Alençon, Argentan, Armenian, Limerick and hollie point.

Cutwork lace Constructed by the removal of threads from a woven background fabric. The remaining threads are then worked on with embroidery. Types of cutwork lace include Battenberg, broderie Anglaise and Carrickmacross.

Bobbin lace Made using bobbins and a pillow. The bobbins hold the threads, which are laced together and held down onto the pillow by pins. Types of bobbin lace include Antwerp, Flanders, Bayeux, Chantilly, Genoese, Venetian, Maltese, Bruges, Brussels and Milanese.

Lace knitting Technically knitting with many 'holes' in the design work that create the lace effect. It is considered the highest form of knitting and was especially popular in the nineteenth century when Queen Victoria practised it. In parts of Russia lace knits form part of the wedding dowry, the finest of which can be pulled through a wedding ring.

Machine-made lace Any type of lace made by mechanical methods rather than by hand.

Tatting A type of lace construction first introduced in the early nineteenth century to imitate needle-lace work. It is created by a series of chain knots and loops, mainly used as lace edging, collars and doilies.

As a physical material, black lace has diverse cultural implications in relation to sexuality, death and gender. In these artworks by Anne Wilson the webs and networks of found black lace are deconstructed to create large horizontal topographies or 'physical drawings' that are both complicated and delicate. The structural characteristics of lace are understood by unravelling threads; mesh structures are also reconstructed through crochet and netting. Lace fragments are also scanned, filtered and printed out as paper images. These computer-mediated digital prints are then re-materialized by hand stitching and are placed in relationship to the found and re-made lace in the topography.

Macramé

Macramé is created by the interlinking of knots. It is believed to have Arabic origins, and was used to decorate the excess lengths of yarn along the edge of hand-loom textiles. It was taken to Spain with the Moorish conquest and eventually spread to the rest of Europe, reaching England by the late seventeenth century. It may also classify as a form of lace making.

Macramé was a popular pastime among British and American sailors all through the nineteenth century; the preference was for substantial square knots, which they used to make hammocks and belts.

As well as cotton and hemp, leather is often used. Most friendship bracelets are a form of macramé.

James Long subverts the craft connotations of macramé in this outfit that features the intricate knotting technique worn over a silk tulle T-shirt for his menswear collection 'Arabian stallions'.

Dyeing

Dyeing is the process of transferring **colourant** to fibres, yarns, fabrics or ready-made garments. Colourants take the form of **dyes**, which are in liquid form, or **pigments**, which are in fine powder form.

Until the mid-nineteenth century the primary source of colour dye and pigment was animal, plant or mineral; the plant kingdom being the most prolific provider in the form of berries, roots, bark and leaves. These natural colourants were used with very little, if any, processing. The first synthetic dye, a **mauvine** or aniline purple, was invented by accident in a failed medical experiment in 1856.

The Industrial Revolution was the catalyst for the mass development of the textile industry, and in turn the development of synthetic dyes. This resulted in a larger range of colours with a higher level of colour consistency. In addition to this the colours were more stable under continuous washing and wearing. Today, different classes of dye are used for different generic fabric types, and also for different stages of textile production.

Yarn dyeing

Yarn is dyed to a colour of choice before it is either woven or knitted into a fabric. The two most common ways to **yarn dye** are at package form for cotton yarns and at hank form for wool and **acrylic** yarns.

Yarn-dyed fabrics tend to give a much better level of **colourfast**ness in wearing and washing than **fabric-dyed** items. Any fabric with a stripe, check or other type of design woven into it will be yarn dyed. Good-quality suiting fabrics and shirting fabrics are almost always yarn dyed, even if they are of a solid/plain colour.

Yarn-dyed fabrics are almost always more expensive than their fabric-dyed equivalents. The process of yarn dyeing takes longer and the minimum quantities to be ordered are always far greater than with fabric-dyed orders. Within the design process the selection of colours for yarn dyeing also has to be done much earlier in the season, because the mill **lead times**, to weave and then finish the fabric, are far greater.

Before a larger sample batch of yarn is dyed – known as a **dye lot** – small pieces of yarn windings are sample dyed to colours for approval. These samples are known as **lab dips**, and designers and merchandisers, as well as **technologists**, may all be involved in the approval process.

Markus Lupfer modernizes the technique of dip dyeing by teaming it with a monochrome optical print.

Fabric dyeing

Fabric dyeing is also referred to as **piece dyeing**, and in this instance the fabric is dyed after it has been woven. The advantage of fabric dyeing is that you are able to buy much smaller quantities than is necessary for yarn-dyed equivalents, making it much easier and far less expensive to carry an extensive colour palette of fabric in stock. Furthermore, the lead time involved is far shorter. For the fabric supplier or **converter** there is less of a risk, because the fabric can remain in its **greige** – undyed – state indefinitely.

Piece-dyed fabric is perfect for solid colour, woven cotton goods, as well as knitted cotton fabrics such as lightweight **jersey** and interlock fabric, heavier interlocks (sweatshirts) and fleece loop-back fabric. Plain coloured swimwear and underwear fabrics are often piece dyed. Woollen fabrics for heavy outerwear, if of a solid (plain) colour, are usually also piece dyed.

Before a final dye is agreed, lab dips are made by dyeing **pieces** of fabric in a small vessel or beaker. Three shades of the requested colour are submitted for designer approval before dyeing the sample lengths, which are usually done in 50-m **vats**. Bulk production dyeing would follow after an approved sales order.

(top) Piece-dyed fabrics on drying racks. For solid colour fabrics piece dyeing is far less expensive and also less time-consuming than the alternative yarn-dyeing process.

(above) Before placing a bulk order for either fabric or yarn, a colour lab dip must be approved. Several variants of the hue are presented to the client for colour matching and approval. Once the selection has been made, both the factory and the client keep a sample swatch, which is used to quality check against the bulk production.

(above) Hand dyeing fabric in a traditional dye shop in India. This form of hand dyeing is today only used for small dye lots and specialist fabrics. Constant immersion in the liquid dye has permanently discoloured the dyer's hands.

(right) Dip-dyed fabric lengths hung up to dry in an Indian workshop. In the developing world, piece-dyed fabrics and special dye treatments such as tie-dye are often processed in small lengths in a similar environment.

Garment dyeing

Garment dyeing, the dyeing of a ready-made garment, is the least colourfast method of dyeing, but it does give a very specific visual look. This technique also gives the manufacturer greater product colour flexibility, because ready-made garments can be made and kept in stock, then dyed to specific colours. The most common product in this category is likely to be low-cost shirts and tops.

Garment-dyed products tend to have a residue of dye sitting along the raised seam edges, and if the sewing threads used to assemble the garment are of a different colour and composition they will resist the dye, resulting in contrast **top-stitching**.

Resist dyeing

Resist dyeing refers to various methods of patterning fabric by preventing dye reaching certain parts of it. Common methods include the application of wax or paste and stitching areas together. An alternative method is to use a chemical agent within a dye that will repel a second colour when applied.

Wax and rice paste

Wax or rice paste is painted or applied to the fabric, forming a design, prior to dyeing. Once the resisting agent has dried it is removed by ironing to reveal the colour underneath. This can be repeated numerous times to build up a complex design of several overlaying colours.

Several variations of this method can be found among different cultures around the world, for example **batik** from Indonesia, Malaysia and India; and roketsuzome, katazome, yuzen and tsutsugaki from Japan.

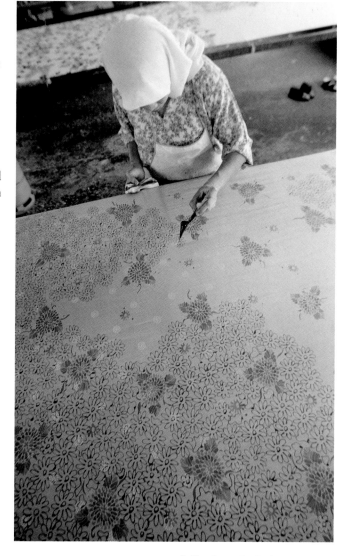

Batik, a type of resist dyeing, is an ancient craft and can be an intricate and labour-intensive process. It involves the use of molten wax or rice paste, which is applied directly onto the fabric and allowed to dry. This prevents the dye from reaching the treated part of the fabric. Intricate multidimensional effects can be built up by repeating the processes.

Multicoloured batik silk design by textile artist Isabella Whitworth. Here, the batik wax resist technique is expressed in a painterly and free-form approach showing the characteristic 'crackle' that occurs when dye seeps into cracks in the cooled wax.

Stitching and tying

Fabrics can be stitched or tied in specific areas to shield them from dye. Variations of these techniques from different cultures include ikat from Indonesia and Malaysia; **tie-dye** from India; and adire from Africa.

Chemical resist

A resisting agent is added to the first dye colour that is applied. When the second colour is applied it will be repelled where it crosses the first colour. This is a common method used in T-shirt printing.

Mordants

A **mordant** is used after some dyes as a method of **fixing** the colour to the fabric. Historically mordants were used as a means of altering the colour and intensity of natural dyes, as well as to improve their colourfastness. Environmental concerns have now restricted the use of some types of mordant, in which case they have been replaced with **reactive** and metal complex dyes that do not require a mordant.

Reversing the dyeing effect

To remove unwanted dye a process called **stripping** destroys the dye by the use of a powerful reducing agent, which may damage the substructure of the fibre; the alternative is to **over-dye** to a darker colour, such as navy or black.

Twist-dyed silk scarf by Isabella Whitworth. The silk fabric is tightly twisted in one direction and tied, stretched, folded in half, twisted in the counter direction and tied. Dye is applied and allowed to absorb through the layers. When dry the fabric is untied to reveal the final design.

Anand Kabra engineers the placement of tie-dye motifs in this indigo and yellow silk embroidered tunic dress to striking effect.

Acid dye Class of dye used on protein fibres such as silk and wool.

Alum Mordant for natural dyes.

Aniline dye The first synthetic dye, made from alcohol and coal-tar derivatives.

Azo or azoic dye Petroleum-based dye typically used on cellulose fibres.

Basic dye Class of dye used on some synthetic fibres.

Batch dyeing A large batch of yarn is dyed in the same vat. The batch is called a dye lot.

Bleeding Loss or transfer of colour.

Changeant An effect whereby the colour appears to 'change' depending on the angle it is viewed from. Also called two-tone or shot effect.

Chrome dye Class of dye used on wool.

Continuous dyeing Processing fabric in sequence through all dyeing stages to give continuous output.

Direct dye Class of dye used on cellulose fibres.

Disperse dye Class of dye used on some synthetics, such as polyester and acetate.

Fugitive Colour that washes out or 'bleeds', ie not colourfast.

Hank dyed Dyed as yarn in hank format.

Indigo Possibly the only natural plant dye still in mass use.

Match Two samples in which the colour match is commercially acceptable.

Mordant dye Alternative to chrome dye.

Off-shade Not an acceptable match.

Ombre Graduated colour from light to dark.

Reactive dyes Class of dyes used on cellulose and protein fibres.

Shading Defective dyed fabric featuring lighter and darker shades.

Shot A fabric that appears to change colour when viewed from different directions, an effect of cross dyeing yarn.

Strike-off Preliminary small sample for approval of colour and print.

Tendering Adverse reaction of dye to light.

Vat A dyeing vessel

Vat dyes Common cotton dyes.

Surface decoration

This generic term refers to any form of decoration applied to a ready-made fabric to embellish it with texture and/or colour. The two most important methods of surface decorating are printing and **embroidery**.

Printing

Printing is the process of creating a design on fabric by the application of colour. This may be a simple single-colour process, or a complicated multicolour design – five colours is the maximum for mass-market printing. Printing mediums used to transfer colours onto the fabric include wooden **blocks** – by hand or machine – stencils, engraved plates, **rollers** and **silk screens**. Roller printing is the most common for mass-market fabric.

Hand-block printing
The blocks are engraved with the design, which is used to transfer the dye onto the fabric. The registration of each repeat design is carefully positioned by hand.

(above) Giant T-shirt photographic silk-screen print on an oversized 100 per cent cotton jersey dress by Undercover.

(left) Trompe l'œil enlarged 'bias weave' silk-screen print by Ioannis Dimitrousis.

(top) Indonesian hand-block printing.

(above) Batik treated fabric overprinted using copper blocks.

Silk-screen printing

This is the original hand-printing technique and is based on stencilling. A fine woven mesh (originally silk) is stretched over a frame and an impermeable stencil is applied to it. The surface to be printed is then placed underneath and ink or dye is drawn across it and thereby forced through the areas of open mesh circumscribed by the stencil. A series of such screens can be used for successive layers of colour.

The screen-printing process. A film positive is used to expose and harden light-sensitive emulsion to create the stencil design.

A fine mesh is stretched over screen frame.

Ink is pressed through the stencil with the squeegee to make the print.

Print House Inc. is a state-of-the-art manufacturing facility providing full-service product development for screen-printed clothing.

(top) Traditional hand silk-screen printing.

(above) Mechanized silk-screen printing for lengths of fabric.

(left) Mechanized silk-screen printing for individual garments, most commonly T-shirts.

Direct printing

Direct **printing** is today's most-used industrial printing method. Colourants consisting of dyes, thickeners and mordants for fixing the colour are printed directly onto the fabric.

Mordant printing

A mordant – dye fixative – is pre-printed as a pattern prior to dyeing the fabric. The colour adheres only where the mordant has been printed.

Resist dyeing

A resist substance such as wax is printed onto the fabric, which is then dyed. The waxed areas will not take the dye, leaving uncoloured patterns against a coloured **ground**.

Discharge printing

A bleaching agent is printed onto previously dyed fabrics to remove some or all of the colour.

Digital printing

Digital printing is ideal for short runs or engineered prints, as it has a quick turnaround, and does not require start-up costs or costly **strike-offs**. Using pre-treated fabric and inkjet technology to print reactive dyes, it allows multi-hued photographic images or original artwork to be printed without minimum print-run restrictions.

Useful printing terminology

Devoré A fabric containing two or more fibre types is printed with a substance that burns out or destroys one or more of the fibres. The result is usually a fabric that is partly sheer.

Flock print An adhesive agent is printed onto the fabric and flock particles are applied.

Glitter print An adhesive agent is first printed, followed by glitter particles.

Ground colour The base colour of the fabric, or predominant colour of the print.

Half tone Colour graduation within an area of a single colour.

Metallic print Printing with metallic pigment.

Over-print A design motif printed over an existing all-over print.

Pigment print A print made from pigment and binder rather than dyes. Tends to sit on the fabric rather than being absorbed.

Placement print An image printed in a designated position on a garment.

Repeat One complete unit of a design. A small repeat has an all-over effect, while large-scale repeats need to be carefully considered for positioning before cutting the fabric.

Run Complete length of printed fabric.

Transfer print The colour image is transferred from one material, or paper, onto the garment or fabric, usually by heat.

Hallucinations from the 'State of Mind' series by Myka Baum. Vinyl placement print on 100 per cent cotton sweatshirt.

Devoré

The technique of devoré (from the French *dévorer* 'to devour') is also known as 'burn out'. It describes the effect achieved when part of a fabric composition is eaten away by the application of a corrosive paste to produce a design. The acidic dévorant paste will eat away the areas of the fabric that are cellulosic (viscose, rayon, cotton or linen for example). The base weave (silk or synthetic) will remain. The technique is particularly effective with pile fabrics, such as a silk/rayon velvet, where the contrast between the sheer silk ground and the texture of the pile is pronounced.

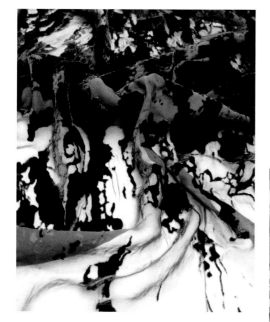

Original devoré design on a silk velvet fabric by Hayley Cheal.

(above) A trompe l'œil photographic digital print of an enlarged knit, printed on a supple silk dress by Bora Aksu, plays with our visual expectations of texture.

(left) Original and silk-screen print on dip-dyed silk and viscose satin by Hayley Cheal.

Embroidery

Embroidery is a form of surface decoration made using threads and yarns in various stitches and combinations of stitches. The process may also include the addition of beads and sequins, as well as other applied decorative **trimmings**.

There are many roots to the origins of embroidery, and similarly many differing styles reflecting various cultures and geographic regions.

Embroidery is classified depending on its under-fabric, or according to the relationship of the stitches' placement to the fabric. Further divisions indicate whether the stitching is on top of the fabric or through it.

Freehand embroidery

The designs are applied without regard for the weave structure of the base fabric; it is also a form of surface embroidery. **Crewel-work** and traditional Chinese embroidery are two examples of freehand embroidery.

(above) Thickly worked wool yarn embroidery applied on wool crêpe creates a customized textile in this dress by Ashish. The dress features a shaped bodice top and full skirt reinforced with a silk tulle underskirt.

(right) Unique jacket featuring original silk thread Uzbek Suzani embroidery by Tamerlane's Daughters. Designer Karina Duebner incorporates nineteenth-century textiles into contemporary designs, creating modern heirlooms.

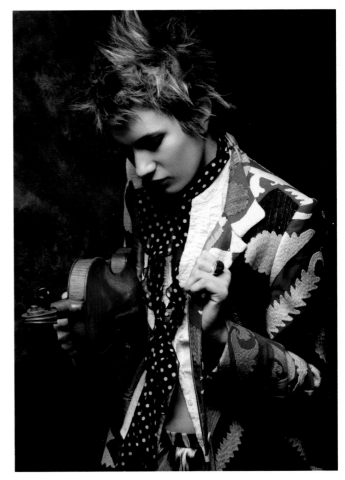

Counted-thread embroidery

The warp and weft threads of the base fabric are pre-counted by the embroiderer before inserting the needle and embroidering thread. Designs tend to be symmetrical. **Needlepoint** embroidery and **cross stitch** are two examples of this style of embroidery.

Canvas work

Threads are stitched through canvas to create a dense pattern and completely cover the under-fabric. **Canvas work** requires the use of an embroidery hoop or frame to stretch the fabric. Needlepoint, **petit point** and **bergello** are examples of canvas work.

Smocking

Smocking is an embroidery technique used to gather fabric, developed in England in the Middle Ages. The gathered fabric is held in place with decorative stitch-work. It derived its name from the tunic or smock worn by the farm labourers who favoured this technique. Before the use of elastic, smocking was used for cuffs and necklines in place of buttons, and gave the garment a degree of stretch.

Up-cycled dress composed of reclaimed Indian cotton crochet lace encrusted with beaded embroidery on a nylon–Lycra blend base by Rachael Cassar. The designer's aim is to produce one-off pieces that comprise 90% recycled materials and to challenge the preconception that luxury and sustainability are mutually exclusive.

(above) Embroidered brocade coat by Josep Font. The encrusted 'freefall' sprinkle of beads and sequins highlights the collar and shoulder area.

(left) Fine grey wool tunic by Carta e Costura showcasing a modern interpretation of the craft of smocking. The fabric is contoured and moulded to the body by graduated elastic shirring, which causes tiny gathers and bubbles in the fabric and lends it great stretch.

Machine embroidery

Embroidery designs can be stitched with automated machines. Today logo badges on T-shirts, sweatshirts and polo shirts make the greatest use of **machine embroidery**.

Appliqué

This needlework technique uses pieces of fabric stitched or embroidered onto a base cloth to create a design. The technique is French in origin but extensively used in North America for traditional quilts. West Africa and parts of India and Pakistan are also famous for **appliqué quilting**.

Quilting

The technique of stitching through two or more layers of fabric with a layer of **wadding** in between to produce an insulative and decorative three-dimensional effect.

(above) Nude organza dress with hand-stitched raw-edged appliqués, cut from woven silk-striped fabric. From Vivienne Westwood's Spring/Summer 2009 'Do it Yourself' collection.

(right) Arresting evening dress by Manish Arora featuring a riot of neon butterflies in a three-dimensional appliqué technique.

(above) Oversized stylized leaf motif overdress in black quilted Italian worsted wool by Maria Francesca Pepe, 2007. The organic shape showcases the strong three-dimensionality of quilted textiles, and their unique relationship with the body. The piece is worn over a hand-dyed and washed silk dress.

Finishing processes

There are many processes that can be applied to fabrics after they have been made, from traditional operations such as **brushing** the surface to make it feel warmer and to compact the weave, to chemical impregnation, making the fabric **water-repellent**, or even adding **fire-retardant** properties. Most of these treatments are for woven fabrics, but also include knitted fabrics, and are executed at the manufacturing **mill**, although some specialist finishes may require the fabric to be sent out to a specific finishing plant.

Waterproofing treatments

These treatments are applied to the fabric to enhance its rain- and general weather-proofing properties. It is important to understand the difference between the terms 'proof' and 'repellent'. Water- or rain-proof implies there will be no ingress of water; this term applies to both the fabric and the manufacturing process of the garment. The manufacturing process that makes a garment waterproof requires either seam-taping to stop water ingress through the stitching holes or, alternatively, the inclusion of a membrane fabric. This is a middle layer referred to as a drop liner, which sits between the outer fabric or shell and the inner lining.

Oiling and **waxing** wear away with time and will need to be reapplied.

Enhancing treatments

There are many treatments that change the basic appearance of the fabric.

Milling and washing are generic terms for numerous specific variations all of which will give quite different effects. These treatments are often an inexpensive way to give added design value to base fabrics. Denim is a fabric that benefits from experimental washing treatments.

Brushing will raise the surface of the fabric and give a softer colour bend; **calendering** and **mercerizing** will add lustre to a fabric.

Additive treatments

These are treatments that enhance the performance or endurance of a fabric or yarn. Some treatments will make a fabric easier to care for; other treatments will inhibit the fabric's natural tendency to crease. Fire-retardant treatments are often required on children's nightwear and on display fabrics.

Examples include antibacterial, anti-soiling, easy-care and crease-resisting fabrics.

Useful finishing terminology

Antibacterial Inhibits bacterial growth.

Anti-soiling Makes stain removal easier.

Blowing Steam is blown through the cloth to remove creases, and gives a specific look to the fabric.

Bonding Two layers of fabric are attached or fused together, with or without a middle layer, for depth and warmth, for example foam sandwiched between two layers to provide structure and insulation.

Brightening agent Increases whiteness or brightness of fabric.

Calendering Process of adding lustre and smoothness to fabric by passing it through heated steel rotary cylinders.

Chemical finishes Any number of treatments applied to give a specialist finish.

Crease-resistant A treatment that improves fabric recovery.

Easy-care Minimal ironing needed to finished garment.

Emerized Emery-covered rollers produce a suede-like finish to fabric.

Enzymes Naturally occurring proteins that catalyse chemical reactions

Milling A process that blends colours, obscures weave and makes the fabric more compact.

Mill washing Any of a number of washing treatments that softens and ages fabric.

Oiling (cloth) Water-repelling treatment applied to fabric.

Pre-shrunk Fabric that has been shrunk at the weaving mill and should not shrink further.

Scouring Process of removing the grease and natural fats from yarn, giving fullness to the fibre and bulking up the fabric.

Shower-proofing Any number of applications to proof fabric against water.

Waxing Impregnating fabric with wax to make it shower-proof.

Introducing colour

Colour is a powerful communicator, as complex as language or music.

Colour is fundamental to the way we experience the world; it is central to our visual and emotional sense of our surroundings. Colour is the first thing we notice, usually perceived before shape and detail, and as children we are primarily stimulated and most responsive to high-**contrast** combinations of colour. Colour can provoke strong emotive associations and reactions, even making things feel warm or cool, exciting and stimulating or soothing and tranquil. Colour has the suggestive power to affect mood and enhance our experiences. It enriches our sense of the world and how we perceive it by helping us to interpret our visual language. It may camouflage us in times of danger, and is an effective tool, a code that may alert us to hazardous situations and steer us to safety, even if only subliminally.

Colour theory

The ancient Greek philosopher Empedocles (492–431 BC) was the first person to formulate a colour theory. It was his hypothesis that colour is not the property of the object, but that it exists in the eye of the observer. This seemingly philosophical leap of understanding was proven centuries later. The science of colour is also known as **chromatics**, which takes in the perception of colour by the human eye and brain, the origin of colour in materials, colour theory in art and the physics of electromagnetic radiation in the visible range – or what we commonly refer to as light.

Colour and light

Colour from the viewer's perspective may be referred to as a 'sensation', but it is technically contained within light. The individual's perception of colour is synthesized in the mind. The concept of colour is a reaction to the sensation of light, which is transmitted to the brain through the eye. Light is made up of waves of energy, which travel at different wavelengths; the brain interprets these into the complex nuances of colour and processes these minute differences in wavelengths.

Pigment is pure colour, but even the colour of a pigment is essentially the colour of the light it reflects. Whenever we look at a colour we are viewing coloured light, because pigments have a special ability to absorb specific wavelengths from the light that falls on them, and to reflect others to the eye.

A white surface will reflect all light rays that strike it, while a black surface will absorb them. A coloured surface, such as red, will reflect the red light, but absorb all the other light rays. It could be said that white is pure light, while black is the total lack of light, and both are not actually colours.

Physicist and mathematician Sir Isaac Newton (1642–1727) pioneered the study of light in laboratory conditions and formulated a logical framework for understanding colour. The proof of Newton's theory, that sunlight is composed of the colours of the spectrum, is apparent each time a rainbow is formed, or when the sun's rays are dispersed on the skin of a bubble, or by a film of oil on a puddle.

Visible spectrum

When a ray of light enters a prism, the array of colours that is refracted through the prism appears in the following order:
Red
Orange
Yellow
Green
Blue
Blue-violet
Violet

(opposite page) Room sized installation, 'Tribute', by Alain Guerra and Neraldo de La Paz, constructed from a rainbow-hued heap of discarded clothing.

(right) Design duo Basso and Brooke create an extravagant explosion of sunset colours by using analogous hues from the 'warm' section of the spectrum in this multi-layered evening gown.

These constituents of light are known as the visible spectrum. Each colour has a different wavelength. When light strikes a surface certain wavelengths are absorbed, and others are reflected by its pigments or colouring. Most light sources emit light at many different wavelengths, a process that gives a surface its colour.

In 1860, Scottish physicist James Clerk Maxwell (1831–1879) showed that light was a form of electromagnetic energy. The eye is able to receive light waves between 400 and 800 million cycles per second, and we perceive these cycles as colour. Violet is the shortest and red the longest.

Hue

The first dimension of colour is **hue**. A hue is the name or type of a colour. When we refer to a colour by its name we are referring to its hue. A pure hue is one which has no other colour mixed in.

Certain hue combinations conform to standard categorizations.

Monochromatic: Of a single hue.

Analogous hues: Colours that are adjacent to each other in the spectrum.

Complementary hues: A pair of opposite colours as viewed on a **colour wheel**. Mixing complementary colours lowers the **saturation**, or richness, and **value**, or **luminosity** of the resulting colour, in other words it has a darkening effect.

Triadic hues: Any three equidistant colours on the colour spectrum when it is configured as a circle of hues. Red, yellow and blue form the **primary triad**. When the full spectrum of colour is presented as a wheel the relative positions of red, yellow and blue conform to a perfect equilateral triangle.

Colour groupings and systems

The various terms used within the colour-wheel models.

Primary colours
The term **primary** refers to a colour that cannot be made from other colours. Red, yellow and blue form the primary triad.

Secondary colours
Secondary colours are the result of mixing two primary colours, for example blue and yellow mixed to produce green. The **secondary triad** consists of green, orange and violet.

Tertiary colours
Tertiary colours result when a primary and an adjacent secondary colour are mixed together.

Subtractive colour system
The **subtractive** method of creating colours is based upon pigments or dyes, and explains the way these colours mix by absorbing some wavelengths of light and reflecting others.

Additive colour system
This is the process of mixing coloured light, as in theatrical or retail applications. An **additive system** begins with no light – black – and light is added to make colour.

Partitive colour system
The **partitive** colour model is based on the viewer's reaction to colours when they are placed next to each other.

Ensembles of garmets in monochromatic colours.

Colour wheels

The colour spectrum can be organized into wheels to help rationalize and predict colour interactions. Colour wheels are the first basic tools used in the analysis and discussion of colour. There are many variations on the visual organization of colour, some are simple in format and others highly complex, but their principles are all linked.

Pigment colours

In subtractive, or pigment, mixtures, the primaries are traditionally said to be red, yellow and blue. If two primaries are mixed, they theoretically produce the secondaries orange, green and purple. If all three are mixed, they theoretically produce black.

The pigment and process wheels

On the conventional 12-colour wheel of pigment hues, the primaries are red, blue and yellow; the secondaries are orange, green and purple; and the tertiaries are mixtures of adjoining primaries and secondaries. If colours are mixed with their complement (the hue lying opposite on the wheel), a neutral grey should be created, as indicated in the centre. The 12-step **pigment wheel** is the basis for working with subtractive colour; textile artists will use a subtractive wheel to create colours of yarn and textiles by dyeing.

The 12-step **process wheel** also deals with subtractive colour but the three basic primaries are purer – yellow, magenta and cyan – that upon mixing also result in purer hues. This arrangement is the standard employed in colour printing and photography, as well as pigment manufacture.

The Itten wheel

Devised by Swiss teacher and artist Johannes Itten (1888–1967), the **Itten wheel** shows a logical and easily remembered format for working with colour pigments. Itten was captivated by colour from both a scientific and a spiritual point of view, and taught at the influential Bauhaus School in Germany in the 1920s. He observed that colours can be classified as warm or cool shades, and how the two combined can affect each other. Theoretical elements, including the Itten colour wheel, generated from the Bauhaus teachings still inform art instruction around the world today.

The Itten colour wheel organizes the basic theory of the interrelationship between the primary, secondary and tertiary colours in a practical graphic format. The triangle in the centre shows the three primary colours, yellow, blue and red, which cannot be created by mixing any of the other pigments. Surrounding them are the three secondary colours, which are produced by mixing the primaries. The wheel that encircles the primaries and secondaries is divided into 12 sectors. Six of these are primaries and secondaries, and between each of these is another colour. Itten referred to these as tertiary colours. A tertiary colour is the result of mixing a primary and a secondary colour.

(above) The Itten colour wheel organizes the basic theory of the interrelationship between the primary, secondary and tertiary colours.

(left) The 12-colour pigment wheel.

The Munsell wheel

Albert Munsell (1858–1918) developed a partitive colour system (below) based on five primary hues, or as he referred to them, principal colours of yellow, red, green, blue and purple. These primaries are based on **after-image** perceptions – when the brain supplies the opposite colour after staring at a particular hue – that derive from hues we see in nature.

Light colours

These colours are additive rather than subtractive (like pigments). If primary-coloured lights – red-orange, green and blue-violet – are projected in overlapping circles, they mix to form the light secondaries yellow, magenta and cyan. In additive mixtures, the secondaries are paler than the primaries. Where all three primaries overlap, they produce white. This system is used for lighting and also forms the basis for video and computer graphics.

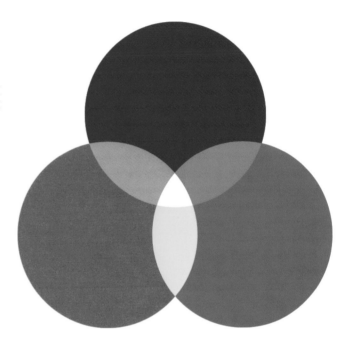

The visual wheel

The 16-step **visual wheel** (below) was arranged by the Italian artist Leonardo da Vinci (1452–1519), whose understanding of complementary colours greatly influenced Renaissance painting. It is a partitive and subtractive colour wheel.

Light colours are additive (above), and react differently to pigment colours, which are subtractive (below).

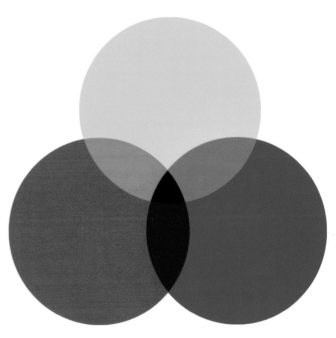

Perception of colour

Our perception of colour is fundamental to our ability to define our world and our emotions. Experience teaches us to connect certain colours with cool or warm sensations. Colour can help us identify freshness and levels of ripeness or decay, can be an indicator of potential illness, and help us recognize fear, anger or embarrassment.

Mind and matter

Three elements are needed to appreciate colour: a light source, a subject and a viewer. The brain interprets as colour the waves of light that are received by the lens of the eye. The information received by the eye is conveyed to the brain, so the perception of colour is therefore a mental, psychological and physical phenomenon. Our perception of colour is affected by the context it exists in: what surrounds it, what other colours are next to it and the lighting conditions under which it is seen. It is the human eye in conjunction with the brain's ability to synthesize that informs how we distinguish the type of colour seen.

Our ability to perceive texture, distance and three-dimensionality is affected by colour: generally darker colours appear to recede, or make things look smaller, while lighter colours tend to have the opposite effect.

Yellows and greens tend to be seen before other hues, while reds and violets are the most difficult to perceive.

Cultural reference

The meaning or emotional impact a colour imparts will vary across different cultures and can fluctuate over time, acquiring both positive and negative connotations throughout the ages. Fashion also exerts a significant influence on the associations we make with various colours. Anyone involved in the use of colour for the development of fashion products needs to be conversant with the 'codes' that different colours can communicate.

Symbolic colour associations rely on an audience that shares the same cultural experiences. The idea that blue, green and violet are 'cool' in temperature, and red, orange and yellow are 'warm' colours is shared by many cultures worldwide. This association is rooted in our shared physical experience with water, shadow and icy climates, or fire, sun and deserts. The meaning of colour seems to be generated from a psychological reaction to a physical experience.

Gathering and stuffed forms enhance the pulsating optical effects of this Op-art inspired synthetic Lycra-blend dress by Aiwa Yau.

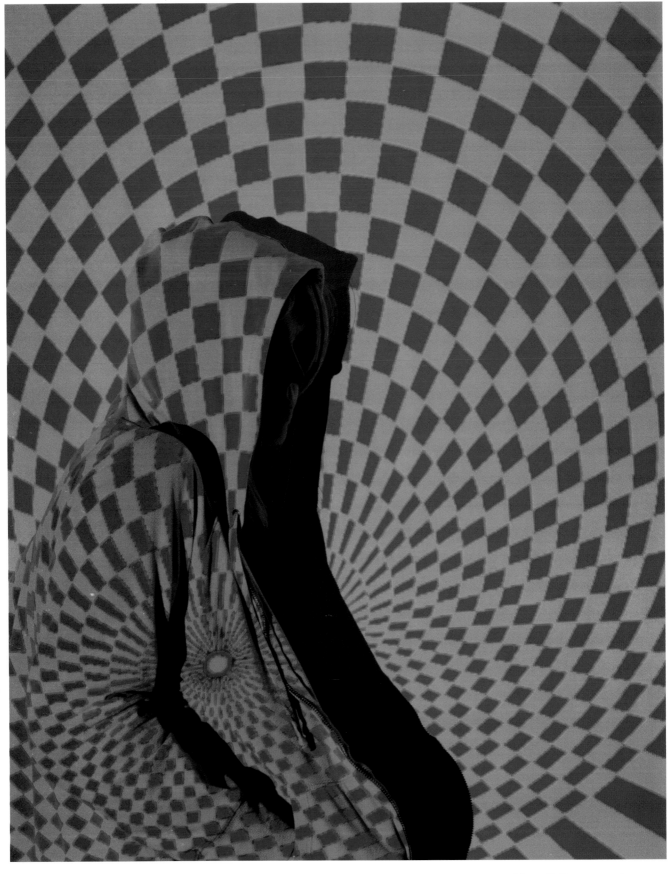

Chromatic Convergence by Myka Baum illustrates the principle of simultaneous contrast.

Colour communication: the vocabulary of colour

The human eye can differentiate between several million colours of varying hue, saturation and **tone**, and we recognize that colour has more than one visible quality by the adjectives we use.

The vocabulary used to describe colour is often imprecise. We say red, but red can be yellow or bluish in cast, shockingly intense, cloyingly dark or tender and bordering on pink. Differences in colours are not adequately communicated by a broad colour name alone. Therefore, colour names, such as red, are often coupled with evocative adjectives that enhance the communication of the colour 'feeling', for example hellfire red, cherry red or blood red.

Cultural necessities

Thinking about colours as moods and feelings inspires evocative or emotive language and descriptive adjectives that can provoke recognition of very specific colours.

Many thousands of colours have been apportioned names, but these are generally limited. The basic colour vocabulary of even the richest language is surprisingly small, often fewer than a dozen words. All other colour terms are arrived at by qualifying a basic word with the addition of 'light' or 'dark', or by illustrating the colour by referencing it to an object or material, such as ivory, lemon, coffee or mahogany.

No one knows exactly how precise colour terms developed in different languages, but there seems to be a correlation between the importance of a particular commodity, or the need to describe environmental factors, and the complexity of descriptive colour terms. Where precision is found in colour language it is often influenced by a society's environment, for example, desert tribes have a large range of terms for yellows and browns, conversely Eskimos possess a wide vocabulary that enables them to differentiate the colours and variations of snow and ice. The Maoris have over 100 words in their vocabulary for what we would call 'red'. Many African tribes have extensive colour vocabularies for their most significant possessions, cattle. Old Germanic people's reliance on their horses is reflected in their many horse adjectives, a tradition that has passed into English, which also boasts a large variety of descriptive words for the colouring of horses, including roan, bay, chestnut, piebald and skewbald. In most cultures human hair and skin colour are also descriptors that can reflect quite complex shade variations to establish a person's heritage or caste.

Colour trends

The consumer's first response is to colour. Selecting colours and forming a defined colour palette is one of the first considerations when planning a range or collection.

Many industries depend heavily on our constantly changing taste in colour. The prediction of colour trends involves an ongoing assessment of all the subtle factors that influence consumer tastes.

Crazes in colours can be associated with a certain lifestyle. A group of colours can express a cultural attitude or inspirational lifestyle fantasies such as 'sporty', 'classic' or 'ethnic'. The most enduring colour trend of the twentieth century began in the late 1980s. Inspired by the stark aesthetic of a new wave of Japanese designers, black relentlessly encompassed all levels of fashion, and became no longer a colour to be associated with mourning or glamour, but the ultimate expressive 'non-colour' for all aspects of contemporary urban life.

Simultaneous contrast

The effect produced by placing colours of the same intensity together is known as simultaneous contrast (see opposite page). Colours that oppose each other in the spectrum can create striking optical effects, appearing to flicker, shimmer or even undulate depending on the proportion and sequence they are used in. This effect will only be fully apparent if both hues have the same intensity. The value of each colour can appear to change in relation to the colour it is placed next to. In prints or stripes this can cause an optical 'flicker'.

Colour forecasting

The textile industries collaborate with a range of experts for guidance on trend direction. Part of the symbiotic relationship between fashion and textiles is rooted in trends, and these influence the preliminary stages of the development of colour palettes.

For the first view of the new season's trends, the fabric fair **Première Vision** is held twice-yearly in Paris. Here consultations with industry professionals serve to predict and formulate future trends in colours and fabrics. The principal colour organisations are renowned for their precise and accurate colour predictions. They are made up of international expert colourists that assure a global perspective on colour forecasting. The principal colour consultants are the **Colour Group of Great Britain**, the **International Colour Authority (ICA)**, the **Color Association of the United States (CAUS)** and the **Colour Marketing Group (CMG)**. Colour forecasters analyze and interpret the underlying social, cultural and consumer preferences for colour 'moods' or families and make projections for the future. They do not impose colour selections upon markets, but are adept at analyzing and interpreting underlying trends that indicate the moods and preferences of consumers. Most predicted colour palettes are ready to be distributed to the textile and fashion industries at least one or two years in advance of the retail selling period.

Matching colour

The designer, product developer, merchandiser and retailer need to be aware of the role that light plays in the perception of colour. Every colour we view is modified and defined by its surroundings and by the type of light that illuminates it. Different types of light can radically alter the way a colour looks. A fabric that looks greyish green under a fluorescent light in a retail environment can look bluish green under a domestic light, in context with other colours. The lighting in a retail environment can affect the way a colour is seen, therefore colour matching for this purpose needs to be well considered in order to avert potential merchandising disasters.

Artificial light is also known as reduced spectrum lighting because it is deficient in some colour frequencies. Incandescent bulbs give a warm light that favours the yellow, orange and red frequencies. Warm colours will therefore look more vivid when viewed with this light. Fluorescent light conversely favours the cool frequencies of blue and green colours; this light source will make the colours appear livelier. Light naturally behaves in a random and chaotic manner. Sunlight or electric light, for example, can scatter a mixture of wavelengths in all directions. If various components of product ranges are manufactured in different countries and the colour matching is done under light sources that differ from those of the retail environment, the resulting colours can appear dramatically different.

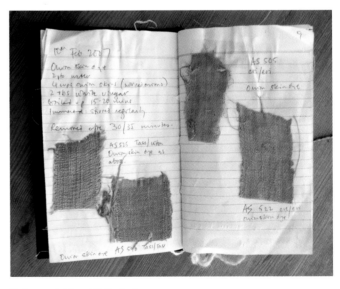

Colour matching. Artist Isabella Whitworth has experimented with natural dyes to complement the ethically-farmed semi-wild Eri silk. Her swatchbook documents the recipe as 4 cups of onion-skin, 2 parts water and 2 tablespoons of white vinegar, boiled for 15–20 minutes and allowed to stand for a further 30 minutes.

Eco considerations

Consumers are becoming increasingly aware of the impact that their purchasing habits may have on the environment. Colour forecasters identified this attitude in the 1990s and it informed the trend for 'natural state' fabrics: undyed, unbleached textiles and a feel for softer, more 'real' colours.

The environmental and social impact of producing and finishing coloured textiles can be immense and there is no doubt that certain chemicals, dyestuffs and finishing processes have a negative impact on the environment. The toxins discharged by chemical dyes and the waste of natural resources involved in processing are a major consideration when sourcing textiles. Recent years have seen non-governmental organizations (NGOs) driving legislative change that resulted in 22 carcinogenic **azo dyes** being banned in Europe. Informed choices by consumers and commitment by developers of products can help protect the environment.

The surface of the material that a light source falls upon can also affect the way we perceive the colour of that material. Corduroy, velvet, satin and **bouclé** tweeds all have very different surface textures that will affect our visual perception of colour due to the level of absorption or reflection of light upon the fabrics' textures. If a surface is rough or porous, it will absorb a greater proportion of light waves hitting it, and the colour will look darker, while a shiny surface will reflect more of the light and will therefore appear lighter.

Commision Internationale de L'Eclairage (CIE) is an organization that was founded in 1931 at the International Commission on Illumination, following the exploration of the need for a standardization of colour. This system was based on lights. A colourimeter was used to measure three variables of any colour, the luminance (intensity of light given off), the hue and the saturation. Together these values determine the 'chromacity' of a colour. The advantage of the CIE system is that it provides the industry with the means of accurately and consistently matching colours of barely perceptible differences. This objective standard eliminates differences in human interpretation. The **SCOTDIC (Standard Color of Textile Dictionnaire Internationale de la Couleur)** and the **Pantone Professional System** are also widely used in the fashion and textiles industry.

Combining colour

Colours are rarely seen or used in isolation. When working with colour try to transcend the received wisdom of which colours should and should not be seen together. Fashion constantly demands a new perspective on colour and needs to express new ideas. When colours share similar visual qualities we perceive them as harmonious or unified. Colours when juxtaposed can play tricks with our perception of them; they can appear to alter in cast, tone or even size.

A colour moodboard compiled to develop an autumnal palette.

Creating a colour palette

Selecting colours and formulating a colour palette is one of the first considerations in the design and planning of a fashion range. A colour palette (or gamme) is a grouping of colours that show the colour offering of a fashion range. Some of the colours in the palette will take precedence and be used as base colours – these may be the darker shades or neutrals – while others will be used more sparingly as highlight colours or within prints. It is important to be aware of the effect that certain colours can have against skin tones and how the strategic use of colour can create optical effects on the shape of the body.

Inspiration for a fresh approach to colours and forming palettes can be found in the most unlikely sources.

Compiling a colour library involves drawing from diverse inspirational sources such as paintings, photographic imagery, paint samples, coloured yarn, found objects and myriad textures and materials.

Colour resourcing requires the collection of examples of colours. The direction the palette will take is often derived from a combination of the inspirational material gathered while researching a collection, coupled with trend information.

Connecting colour choices to an inspirational mood or 'feeling' helps to define the character of the individual colours and how they relate to each other in a collection. For example, the mood may be for a grimy, urban, degraded-looking neutral palette contrasted with accents of acidic neons. Colour selections can be refined by comparing shades from an archive and matching to professional colour systems. Awareness of the minute differences between shades helps create sophistication within tones.

Fashion demands novelty, and colours we think we have seen before need to be revisited; their tone, cast and intensity reinvented and placed in fresh combinations.

(opposite page) Monochrome shadows form subtle variations of grey. The palest can be clean, pearly, luminous and discreet. Faded and gentle tones have a dusty, ashy and powdery feel. Mid tones are flinty, mature, refined and serious. Cast with other hues grey can take on a deceptive mercurial liveliness.

Useful colour terminology

Achromatic No hue present, without chroma.

Chroma The saturation or brightness of a colour. This term can also define the purity or strength of a colour.

Chromatic Having a hue.

Chromotherapy The use of colour for healing purposes.

CMYK system The four-colour screen system used to reproduce colour photographs: cyan, magenta, yellow, black.

Colour harmony Colour relationships, colours in proportion to each other.

Contrast The visual difference between colours. For example black and white are high-contrast colours.

Co-primary triad The result of the primary triad when split into three pairs consisting of cool and warm versions of each hue.

Muted colour A subdued version of a hue.

Neutral Colours based on the tertiary hues.

Pastel A colour tinted with white to produce a pale version of a hue.

Secondary triad In subtractive colours: orange, green and violet. They are referred to as secondary, because combining two primaries can make them.

Shade The colour resulting from adding black to a hue.

Tint The colour resulting from adding white to a hue, or a colour appearing to weakly modify another, for example 'grey with a green tint'.

Tone A 'greyed' colour.

White exudes ethereal purity and ultimate light. Modern whites are shimmering, reflective and tinged with dilute blue and ultra violet. Naturally sun-bleached, starchy and chalky hues have a transient brightness. A creamy or misty cast is evident in antique whites.

The startling, almost chemical, astringency of citrus yellows and acidic chartreuse are tempered and softened by gilded flaxen tones and orange-tinged saffron which convey egg yolk, custard and sun-baked days.

Naturally fresh and verdant chlorophyllic greens can possess an intensely invigorating effect that, when deepened, can verge on poisonous. Verdigris and saturated glowing emerald denote sophistication, and cast with blue become elegant jade. Ripened, muddied and mouldy tones appear in olive, khaki and lichen.

57

Pale, insouciant diluted pinks are flirtatious, powdery and intimate. Flushed with pigment they become florid and hyper real. Lurid pinks can appear to pulsate with a searing flamboyant appeal akin to red. Tinted with violet, pink can be saccharine and cloying. Tinted with yellow, pink becomes fleshy, limpid and tender. Ripe, reddened tones of orange convey a juicy fruitfulness with an intense glowing warmth. Tinted with browns they mature into earthy, autumnal, rusted and bronzed tones.

Full-spectrum saturated scarlet raises the pulse in its most fierce and fiery shades. Intense ruby and vermillion deepen to become rich crimson and claret.

Blued reds develop into maroons and border on purple. Reds sullied with browns and violets take on a rustic appeal, developing complex shades such as puce.

58

Icy or salt-bleached tints of blue convey a languid ozonic clarity. Pale, liquid and patinated hues are almost reflective. Intensely saturated blue can be electric and invigorating. Shades with a violet cast inject warmth, and iconic indigo denim spans shades from the merest tint through to the deepest, blackened navy.

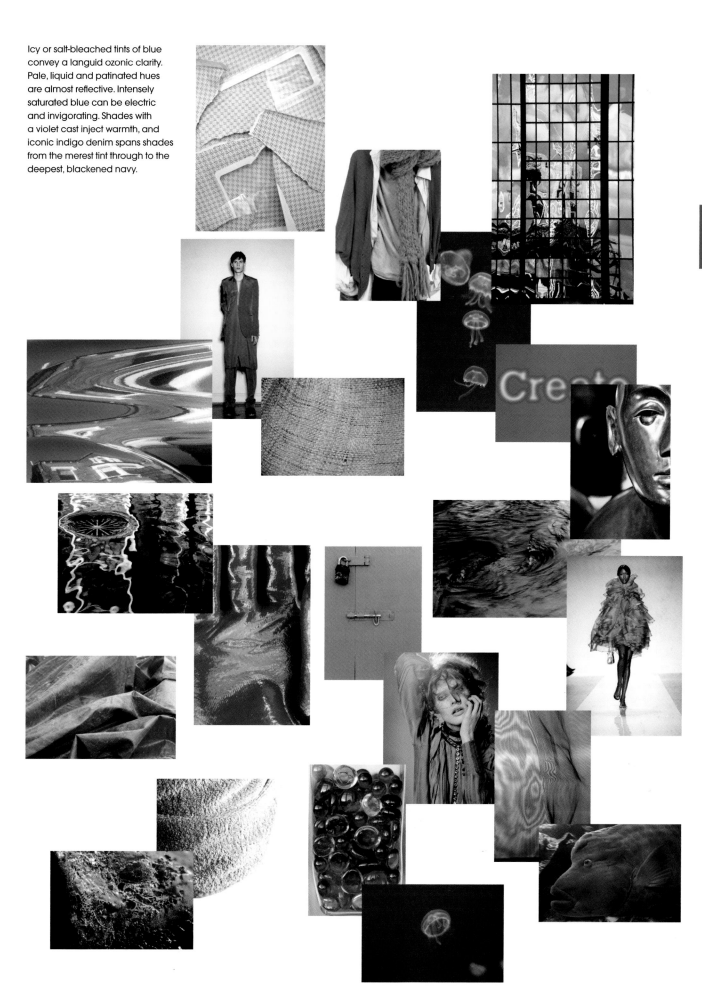

59

Section 1 Animal fibres

Wool

Wool is the ultimate natural chameleon fibre, embodying many diverse aspects.

Wool can be satisfyingly soft, warm, cosy and sensuous, or rugged, tough and functional, while its inherent drapability allows its finest fibres to appear lustrous, sleek and elegant.

The history of wool

Our relationship with this historic fibre is almost as old as civilization itself, and wool's unique thermally responsive and insulating qualities remain as relevant today as at any time in history.

Early history

The use of felted wool for clothing can be traced back tens of thousands of years. Taking inspiration from the matting of the fleece that occurs naturally on the animal's back, primitive cultures worldwide developed processes of wetting, massaging and pressing the wool to produce a dense, matted felt 'blanket' that could be cut or manipulated into varying thicknesses, or moulded into shape. Felted wool was commonplace in China and Egypt long before the technologies for spinning and weaving were developed.

However, wool was the first animal fibre to be woven, and by Roman times wool, together with linen and leather, clothed Europe. Cotton was seen as a mere curiosity, while silk was an extravagant luxury. It is believed that the Romans invented the carding process to brush, tease and comb the fibres into alignment to facilitate the smoother spinning and weaving of the yarn. It is also believed that the Romans started the selective breeding of sheep to provide better and finer qualities of wool.

(right) A contemporary expression of a historic process, this red merino wool 'boxing' dress is hand felted by US-based German artist Angelika Werth. The boxing dress was one of a series of twelve 'Madeleines' conceived by the artist to express specific personalities. Her interpretation of a baroque-inspired dress exploits the sculptural nature and robust qualities of traditionally felted fine merino wool.

(opposite page) Merino wool rovings dyed in rainbow hues, by Wild Turkey from upstate New York. Roving is the term given to the continuous staple wool fibres that are a result of the carding process that prepares the fibres for spinning. This colour range shows the lustrous sheen and brilliant saturation of colour that is associated with premium-quality fine-grade Australian merino wool.

Pre-industry

By the beginning of the medieval period the wool trade was the economic engine of both the Low Countries and central Italy, and relied on English wool exports for cloth production. Wool was, at this time, England's primary and most valuable export commodity. Pre-Renaissance Florence's wealth was similarly built on the textile industry, which guided the banking policies that made Florence the hub of the Renaissance.

By the time of the English Restoration, in the mid-seventeenth century, English woollens had begun to compete with silks in the international market. To help protect this lucrative trade the Crown forbade its new American colonies to trade wool with anybody other than the 'mother' country.

Spain's economy was similarly reliant on this valuable export, to such an extent that the export of **merino** lambs was only permitted by royal consent. Spanish merino sheep, with their finer quality fleece, became the most desirable breed. A great majority of today's Australian merino sheep originated from here, via a circuitous route as part of a gift to the Governor of the Dutch Cape, and then onto Australia, where the vast areas of dry pastures perfectly suit fine-wool sheep breeds. The Spanish also introduced sheep to Argentina and Uruguay, where the climate and pastures were favourable for their growth and expansion, and today they represent a sizeable percentage of the two countries' export revenue.

Modern times

By the mid-nineteenth century the Industrial Revolution had turned Bradford in Yorkshire into the centre of the industrialized world's spinning and weaving industry. Bradford's insatiable appetite for fine woollen fibres is said to have built and maintained Australia's colonial economy. By the beginning of the twentieth century Australian sheep rearing and its wool trade had usurped Europe's industry, and to this day Australia remains the most important global producer of wool.

The end of World War II was a catalyst for many socio-economic and political changes. Man-made materials were in tune with the modern world of working women, busy lifestyles and greater social mobility. New sporting and leisure pursuits encouraged the use of easy-care fabrics. The synthetics first developed between the 1930s and 1940s were in general use throughout the 1950s and 1960s, and were considered sophisticated and in tune with postwar values.

Acrylic was developed as a substitute for knitted wool, while **polyester**, or **Terylene** as it was known in tailoring, was the perfect medium for drip-dry, non-iron, easy-care lifestyles.

By contrast, by the mid-1960s new socio-political movements were emerging in North America and Western Europe; the flower-power movement questioned Western values and especially materialism. In the search for a new world order many alternative lifestyles and cultures were embraced. One outward sign of this was in a revival of traditional crafts. Wool and cotton, both natural and traditional fibres, were favoured, preferably if **homespun** and ideally with an organic pedigree. It may be said that the hippy movement was instrumental in jump-starting the wool revival.

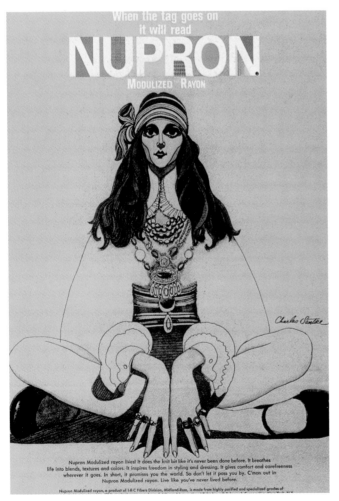

The hippy movement of the 1960s questioned Western values and was instrumental in jump-starting the revival of fortune for natural fibres. Fabrics with an organic pedigree became *de rigueur*, an irony lost in this advertisement of the period using hippy imagery to promote synthetic fabrics.

Looking to the future

While wool's heritage and association with reliability and quality may be one of its defining strengths as a commodity, contemporary consumers are now increasingly sophisticated and demanding, with myriad lifestyle issues that fabrics and fashion must strive to address. In the drive to be responsive to contemporary needs and also remain relevant, scientists and textile designers are researching and developing new technological solutions to extend the existing attributes of this important, traditional fibre. Technological advances in textiles can provide natural fibres with adaptive aspects, which give an already desirable raw material specific enhancements and new benefits, allowing it to remain competitive and aspirational. Current research aims to develop innovative treatments that will enhance, extend and manipulate wool's properties in order to respond to the increasingly shifting requirements of the twenty-first-century consumer.

New-generation wool technology is no longer cost driven, but is about adding alternative fibres, be they synthetic or high-tech, as visual, tactile or practical enhancements to give an alternative aspect to wool. In the two decades after World War II synthetics and natural fibres had no shared common goals, and there was a cultural class divide between the selection of one over the other. Today, natural fibres and synthetics can blend harmoniously, both from a fibre and social viewpoint. Adding 2 per cent **Lycra** will give fine-wool suiting a 'memory', while **Lurex**, for example, can liven up a flat worsted suit fabric; the options are endless.

Modern interpretations of wool can provide the designer with a broad, tactile vocabulary that can express a wide range of design requirements, from classic, traditional and authentic themes, through to the most challenging futuristic explorations in performance fabrics.

Once upon a time wool care, for the consumer, meant careful hand washing, a dedicated cleaning agent and towel drying. Today's consumer is able to enjoy the beauty of woollen products while caring for them in much the same way as they would many other fibres.

The chameleon qualities of this versatile fibre can express and respond to myriad fashion personalities, from urbane, contemporary modern luxury to functional and technologically advanced sportswear.

65

Classifying wool

Fine
Under 24.5 microns

Medium
24.5 to 31.4 microns

Fine cross bred
31.5 to 35.4 microns

Coarse cross bred
35.5 microns plus

The diameter of the wool fibre is measured in microns (see page 68).

Wool ready for grading classification and carding at Coldharbour Mill, Devon, England.

Wool fibre

The natural properties of wool make it flexible, resilient, insulative, absorbent, hygienic and mouldable.

Wool is an organic compound composed of **keratin**, an animal protein that is also found in hair, nails, feathers and horn. As distinct from hair or fur, wool has many tiny overlapping scales, all of which point in the same direction.

The predominant natural colour of wool is a creamy white, although some sheep breeds produce other natural colours, such as brown, black and silver, as well as some random mixes.

Wool fibres, while still on the animal, are coated in a grease that contains lanolin, a slightly yellowish substance. The lanolin is removed and collected during the washing process of raw wool, and used in products such as cosmetics, skin ointment and waterproofing wax. On occasion the wool may be processed without the removal of its natural oil, in which case it retains excellent water-repellent qualities. Traditional **Aran wool** does not have its lanolin removed and was originally used by Scottish and Irish fishermen because it offered excellent protection from the elements.

Crimp

Wool fibres have a **crimp**, a natural wave that allows air to be trapped within the structure, giving wool its natural insulating quality. Fine merino wool may have as many as 100 crimps per inch, while a coarser **karakul** may have as few as one or two crimps per inch. In the spinning process the crimps of the fibre wrap around each other, increasing wool's already excellent tensile strength, which can be stretched from 25 to 35 per cent of its length before reaching breaking point. The springiness of the crimp gives wool its inbuilt recovery, or 'memory', enabling woollen clothes to maintain their shape. Hanging a creased suit in a damp or steamy environment will allow the creases to drop out in very little time without any need to press or iron.

(above left) The three-dimensional stitch work of this traditional Aran sweater helps to trap the air for added warmth. Aran wool has not had its natural lanolin removed.

(left) Wool fibre under magnification, showing the many tiny overlapping scales all pointing in the same direction. The natural wave or crimp allows air to be trapped within the structure and lends the fibre its natural insulating quality.

(above) This deconstructed Aran wool knit by Natalie Jacobs modernizes the traditional knit technique by displacing the direction of the knit and dispensing with formed sleeves.

Resilience

The exterior of the wool fibre is hydrophobic and tends to repel water, while the interior of the fibre is hydroscopic and attracts water, which means it can absorb up to 30 per cent of its bulk weight in moisture vapour without feeling wet. This gives wool its comfort factor, because it can still feel warm while wet, which is one of the reasons nomads, herdsmen and fishermen living and working in harsh intemperate climates use it.

Wool has natural flame-resistant properties so needs high temperatures before igniting, and does not disintegrate until about 90°C.

Wool that has been felted and treated with lanolin is water-resistant and air-permeable, as well as being slightly antibacterial, which helps the wicking away of odour; airing a woollen product will remove much of the build-up of odour, eliminating the need for constant laundering.

Merino Perform™ Advantage fabric

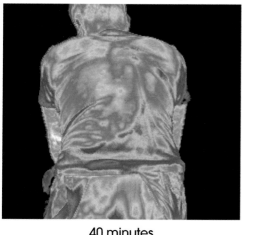

40 minutes

Synthetic fabric

40 minutes

23°
24°
25°
26°
27°
28°
29°
30°
31°
32°
33°
34°

Sheep

Sheep are universally domesticated animals that produce a unique fibre. They can be separated into two principal types: **hair sheep** and **wool sheep**. Wool sheep are then subdivided into three further types.

Hair sheep

Hair sheep are the ancestors of today's domesticated sheep. These originally had coarse hair and a downy or woolly undercoat. Through years of selective breeding the hair disappeared and the woolly undercoat developed to became the outer fleece we recognize today. It is estimated that today only about 10 per cent of the world's sheep population are hair sheep, the majority of which are to be found in Africa. Hair sheep are used for meat consumption and the manufacturing of leather. Sheep leather is referred to as sheep **napa** (or nappa) and lamb is referred to as lamb napa.

Wool sheep

Wool sheep are subdivided into three main categories:

the down breeds or short wools, which prefer warmer, drier climates;

the long wools, which thrive in the wetter regions, with their richer pastures;

the mountain breeds that exist comfortably on exposed hills. The land and pastures that feed the sheep influence the properties of their fleeces. Wool sheep are bred for wool production and also for meat.

A Sportswool™ garment viewed under a thermal imaging camera shows the natural thermally responsive regulating aspects of the fibre. It helps to raise the body's temperature when in a cool climate, and cools the body when the ambient temperature rises.

Wool production

Over 60 per cent of global production is destined for the clothing industry. Australia is by far the largest producer of wool, of which the majority is from merino breeds. New Zealand is the second largest producer, mainly from cross-bred varieties. Organic wool is becoming popular but represents a very small percentage of global production.

Sixty per cent of all global wool production is destined for the clothing market.

Shearing

The fleece of a sheep is carefully shorn and removed in one piece. **Shearing** represents the single greatest expense of the entire wool-production cycle, constituting approximately 20 per cent of the total cost. The best lambswool is obtained from the first shearing, taken at about six months of age when the fleece is at its softest and finest. Thereafter sheep are shorn at yearly intervals.

An alternative to shearing with hand blades or electric clippers is the protein injection. A retaining net is fitted over the sheep before injecting a protein substance that forms a natural break in the wool fibre. After a week the net is removed and the wool fleece pulled off by hand.

After shearing the fleeces are thrown clean-side down onto rotating tables in the shearing sheds, where impurities and any foreign matter are removed.

Wool classes

Prior to spinning, wool is separated and graded into different quality classification categories known as **wool classes**. The diameter of the fibre is measured in **microns** and is the principal component in determining the classification category. Generally, anything under 25 microns is used for light clothing, while medium grades are used for heavy outerwear and coarse grades for rugs. Finesse, crimp, fibre length, cleanliness and colour are other key ingredients for consideration; grading is also dependent on the breed of sheep and the end purpose of the wool. At this stage, and until the wool has been **scoured** and cleaned, it is referred to as **grease-wool**, or wool-in-the-grease. Finally the wool fibres are compressed into bales ready for packaging and transportation to the mills that will carry out the next round of processes.

Wool scouring

Scouring is an essential cleaning process that removes both the grease and debris from the wool prior to spinning. Scoured wool is usually about 70 per cent of the weight of pre-scoured or grease-wool.

(left) Drafting with view of pin feed at Lightfoot Farm, Maine, USA.

(below) Bobbins of rovings ready for final spinning into yarn. The wool is from a breed of domestic Dorset Down sheep and is in its natural colour. Coldharbour Mill, Devon, England.

Shearing and classifying
Referred to as grease wool throughout these stages

Shearing

↓

Removal of foreign matter

↓

Classification for quality purposes and possible end user. Compressed into bales for transport to spinners.

↓

Spinning mills
Scouring—Carding—Drawing

↙ ↘

Woollen spinning	**Worsted spinning**
Drawing	Combing
Twist	Drawing
	Twist

Carding, combing and drawing

Carding, combing (see page 13), and drawing are three independent processes that together form part of what is termed the **spinning process** – which also includes spinning itself. All of these processes are carried out in a spinning mill, which may be simply referred to as the 'spinners'.

Drawing and finisher drawing

The two processes of **drawing and finisher drawing** may be applied to both woollens and worsteds to further improve the evenness and regularity of the yarn, prior to final spinning. Woollen spun yarn will also need to go through **condensers** to separate the **web** or **batt** (multiple sheets of fibres) into predetermined weight strands. Each technique gives a uniquely different character, in both appearance and feel, to the fabric and end product. The choice of selecting one over the other is purely a creative decision.

Wool yarn count

Yarns are bought and sold by weight, not by length. Because of this, sizes (numbers or count) are used to express a relationship between the weight of yarn and its length. This relationship also reflects the diameter or thickness of the yarn.

Wool count refers to the number of hanks of yarn (each 560 yards or 512 m in length) that it is possible to spin from one pound of clean wool. The finer the count the more wool it is possible to obtain from one pound. The number of hanks produced gives the wool its count.

In tailoring-fabric terms, the prefix super refers to fabric that has been woven from yarns counted as 100 or more. Therefore a super 120s fabric has been woven from finer yarns than a super 110s fabric. The finer the wool count the softer the fabric is to the touch.

Spinning

The final stage of the spinning process is the application of twist to the yarn, giving it greater tensile strength and added flexibility in preparation for the subsequent knitting or weaving processes. Adding twist can also be a way of achieving myriad different visual effects. Twisting several shades of a colour together will produce a tone-on-tone mélange effect, while twisting together complementary colours can result in innovative colour solutions. Alternatively, different types of yarn can be twisted together to achieve more complex textures. Twisting a Lurex yarn with a traditional woollen yarn gives an element of shimmer that takes a traditional woollen or worsted fabric into another dimension. Yarns spun of differing thicknesses will, when woven, give interesting and complex textural surfaces.

Linton tweed fabric is hand checked before despatching to major fashion houses, such as Chanel.

(above) Wool tweed in classic colour palette of rusty reds and greys reinterpreted in a modern chunky sweatshirt shape and matching shorts by Ashish for Autumn/Winter 2008.

Twisting yarns of differing natural fibre sources is an interesting proposition from both a fabric and fashion perspective, as well as being a potential marketing lever for a brand. Twisting silk and wool together offers interesting retail marketing possibilities, expounding the contrasting but complementary qualities of both fibres. By contrast, a brand that is at a price-competitive level of the market could use a cashmere and wool mixture and market the luxury aspect of the product while not dramatically increasing the price.

In the search for something new to offer the designer, and ultimately the end consumer, traditional woollen yarns have been twisted with everything from cellophane to **metallic yarns** in the quest for creativity and to promote the use of traditional fibres with added technology.

Woollen spun yarn

Yarn that has gone through the carding and drawing processes is referred to as **woollen spun yarn**. As a result of these processes the fibres tend to lie in all directions, giving a fuzzy, textured appearance. Woollen spun yarns are perfect for knitwear of almost any machine gauge, producing sweaters that are soft, supple and comforting, while woollen spun fabrics tend to have a coarser **handle** with a less visible fabric structure than worsteds (see below). The fibres used are thicker and less even in length, making woollen spun fabrics a perfect medium for textured surfaces with high tactile fabric interest, such as tweed.

(above) Sleek, androgynous styling exemplifies a take on the modern urban uniform, here in a fine wool and polyester mix suit by Kostas Murkudis.

(right) Y.3 jersey dress with exceptional stretch, by Yohji Yamamoto for Adidas, exemplifying wool's flexibility and adaptability.

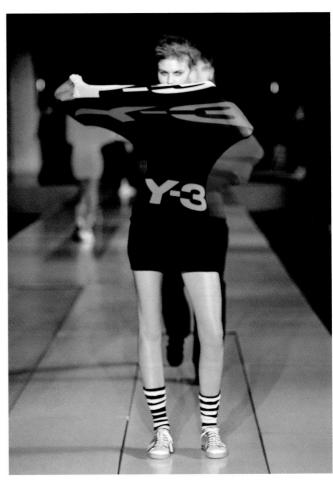

Worsted spun yarn

Yarn that is carded, drawn and in addition then also combed is referred to as **worsted spun yarn**. The fibres lie almost parallel to each other, so worsted spun fabrics tend to have a flatter, smoother finish and a much more visible fabric structure, and could be described as having a cleaner-cut appearance than their woollen spun equivalents. They are used for fine tailoring and dressweight fabrics, as well as some specialist knitwear, where a flatter, less 'woolly' texture is desired. The fibres used are finer and more even in length, making worsteds a perfect vehicle for fine tailoring.

Worsted wool

Worsted wool is the ultimate cloth for expressing precise and urbane classic tailoring. New wool blends lend contemporary deconstructed tailoring a drapeable and supple elegance that moulds to the body and is supremely comfortable.

Traditional wool tweeds can provide an authentic rugged durability or a soft and comfortable sporty feel in softer yarns. New fibre technologies have enhanced the natural thermal properties of wool and make it an ideal choice for performance and fashion sportswear.

(left) A fine grey worsted wool suit by Kris Van Assche highlights the natural drape of this classic tailoring fabric, conveying ease and elegance.

(top) Worsted suit by Edward Sexton, 2008 collection. In the late 1960s Edward Sexton and Tommy Nutter rejuvenated the once stuffy Savile Row with the spirit and verve of swinging London, and attracted a new wave of rock and pop celebrities.

(above) A classic 1964 Chanel jacket believed to be cut from Linton tweed. Chanel loved the heritage and practicality of British tweeds and collaborated with mills to modernize them with lighter yarns and unexpected colour.

Producing fabric: weaving and knitting

Once the yarns have been spun they are ready to be either knitted or woven into fabric. Specialist knitting factories and weaving mills will use selected yarns to produce the woollens, worsted fabrics or knitwear. Bi-annual yarn **trade fairs** will showcase their latest developments and new fashion colours. These trade fairs are ideally suited to knitwear and fabric designers, much more so than fashion designers. Each season's trade fairs are really the start of a new season's collection.

Wool fabrics

The fabrics listed here represent the most popular woollens and worsteds in use, and would give the designer or merchandiser an extensive selection for designing a range or building a collection. The list, however, is not exhaustive. The fabrics are all primarily made from woollen yarns, though some names are shared with other natural and/or synthetic yarns.

Textured traditional

These textured, historic fabrics, with a hand-loom provenance, express an authentic, robust, coarse, rugged aspect.

Tweed Generically describes coarse-textured woollen spun fabrics from Scotland, Ireland and Yorkshire, although Scottish in origin. Today they have been made lighter in weight and are available in all fashion colours. Tweeds are often prefixed with the town or area from whence they originated.

Harris tweed Originally hand-loomed tweed using vegetable dyes, from the Scottish Hebrides.

Donegal tweed Originally hand-spun, with coloured slubs woven into the fabric. Now a generic term for any similar fabric.

Cheviots Traditionally twill-woven outerwear fabrics made from Cheviot or cross-bred wool varieties.

Smooth and compact

These woollen fabrics have a lightly pronounced surface structure, a clean-cut touch and firm handle.

Barathea May be of woollen or worsted construction. Very flat in appearance with a very slightly raised surface.

Cavalry twill Twill weave with a more pronounced double twill.

Gabardine Twill weave with clear surface and fine diagonal rib effect.

Serge Even-sided twill weave. Although originally an Italian silk weave, it is now almost exclusively worsted and used for tailoring.

Venetian Firm touch sateen close weave with a slight matt sheen.

(above) Pure new wool tweed jacket by Timothy Everest.

(left) Herringbone is a classic two-colour design formed by the weave structure, which is created by alternately reversing a twill weave at regular intervals to produce the distinctive 'zig zag' effect.

(right) Prince of Wales is a traditional Scottish Glen Urquhart check, usually woven in black and white and featuring a characteristic coloured windowpane overcheck. The design was popularized by the Prince of Wales in the early twentieth century.

(left) This classic red wool Scottish tartan is sharply cut by Gabrielle Miller. The styling and proportion incorporate references to Regency menswear, and folkloric embroidery features on the jacket.

(right) A woven 'regatta' stripe tailored jacket in a smooth wool Venetian fabric takes inspiration from traditional menswear styling. Designed by Abyssinia Sollitt Davis.

Raised surface

Hopsack Plain weave with a pronounced surface resembling its name.

Panama Lightweight plain weave with a very lightly pronounced cross effect.

(right) Two colours are used in a twill weave construction creating a 'star' effect known as dogtooth or hound's-tooth. The same effect on a smaller scale is referred to as puppy tooth.

(left) Tattersall check, a traditional equestrian fabric, derives its name from an eighteenth-century racehorse auctioneers at London's Hyde Park Corner, long before it became London's premier address. Today the term Tattersall applies to fabrics of any fibre and checks of any scale, as long as they maintain the equestrian feel of the original fabric.

Iconic fabric designs

The historic fabric designs shown on pages 72–73 originated in the woollen textile industries of Scotland and England. They have been reinterpreted in other fibres, both natural and synthetic. They are constantly revisited by designers and have become instantly recognizable, even when their traditional status is subverted by re-proportioning and reinterpreting the designs in print, knit and even embroidery.

Shown here are:

Hound's-tooth

Prince of Wales

Glen Urquhart check

Tattersall

Herringbone

Tartans/plaids

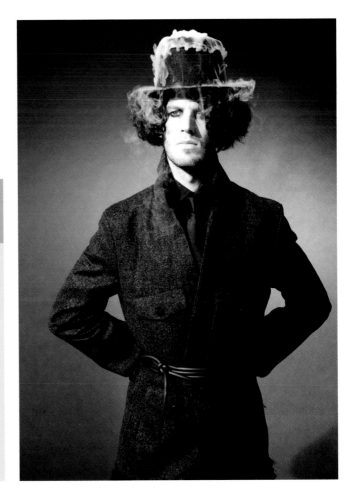

(right) Structure meets free spirit in this men's wrapped and tied jacket by Rui Leonardes. The designer reworks a classic flannel fabric by re-proportioning classic tailoring and interrogating the received wisdom of traditional fastenings.

Insulative

Warm and brushed with a cosy, tactile surface.

Flannel Used generically for many worsted spun fabrics. May be of plain or twill weave with napped surface to one or both sides.

Loden Brushed, raised surface, coating weight, originally from Tyrol. The name also implies a specific shade of green that camouflaged well into the local landscape.

Melton Thick, diagonal-weave fabric with a raised surface. Quite firm to the touch and used for outerwear.

Loopy

Fluffy, airy or granular in texture.

Bouclé The French word for 'curly', the fabric may be woven or knitted. The term is applied to a yarn or finished fabric with a curled surface.

Crêpe An all-over granular effect with a very dry touch.

Moroccan Heavy crêpe effect.

Sensual

Glamorous, light and fluid with expressive drape.

Challis Very lightweight plain weave with a soft touch.

Georgette Lightweight plain weave with a very fine crêpe effect.

Mousseline Generic term for very fine, semi-opaque fabric.

(above) A traditional wool-melton sculptural, arc-shouldered men's jacket by Rui Leonarde. The architectural silhouette is beautifully expressed by wool fibre, the close weave that forms the structure of this cloth.

(above) The bias cut and oversized blouson styling of this coat by Alexander McQueen emphasize the inherent drape and almost weightless character of this brushed wool and mohair fabric.

(right) Sumptuous oversized knit in violet wool by Josep Font, created by stuffing the large-scale plain knit with wadding and re-knitting to form the 'inflated' silhouette.

Luxury wool and lambswool

Luxury wools are considered to have special and more desirable attributes than standard wool varieties. Luxury wool fibres will usually be supplied with specialist labelling, a logo and appropriate brand advertising. This is a shorthand code to communicate the desirability of the product to the consumer. It also gives the confidence and knowledge of the product's key benefits.

Lambswool

Lambswool is taken from the first shearing, when the lamb is about six months old, and is especially fine and soft. It is ideal for extra-fine knitwear, especially when fully fashioned, and for superfine suiting fabrics. In the designing and production of a collection the use of lambswool should carry its own dedicated label.

Merino

Merino wool is a statement of luxury. It is soft and supple with year-round comfort.

The wool from the merino sheep is most prized, and considered the ultimate in wool luxury. The lightness, softness and springiness of its crimp make merino yarn a perfect vehicle for fine-quality luxurious clothing.

Superfine merino is one of the finest and softest fleeces of all, while ultra-fine merino wool is often used for blending with prestigious fibres such as silk, cashmere and alpaca.

An important characteristic of merino wool is the tightness and spring of its crimp, as well as the length of its **staple**, which varies from 6 to 10 cm in length. Each sheep produces between 3 and 6 kg of wool per year. Over time merino breeds have been genetically engineered to produce improved qualities of wool and, more recently, following fashion demand, lighter and finer counts of wool.

Merino sheep are valued for their fine wool. The finer the micron count, the more valuable the product.

Classifying merino

Ultra fine
Under 17.5 microns

Super fine
up to 18.5 microns

Fine
under 19.5 microns

Fine medium
up to 20.5 microns

Medium
up to 22.5 microns

Strong
over 22.6 microns

The merino was originally indigenous to Asia Minor, then introduced into Spain via North Africa by the Romans, where the breed developed and became an integral part of the economy. The sheep were so important to the Iberian economy that from the fifteenth to the seventeenth centuries they could only be exported with royal consent. Merino sheep also flourished in parts of England, France and Saxony, now southeast Germany.

In the 1790s a small flock of Spanish merino sheep was given as a prized gift to the governor of the Dutch Cape (South Africa). Eventually some of these were sold on and in turn transported to Australia, landing in Botany Bay. The temperate climate and lush pastures were perfect for the breed to thrive and prosper. Sheep rearing became so important an economic factor that it was a fundamental influence in Australia's key role within the British Commonwealth, with much of its economy linked to the breeding of merino sheep and the export of their wool.

Merino sheep are now successfully reared in New Zealand, South Africa, Argentina, Uruguay and in the west of the United States; however it is Australia that is the most important producer and exporter of merino wool.

The term merino was originally only used for Spanish-bred merino sheep, but the superior quality of the Australian, and later the New Zealand, strains means that the name is now used to describe merinos irrespective of country of origin.

Woollen underwear

In the late nineteenth century Dr Gustave Jaeger (1832–1917) pioneered 'the scientific theory of hygienic dress', which maintained that wool was the ideal fibre to wear next to the skin. He promoted the wearing of woollen undergarments for optimum health, based on the theories of wool's antibacterial properties. This practice was upheld in many countries, to some extent, through to the middle of the twentieth century.

Retro proportioned knitted hand-framed bodysuit by Finnish art brand IVANAhelsinki, whose ethos and production philosophy are based on ethical and ecological choices.

Australia's merino

Australia has four basic strains of merino.

Pepin: Considered to be the most important strain, thriving in drier inland regions, however its fleece falls into the mid-range of merino wool quality.

Saxon: Prefers cooler wetter regions; it is physically the smallest strain but produces the finest, most prized and most expensive quality of wool.

South Australian: Thrives in the most temperate climate and is physically the largest of the strains. The wool produced falls into the coarsest of the categories.

Spanish: The smallest in numbers and shares similar attributes to the pepin.

And wool is also marketed under the name **Botany wool** to denote wool originating from Botany Bay. The term is suggestive of very fine woollen knitwear and carries its own dedicated specialist labelling.

Merino clothing is made from the very best yarns, however in knitwear the term mainly refers to garments made from worsted spun yarns.

Ria Thomas is inspired by the landscape of the human body, and incorporates traditional knit techniques with a maverick approach to interpreting form in this pewter grey merino wool sweater dress.

78

Rambouillet or French merino

The **Rambouillet** breed is believed to have originated around 1786, when Louis XVI either received or purchased a flock of Spanish merinos from the king of Spain. The sheep were crossed with English long-wool breeds on a royal farm at Rambouillet near Paris, producing a well-defined breed that differed in several important points from the original Spanish merino. They were now of a far greater size, with larger wool **clips** and a longer wool length.

In 1889 the Rambouillet Association was formed in the United States with the aim of preserving the breed. Today about half of the sheep on the western ranges of the United States are of this strain. Rambouillet studs have also been of great importance in the development of the Australian merino industry.

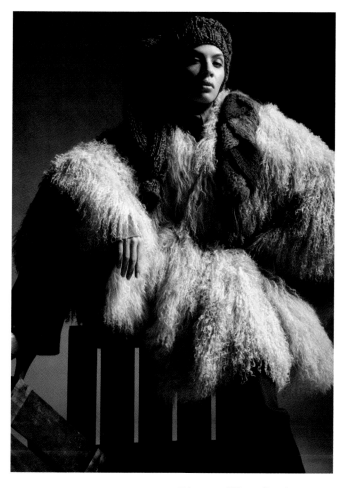

Extravagant Mongolian sheep-wool coat by Huwaida Ahmed. The exceptionally long and curly corkscrew locks are characteristic of Mongolian sheep wool.

Shetland wool

Shetland sheep are the smallest of all the breeds in the British Isles. They are of Scandinavian origin and believed to have been brought over by the Vikings.

From the cold climate of the Shetland Islands, Shetland fleece has a distinctive fine fibre quality in a range of natural shades, from off-whites to reddish brown, grey, dark brown and through to black, colours that traditional Shetland patterns are based on; furthermore the many natural colours of Shetland are in tune with current market demands for ecological yarns that have not been chemically dyed.

Traditionally, Shetland fleece was hand plucked from the sheep at the time when they would naturally shed their seasonal fleece, resulting in fine and soft wool.

Shetland wool conjures up romantic notions of traditional country tweeds and knitwear, often in **muted colours** that camouflage so well with the countryside. Warm, comforting and with a slightly wiry texture, Shetland wool fabric remains popular to this day.

Shetland colours

The different strains of Shetland sheep still carry the Old Norse names, which are also often used to describe the shades or colours.

Bleget Whitish grey.

Emsket Dusky blue to grey.

Eesit Shades of ash.

Moget Light brown, dark belly.

Shaela Shaded wool from dark to light.

Skeget Striped sides.

Skjuret Mixed brown and grey.

Under London label Colenimo, Japanese designer Aya Nakagawa, for the Autumn/Winter 2008 capsule collection, references the attitude of 1950s teddy boys and girls, and plays with feminizing masculine silhouettes and revisiting robust traditional fabrics. Here, a vintage 100 per cent Shetland wool conveys its rugged appeal and shows a contemporary take on the use of authentic fabrics.

(right) Undyed Shetland wool fibre from Hand Weavers Studios. This distinctive fibre comes in a natural colour palette ranging from off-white through to reddish brown, mid- to dark brown, grey and black. In addition to the traditionally crafted iconic country tweeds and knitwear, Shetland wool fabric has now become the perennial favourite of designers, attracted by the romance attached to the heritage surrounding the fibre.

Icelandic wool

In the late ninth century the Vikings brought sheep to Iceland. Over 1,000 years of isolation from contact with other breeds has maintained the purity of their gene pool, resulting in one of the purest and rarest breeds in the world. The sheep are reared in the high mountains where they produce fleeces considered to be among the rarest in the world, their rarity compounded by the fact that their numbers are diminishing annually.

Icelandic wool fleece is double layered, made up of a fine, soft, insulating inner fibre and long, glossy, coarser outer fibre. The inner fibre is as soft as cashmere and classified as fine wool, while the outer fibre is classified as medium wool. The structure of the outer fibre allows water to run down and not penetrate and its irregularity traps air, giving warmth.

Icelandic wool is lighter than most other wool types, and its minimal crimp makes it perfect for worsted spinning, the resulting yarn being lofty in appearance. The two fibres may be spun separately to create yarns of different weights that are suitable for different end uses, or spun together for a yarn that when knitted or woven would give maximum protection from the elements.

The Icelandic sheep has the largest natural colour shade range of any breed, from white to grey to a large selection of browns and black. Some sheep have a differing shade of inner fleece to their outer fleece. Left unshorn the fleece would grow to about 45 cm in a year, and therefore tends to be shorn twice a year.

Karakul wool

Karakul, or Persian lamb as it is often known, is from Central Asia, and is considered to be one of the first domesticated breeds, associated with the felted fabric that predated knitted or woven fabric. Today a large percentage of South African wool is from Karakul sheep. The wool has a tight curly pattern and tends to be in shades of grey to black. As a woollen yarn it is much sought after for expensive millinery, however it is most prized for its pelts.

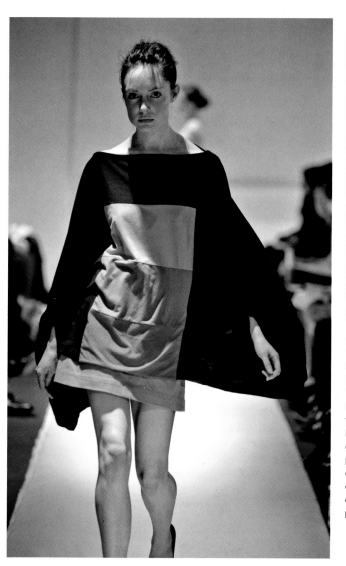

Useful wool terminology

100% virgin wool or 100% pure new wool The product has been produced from fibres that have not been previously processed.

100% wool The product is all wool, but possibly recycled or re-processed.

Mungo Fibrous woollen material generated from waste fabric.

Wool blends A mixture of different wools and/or other fibres.

Colour blocked tunic dress in 100 per cent pure New Zealand merino wool from new luxury eco brand rani jones' debut collection 'Block'. The company differentiates itself from other luxury women's wear labels by combining an innovative approach to design coupled with socially responsible principles and a commitment to exploring all environmental and ethical solutions throughout all the design, production and managerial processes.

Wool market

Australia is singularly the largest wool producer, supplying around 25 per cent of the world's consumption, most of which is exported to make yarn for the weaving and knitting industries. The greater majority of Australian wool is from merino sheep breeds.

New Zealand is the second largest exporter of fine wool, but is however the world's largest producer and exporter of cross-bred wool. The majority of the cross-bred wool (31.5 microns plus) goes to China to supplement its domestic production.

China produces both fine wools and cross-bred varieties. However, due to its importance as a global manufacturing hub it consumes the majority of its domestic production for its own manufacturing industries; the eventual end use is finished clothing for export. It is also a major importer of all wool qualities, which it uses to manufacture end products for export.

Uruguay is the third largest wool producing–exporting country in the world; however it is the second largest producer of clothing-weight wool. Around 10 per cent of its wool production is kept for domestic fabric consumption, which is ultimately also for export.

Argentina and South Africa are also key exporters of wool, followed by Turkey and Iran. Great Britain and Sudan produce around 2 per cent each. The United States – notably Texas, New Mexico and Colorado – produces around 1 per cent of the world's output.

The principal consumers of the good quality merino are Italy, France, Germany, Great Britain and Japan of which Italy and Japan use the very best for their sophisticated fully-fashioned knitwear industries.

Marketing wool

The marketing and promotion of wool is an important issue, which has been addressed nationally by the formation of various wool boards or associations that represent the wool growers of their respective countries. Collectively these offer a guaranteed standard of quality of the raw material that goes to the spinners and in turn to the fabric manufacturers. This quality standard is a selling and promotional tool for the design company, and in turn to the end consumer.

Australia: Woolmark

Woolmark is a registered mark used for branding different types of Australian wool, and is used as a means of guaranteeing a standard of quality. The Woolmark brands and sub-brands are designed to give the consumer confidence and knowledge of the product, as well as communicating the key benefits and promoting an awareness and understanding of the product's full potential. This is essential information for the designer because the choice of fabric, with the appropriate level of brand recognition, may give added value and increase the sales potential of the collection over that of a competitor.

WOOLMARK

The Woolmark trademark logo.

WOOLMARK BLEND

The Woolmark blend trademark logo.

WOOL BLEND

Wool blend logo products are high tech new wool mixes of 30–49% new wool that maintains the natural qualities of wool combined with offering comfort and performance.

WOOLMARK merino extrafine

Pure Merino Wool is premium quality wool. Naturally fine and silky, it is super-soft, lightweight and comfortable to wear.

WOOLMARK COOL WOOL

Logo for new generation of lightweight fabrics and knitwear.

wool plus LYCRA

Wool plus Lycra® is a dynamic mix of new wool and Lycra®.

WOOLMARK Natural Stretch

Logo for pure new wool with enhanced natural stretch. Through a special selection of fibers, this wool gives woven fabrics extra ease of movement, comfort and the elasticity to recover from daily wear.

light wool

Light wool is super lightweight wool that is truly cross-seasonal. Its ultra fine yarns make for the sheerest knitted and tailored clothing.

wool COTTON WOOLMARK BLEND

Wool and cotton logo.

wool LINEN

A special blend of yarns providing all the performance benefits of natural fibres.

GOLD WOOLMARK

The Gold Woolmark denotes an exciting new standard, differentiating luxurious garments made of the finest quality superfine Australian wool.

I.W.T.O.

IWTO (International Wool Textile Organization) is an International organization covering all aspects of marketing wool for all major producers.

The Woolmark logo is a registered trade mark of The Woolmark Company that is owned by Australian Wool Innovation and indicates high quality of woollen products. The Woolmark is an assurance by the manufacturer that a product is made of pure new wool. End products carrying these symbols have been quality tested by The Woolmark Company for compliance with its performance and fibre content specifications (Woolmark indicates 100 per cent). The Woolmark is one of the most recognized symbols globally and represents the world's largest fibre quality assurance scheme.

Ecological and ethical considerations

Wool is, or fundamentally should be, an ecologically sound product, but the increase of production and desire for consistency of quality, together with the concern for maximum return on investment, will mean that some aspects are not as ecologically or ethically sound as today's informed and aware consumer might wish.

The designer or company manufacturing the designs needs to have its target customers in mind when selecting the source of its fabrics. This is not always straightforward, because the supply chain from sheep rearing to fabric manufacturing has many stages that could have ecological and/or ethical implications. How deeply these issues are considered is really dependent on the brand's ethos and the target customer's expectations.

A fabric manufacturer or spinner that uses yarns from ethical and ecologically sound sources will place emphasis on these virtues, especially since the fabrics will tend to be more expensive. The eco-factor may be the **USP** (unique selling point) to justify the price differential. Similarly, sheep farmers that practice a more humane form of animal husbandry as well as sounder ecological grazing methods will also promote these aspects.

Ecological criteria

The International Wool Textile Organization (IWTO) has categorized eco-wool and organic wool for clarification at retail and consumer level. The three categories for classifying eco-wool are: eco-wool; eco-wool products; and eco-wool containing products. The three categories for classifying organic wool are: organically grown wool; organic wool product; and organic wool containing product.

The guiding criteria for ecologically sound wool should consider the following points.

Correct grazing for the flocks Appropriate field rotation minimizes soil erosion and reduces the chance of the sheep incurring internal parasites. Often sheep are crowded onto land, resulting in over-grazing, and thus destroying the vegetation. When a field becomes barren the grower brings in dry feed that can add additional veggie-matter to the fleece, which needs to be destroyed by means of harsh acids that can leave wool dry and over-crimped.

Clean water Unpolluted drinking sources.

A predator friendly environment Using well-trained sheep dogs.

Healthy veterinary practices Using only certain types of medications and supplements.

Soil chemical control Not using herbicides and pesticides on fields that sheep graze on.

Livestock chemical control Sheep are bathed in chemicals to ward off pests and insects, which may leave a residue and contaminate the ground water if used improperly. After shearing, harsh toxic chemicals are often used to clean the wool, as well as bleaching agents to whiten the wool during and after scouring.

Carbon footprint The distance of travel from primary source to final destination.

Hanging On, an exercise in deconstructed Fair Isle knit socks by Myka Baum, from the series 'A Load of Rubbish', inspired by San Franciscan performance artist Michael Swaine.

Recycling wool

The recycling of wool has always been part of the industry's production cycle. Old wool can be mixed with raw wool and wool noil, or alternatively with other fibres such as cotton. This is done to increase the average length of the recycled fibre, because the tearing process involved in its recovery tends to result in shorter fibres, making re-spinning and weaving difficult. Recycled wool is often used as weft yarns on products with cotton warps.

Fibre reclamation mills grade incoming materials into types and colours. The colour sorting means that little, if any, re-dyeing will be necessary, thus saving on energy and pollutants. The textiles are then shredded into **shoddy,** wool that is of inferior quality to the original wool product, made by tearing apart existing wool fabric and re-spinning it. Fibres are blended with other selected fibres, depending on their intended end use. The blended mixture is carded to clean the fibres and mix them together before being spun. Alternatively, the fibres can be compressed for mattress production or shredded to make filling material for car insulation, roofing felts, loudspeaker cones or other similar products.

A buyer or designer will need to check the fabric content label to ascertain the full composition of the fabric. Although it is a requirement that all fibres are disclosed, occasionally a content label may state 2 or 3 per cent marked as 'other fibres'. This is because it is not always possible to know the content of merchandise that may have already been previously recycled.

Make do and mend

The 'make do and mend' [scheme began] during the First and Second [World Wars, at a time as] clothing becam[e scarce]. [We can m]ix or customize our c[lothing to make it our ow]n. The act of repairing [... becomes a stateme]nt in itself, not only c[ommunicating a desir]e to be less wasteful, b[ut establishing a relatio]nship with our cloth[es].

Contemp[orary fashion brands have] embraced th[is concept through resear]ch and development [... darnin]g and patching tec[hniques... marke]t. These brands seek [to emulate the state of weary]ear and its desirable visual [appearance... objec]ts are perceived as authentic and steeped in another's history, even though that history does not always reflect the life experiences of the wearer.

Recycling has long been part of the industry's production cycle. Fibre reclamation mills grade incoming materials into types and colours, thus saving energy on unnecessary reprocessing before shredding into shoddy.

The wool shredder is an important part of the recycling process.

The 'Door to door darning' concept by San Franciscan performance artist Michael Swaine. He started the mobile 'free mending library' fixing clothes, telling stories and provoking the interrogation of our throwaway society.

85

Luxury animal fibres

The allure of these precious 'golden fleeces' is rooted in their exotic and romantic past. Their rarity is inextricably linked with a superlative level of quality and luxury that no man-made substitute can ever match.

The fibres that make up this luxury segment of the market are derived from several different groups of animals. The enduring appeal of these noble fibres is that despite amazing developments in textile technology, their classic luxury status remains unchallenged.

The creatures that produce these fibres have evolved coats of supremely soft and warm material, uniquely adapted to cope with inhospitable extremes of heat and cold. The coats contain the finest of hairs and an all-important under-fleece that is almost heavenly to the touch. Fabrics made from these fibres possess an inbuilt elegance that expresses refinement and the ultimate in luxury.

Musk ox
Qiviut

Angora rabbits

Nigora and Pygora
cross breed goats

Angora goat – Mohair

Camel (Bactrian/2 hump)
Cashmere goat
Yak (Tibet)

Angora goat – Mohair

Alpaca
Llama
Vicuna
Guanco

Cashmere goat
Alpaca

Principal spinning, weaving and knitting manufacturing countries

Principal markets for fabrics and finished products

The animals that provide some of our most valued and luxurious raw materials inhabit a diverse range of climates. Each of the animals shown on this map have coats that possess complex and unique properties that have evolved in response to the climatic challenges presented by different geographical locations, whether in natural or cultivated habitats.

(opposite page) Hand-knitted mohair. Referred to as 'golden fleeces', in acknowledgement of their rarity and desirability, the luxury animal fibres have whisper-light properties that lend them an ephemeral delicacy and exceptional thermal properties.

Camelids

A number of luxury fibres are harvested from a group of animals biologically known as the South American *Camelidae* family, which consists of four types of llama.

Alpaca

Alpaca yarn is ideal for loose spinning to produce a hard-wearing and very light garment, with great insulating properties.

The **alpaca** (*Vicugna pacos*) is a South American mountain animal; however, prehistoric remains have also been found in both the Rocky Mountains of North America and the Sierra Madre mountains of Central America. Principally found in Peru and Ecuador, smaller numbers are also found in the northern parts of Bolivia and Chile.

Superficially resembling a small llama, alpacas were domesticated by the Moche and Inca peoples of Peru, thousands of years before the Spanish conquest of South America. They were a crucial and treasured component of ancient life, used as beasts of burden and for their meat and wool. Now the alpaca is the principal South American fibre-producing animal.

The history of alpaca

In the early 1800s Spain 'rediscovered' the beauty of the alpaca's fleece, and imported the fibre, sending it to France and Germany for spinning.

Alpaca was first spun in England in the early nineteenth century, but was considered to be unworkable. This was in part due to the type of fabric being woven. By 1836, in Bradford, the centre of the English woollen textile trade, alpaca's true potential was realized when it was woven using cotton warps.

The trade in alpaca remained at a domestic level until the early 1950s, when proactive marketing of the processed fibre began.

The United States and Canada first imported alpacas in the early 1980s, followed by Australia and New Zealand later in the decade. The more sophisticated animal husbandry practiced in these countries has proven successful as the alpacas are fast multiplying, and through selective breeding are now producing heavier fleeces and finer fibres.

(above) Sam the suri alpaca, courtesy of Marsha Hobert at Suri Network.

(above) An evocative image of alpaca fibre sorting in Peru. Sorting fibres into colours and qualities is a skilled operation requiring a discerning eye and dexterity of hand.

(left) Contrasting fleeces from the suri and huacaya alpaca. Sorting through the fleece is skilled specialized work, which is done by hand.

88

Section 1: Animal fibres – Luxury animal fibres

Alpaca fibre

There are two types of alpaca. The **huacaya** (pronounced wua'ki'ya) produce a dense, soft sheep-like fibre with a uniform crimp. They are the most common in both their natural South American habitat and in the countries that have since imported them. The **suri** (pronounced soo'ree) have silky, pencil-fine, mop-like locks. Suris make up the remaining 20 per cent of the population and are prized for their finer, longer fibres. Both types are highly valued and regarded to be just below that of vicuña (see page 91) in quality. An alpaca–llama cross breed, **huarizo**, is also valued for its fine fleece.

Fibre from the huacayas is marketed as **alpaca fleece**, while the fibre from suris is marketed as **alpaca suri**.

In textile terms 'alpaca' refers primarily to **Peruvian alpaca**, which is marketed with a dedicated symbol of authenticity. However, the term is also used, more broadly, to describe a genre of fabric. Sometimes Icelandic wool is referred to as alpaca because of its similar visual appearance. Alpaca fleece does have some similarities to sheep's wool but it appears much lighter in weight, silkier to the touch, warmer and less prickly. It has minimal lanolin, making it nearly hypoallergenic. It is also impermeable, thermally responsive and has a low flammability point.

Alpaca production

Alpaca farming is of low impact to the environment and therefore an interesting alternative for some sheep farmers. The animals are sheared annually, producing a fleece grossing about 7kg; after removal of the **guard hairs** the net weight is about 3kg. In their native Andean habitat alpacas are generally sheared once every two years.

Alpaca fibres are processed in a similar way to sheep wool fibres (see pages 69–70).

Colour range

Alpacas naturally range in colour from jet black through warm browns, fawns and cool greys to creamy whites at the lightest end of the spectrum. The large range of colours and shades is a special characteristic of the breed and hence colour sorting is highly skilled work carried out by hand and eye: the most important part of the business. Depending on country of classification, fleeces can range from between 12 to 52 natural colours and shades: Peru classifies 52; the United States 22; and Australia 12.

Fashion demands have made white the commercially most desirable colour, and therefore the most expensive. This has led to selective breeding, resulting in the darker colours being almost bred out of the species. There is now a revival in the demand for the darker shades, which breeders are trying to reintroduce, however the quality is not quite as fine as that of white.

Alpaca's illusion

Alpaca is an enigmatic fibre, prized for its fine, soft and silky-like characteristics. The impression of fineness in alpaca is generated by the low scale height of the cuticle cells, which allows the hand to slide easily over the surface of the fibre.

The second part of alpaca's illusion is the apparent softness of the fibre. Technically it is not soft; in fact the resistance to abrasion of the cuticle cells is more than twice that of wool, a very hard surface. The 'softness' stems from its springiness and resistance to compression: resisting forming into a solid mass under compression gives the impression of lightness of weight. In wool production this is only achieved by scouring.

The enigma of alpaca lies in that it appears fine but is not, appears soft but is actually hard and strong. It has excellent thermal properties with apparent lightness of weight; it is durable and silky in texture.

89

(right) Oversized chunky alpaca and leather crochet coat worn with gunmetal metallic high-waisted knitted trousers by Julia Neil.

(far right) Heirloom inspired alpaca, leather and crystal sweater dress worn with violet cashmere vest and leggings by Julia Neill. Victorian chandelier crystals are integrated into the knit in crocheted frameworks.

Llama

The llama (*Lama glama*) is the largest of the South American *Camelidae* family, believed to have originated in the mountains of North America 40 million years ago and to have migrated south around three million years ago. They became essential pack animals as well as a source of protein for the indigenous Indian peoples of the Andes. The Spanish conquistadors used thousands of llamas as a means of transporting the spoils of warfare.

At present there is only a very small commercial market for llama fibre, and it tends to be favoured by hand spinners for organic and craft clothing.

Llama fibre

The four types of llama are the **curaca** and **ccara**, or classic 'light wool' llamas, and the **tapada** and **lanuda**, or 'heavy wool' llamas. Nearly 70 per cent of the world's llamas live in Bolivia, with a smaller number in Peru. However, because the first llamas imported into Europe were from Peru, it is the Peruvian terminology that is in common use today. Of the Bolivian llamas nearly 80 per cent are of the heavy, woolly-coated type, which have fleeces suitable for making yarn.

Technically **llama fibre** is not wool because it is hollow and has a structure of diagonal 'walls'; however, it is referred to as llama wool. The fibre is strong and light and has good insulation properties. It is thicker and coarser than alpaca fibre, with a diameter ranging from 20 to 40 microns. If the micron count is under 28 it may also be described as alpaca. By way of comparison, merino wool is between 12 and 20 microns.

Llama production

Llamas are low-maintenance animals with little impact on the environment.

They are efficient and adaptable frugal foragers and adjust well to free-choice feeding or once-a-day feeding schedules based on owner convenience. Llamas are shorn either once a year or once every two years. Their fleece comes in four main colours, ranging from white through grey, brown and black, and is grease free.

A llama in its indigenous Andean habitat, dressed in locally handcrafted adornments.

Vicuña

Inca legend states that the **vicuña** (*Vicugna vicugna*) is an incarnation of a beautiful maiden courted by an ugly old king. She would only concede to his advances if given a coat of pure gold. The vicuña's fleece is still referred to as the 'golden fleece', an accolade that is reflected in the stratospheric prices paid for the fabric.

The vicuña was the first of the *Camelidae* family to be domesticated by ancient Andean tribes of Peru. The Incas raised the vicuña for their wool and protected them by law, under penalty of death. The esteem in which these animals were held ensured their mystique, and only Inca kings and the royal court were permitted to wear garments made from vicuña wool.

Endangered and reinvigorated

The huge commercial demand for vicuña fibre and unrestricted hunting in the nineteenth and twentieth centuries resulted in the species becoming almost extinct. In 1960 there were only an estimated 6,000 vicuña left in the wild; it was declared an endangered species in the mid 1970s, and trade of the vicuña fibre was prohibited.

Anti-poaching efforts in Peru, Argentina and Chile, and to a lesser extent in Bolivia, led to a dramatic comeback, and now there are an estimated 130,000 in the wilds of Peru, 30,000 in Argentina and possibly 30,000 between Chile and Bolivia. All four countries relaxed the laws in 1993, and commercial harvesting is now being practised. Vicuña is now a '**cash crop**' that can benefit some very poor communities.

Peru has taken the lead in vicuña conservation. It has introduced a labelling system that shows that a garment has been created through a government-sanctioned **chacu**, an Incan tradition that guarantees that the animals are captured, sheared and released back into the wild; furthermore they will not be sheared again for another two years. The programme ensures that a large percentage of the profit goes back into village communities and to fund further research into the animals' protection.

Poaching, however, still persists, and 25,000 kg of fibre is still annually exported illegally. The animal is difficult to shear, so it is likely in this instance that they are killed for their fleece. To help prevent this illegal export, some countries have introduced a blanket ban on all vicuña fibres and fabrics.

Paco vicuña

The vicuña is the smallest of the wild South American camelids, and lives in the plains, grasslands and mountain regions of the Andes. DNA tests show that alpacas have vicuña ancestry, possibly due to selective breeding 6,000 years ago. Today 80 per cent of vicuña have llama DNA.

More recently, vicuñas have been cross-bred with alpacas, resulting in offspring called **paco vicuña**. Introducing vicuña into alpaca genetics has created a fibre that is as fine as that of the alpaca (14 to 16 microns) but with a fleece longer than that of the vicuña, making it easier to shear. It can also be shorn annually rather than only once every three years. All the other characteristics of the fibre are the same as that of the vicuña, making it just as desirable.

Vicuña fibre

Vicuñas have the finest of all animal fibres, with a diameter of between 6 and 14 microns. The outer guard hairs are about 25 microns, and are easily removed with sticks from the shorn fleece. The wool is very sensitive to chemical treatments, so it is always left in its natural colour, which is a rich, golden honey.

Vicuña fibres are extremely warm, due to the structure of tiny scales that surround the hollow, air-filled fibres, which lock together and trap insulating air.

The fleece yield of a vicuña is approximately 500 grams per year, in comparison to the 7 kilograms of the alpaca.

Vicuña production

A vicuña fleece weighs about 220 grams; it can take one person a week to **de-hair**. After washing, the remaining fibre will be about 100 grams.

Vicuña market

Peru is the principal exporter of vicuña, and garments and fabrics are registered with the Peruvian government authority, the only international body recognized for the task; it also assures quality and purity of fibre.

Current prices for vicuña fabric are from $1,800 to $3,000 per metre. Yarn is priced at around $500 per kilogram, and is the most valuable natural fibre. Italy is the primary global importer of vicuña cloth, while Germany is the primary global importer of vicuña clothing.

Guanaco

A larger cousin of the vicuña, the **guanaco** (*Lama guanicoe*) is found in the high plains of the Andes from the north of Peru to the south of Chile, Bolivia and Argentina. It is fast, wild and of a rich cinnamon honey colour. At the time of the Spanish invasion they numbered approximately half a billion, today they number a few hundred thousand.

The guanaco is double coated with coarse guard hairs and a soft undercoat similar to the alpaca, and is second only to the vicuña in quality. The guanaco is a protected species that needs a permit for hunting, to ensure that the fibre has been obtained from an approved source.

Camel hair

Camel hair has thermostatic properties that keep the wearer warm in winter and cool in summer, and is believed to contain anti-rheumatic and anti-arthritic properties.

Bactrian and **dromedary** are two species of camel, both Afro-Asiatic relatives of the South American family of camelids. The dromedary *(Camelus dromedarius)* is the one-humped desert-dwelling Arabian camel, which was the first of the two to be domesticated. The bactrian *(Camelus bactrianus)* has two humps and was first domesticated some 2,500 years ago in what are today the regions of northern Iran, Afghanistan, northern Pakistan and Turkistan, where temperatures are at hot and cold extremes between summer and winter. Apart from some wild bactrian camels in the Gobi Desert, and feral dromedary camels in Australia, camels are now completely domesticated.

Camel hair for commercial consumption is obtained only from the bactrian camel. The bactrian camels with the best-quality hair live in the extreme climatic conditions of Inner Mongolia (northern China) and Outer Mongolia. Camel hair also comes from Afghanistan, Iran, Russia and Tibet. Camels are not native to New Zealand or Australia but have been introduced to supplement their domestic fibre selection.

Camel-hair fibre

The fibres of the camel's down undercoat are between 2 and 10 cm in length, and do not felt easily. The outer coat has coarse long hairs that are used for carpets and bedding. Among the indigenous peoples of the area, the guard hairs are used to weave waterproof fabric for clothing, to withstand extreme weather conditions.

The mane of the camel is used for **interlinings** for good-quality tailoring. For clothing only the softer undercoat is used, either as pure camel hair or blended with lambswool. If it has been **tri-blended** with wool and a synthetic, then the camel hair is likely to be of an inferior quality, or possibly even recycled.

The very best camel hair is from the underside of a Mongolian baby camel. The fibres are approximately 25 to 60 mm long and 16 to 21 microns in diameter. At this standard it is almost comparable to cashmere (see page 94), and is the result of years of selective breeding. By comparison, adult camel hair has a diameter of approximately 21 to 25 microns.

Camel hair is traditionally used in its natural colour, golden tan with varying tones of red. Contemporary developments in dyeing technology allow it to respond to dye equally as successfully as wool; however, if dyed, it is often preferred in a range of faux natural colours, from blond to brown.

Fine fibre from the Asiatic bactrian camel, processed, cleaned and ready for spinning. As a fibre with a traditional appeal, camel hair is prized for its natural colour of golden tan with varying red highlights.

Camel-hair production

The production of camel hair is a five-step process of collecting, sorting, de-hairing, spinning and finally weaving or knitting.

Camel hair can be collected by combing or shearing, or gathered by hand when it sheds during the moulting season, which lasts for about six to eight weeks during late spring. The camel sheds its un-needed winter coat in clumps of outer hair and inner down, which grows back in the autumn.

The hair is sorted by separating the coarse hairs from the fine, soft hairs, then washed to remove all dirt and debris. The de-hairing stage is a mechanical process that removes the balance of the coarse hairs, dandruff and any vegetable matter, before sending the raw fibre to be spun, prior to weaving or knitting.

Camel-hair market

Italy is the principal destination for camel-hair fibre; the superfine baby camel-hair fibre goes to **Biella**, northwest of Milan, a centre for spinning and weaving fine woollen and worsted fabrics. The remainder goes to **Prato** near Florence, which is another important centre for Italian fabrics. The principal final destination of camel-hair clothing is the United States: no other global market has developed the same appreciation for camel-hair clothes, especially within the menswear sector.

(above) Baby camel-hair jacket by Timothy Everest.

(left) The distinctive red-cast golden tones of camel hair convey enduring associations with classic luxury outerwear. The natural colour palette of camel hair can span pale, sandy blonds and tans through to quite vibrant or deep ginger tones. The fibre itself responds well to modern dye technology but it is usually dyed in a range of faux natural colours to enhance or deepen the natural warm golden tones that make camel hair so desirable.

Goat fibre

Goats are from the *Caprinae* subfamily of the *Bovidae* family of animals, and are relatives of sheep. The domesticated goat is a subspecies of the wild goats of southwest Asia and eastern Europe, and is among the oldest domesticated species, dating back over 10,000 years.

Most goats have the capability to yield fibre; however, the most important fibre-producing goats are the cashmere and **angora goats**. Additionally, within the last few decades three hybrid goats have been developed that also produce commercial quantities of fine fibre.

The proud and elegant cashmere goat shows off its fine and valuable coat. In Mongolia and parts of China the age-old method of hand combing the fleece is preferred to shearing, which is a faster process but results in a coarser hair content and a lower pure-down yield.

Cashmere

Cashmere goats originated high up in the plateau regions of the Himalayan mountains. The local Kashmiri population would spin the fibre from the goat's downy undercoat, weave it into fine fabric and make it into shawls known as **pashmina** – a term derived from the Persian word *pasham*, meaning 'goat wool'. The pashmina shawls were highly valued by the colonial British who ruled Kashmir during the eighteenth and nineteenth centuries, and were exported all over Europe. The fabric from which they were made was referred to as cashmere, named after the province of Kashmir from where they originated.

In India and Pakistan the fibre is still referred to as *pasham*, while the rest of the world knows it as cashmere, a name synonymous with luxury. Unfortunately, by association with inferior man-made copies, pashmina now commonly refers to a style of shawl, as opposed to the rare fibre itself. A genuine pashmina shawl is still hand-spun and made of pashmina wool – cashmere.

Cashmere fibre

Cashmere is not a breed of goat, but a description of a goat that has been carefully bred to produce a fine downy undercoat, the cashmere fibre. Many different breeds can produce cashmere to some degree; however, it is the **Himalayan mountain goat** *(Capra hircus laniger)* that is popularly known as the cashmere goat.

For goat fibre to be considered natural cashmere it must be under 18.5 microns in diameter. No more than 3 per cent of the down may be over 30 microns. The ratio of fine down to coarse guard hair needs to be above 30 per cent. The fibre should measure at least 3.175 cm long, be low in lustre and have a good crimp. Cashmere from Outer Mongolia and the Inner Mongolian parts of China is of the best quality. Much of this is due to the extreme climate of this sub-Siberian land, which seems to encourage the goats to grow a finer, denser under-hair.

Through years of selective breeding, Chinese goats now yield the most amount of fibre, producing over 1 kg of raw fibre per goat, of which the under-fleece (the cashmere) is about 500 g. The 50:50 ratio of cashmere down to guard hairs represents an excellent yield; in some countries the goats yield approximately 500 g of raw fibre of which only 150 g is the all-important under-down. This 30 per cent ratio of guard hair to under-down is the minimum allowed for classification as cashmere.

It is a misconception that the best cashmere down comes from the neck and belly; these are, in fact, the dirtiest parts, because they tend to collect debris. The best fibre comes from the saddle of the goat, from the sides and back and from the shoulders to the rump. The fleece has long coarse outer hairs and extremely fine, soft and silky under-hairs that are 25 to 80 mm long with a diameter of 12 to 19 microns. The natural colours of cashmere range from light fawn to brown; however white is the most sought-after colour.

The fibres are very adaptable and can be spun into either fine or thick yarns, and similarly be woven into light or heavyweight fabrics. The guard hairs are almost worthless because they cannot be spun or dyed. They are used for brushes and interlining canvas. Like wool, cashmere has a high moisture content that allows the insulating properties to change with the relative humidity in the air. It is, weight for weight, warmer than wool.

(right) Quirky British retro styling and a sophisticated colour palette showcase the contemporary appeal and premium quality of Johnston's of Elgin products. Johnston's are the only remaining vertical mill in the UK, which transforms cashmere and other luxury fibres from the raw fibre through to the finished garment.

In this design by Markus Lupfer for Armand Basi modern understated luxury meets contemporary styling. The top is 100 per cent cashmere and the trousers 100 per cent wool.

Practical luxury

Classic men's underwear styling reinterpreted in a superfine cashmere knit by Casa de Cashmere. Contrary to popular belief cashmere fibre is relatively robust and responds well to either hand or delicate machine washing.

Cashmere production

Although an important and profitable fibre, global cashmere production is believed to be around 1 per cent of the total textile market, putting into perspective the uniqueness of this luxurious fibre.

The traditional method of harvesting cashmere is hand combing, which remains the preferred technique in Mongolia and parts of China. In Iran, Afghanistan, Australia and New Zealand the cashmere fibre is removed by shearing, which is a faster method but does result in a higher coarse-hair content and a lower pure-down yield. Combing is carried out using a coarse comb, which is pulled through the goat's fleece to remove the loose tufts. This usually happens in spring, when the animal is naturally shedding its winter coat. Hand combing can take between one and two weeks to complete, but does result in a far better yield, as well as finer and softer fibres for future harvesting.

The fibre is collected from the farmers and sorted by hand and eye in factories within the same regions as the goats are herded. Efficient sorting is crucial to the production of cashmere, and the fibres need to be graded by quality and colour: it is essential that no dark fibres be mixed with white fibres. Once sorted, the fibres are washed to remove coarse hairs, dirt and vegetable matter.

The de-hairing stage removes the coarse outer guard hairs from the soft under-down, which is the all-important component then used for spinning. The technology for de-hairing cashmere was developed in the nineteenth century in Bradford, Yorkshire, then the centre of the British woollen textile industry. Its pioneer, Joseph Dawson, guarded the secret of this complex process, which ensured exclusive production. The technology has since spread, breaking the monopoly of a few specialist cashmere spinners. Investment, as well as European and Japanese technical expertise, has now brought Chinese de-hairing to a high enough standard of quality for the cashmere knitters of both Scotland and Italy.

The fibres are then traded internationally. The majority are sold to Italy, Japan and Scotland, the three principal countries renowned for sophisticated and innovative cashmere spinning, knitting and weaving. **Johnston's of Elgin** of Scotland is the oldest cashmere mill still in operation.

Cashmere market

The annual global yield of pre-cleaned fibre is approximately 10,000 tons; after cleaning the remaining pure cashmere is approximately 6,500 tons. Today about 60 per cent of the world's raw cashmere production comes from China. Outer Mongolia contributes about 20 per cent and is the second largest global producer. Iran, Afghanistan, India, Pakistan and a few Central Asian republics produce the remainder.

Mohair

Mohair, from angora goats, is a luxury fibre that is desired all over the world. It is admired for its lustre, its softness and its strength, and may be one of the oldest animal fibres still in use.

The history of mohair

Angoras are an ancient breed of goat, and the first records of them being used for fibre purposes date back to the fourteenth century BC. Some believe they were native to the Anatolian plateau region of what is now modern Turkey, while others believe their true origin is the Himalayan plateau, the regions around Tibet and Mongolia. Legends tell of the goats trekking westward to Anatolia in great nomadic caravans with Suleiman Shaa when fleeing the advances of Genghis Khan and his Mongol armies around 1240 to 1245. They finally settled in the region of Ertena or Angora, now part of modern-day Ankara and its surrounding land. The sultans of the Ottoman Empire banned the export of the raw fleeces to try to keep the precious fibre exclusive.

The Holy Roman Emperor, Charles V, came across the angora goats in the 1550s at the time of his ongoing conflicts with the Ottomans. He tried to introduce the goats into Europe but the attempts were not successful as the breed is neither hardy nor prolific, and has high nutritional requirements.

Until 1847 the Ottoman province of Ankara was the only producer of angora goats and fibre. They were then imported into the United States and South Africa. Some were later bred on Navajo Indian Reservations, where the purity of the stock was compromised through interbreeding, resulting in angoras with fleeces of different colours. It is believed that current **coloured angoras** originate from these mid-nineteenth-century hybrids. In the twentieth century the goats were imported into Australia, but only reached Great Britain in the early 1980s.

The fleece of the angora goat is known as mohair. The desirable and valuable mohair fibre is protected firstly by a coarse outer kemp fibre and secondly by an intermediate medullated fibre.

Mohair fibre

Mohair fibre is white, smooth and lustrous with a high tensile strength. It is composed of keratin, a protein substance. A cross section of mohair will be slightly elliptical compared to wool, which is rounder. The scales on the fibre are larger but lie flatter, making the fibre smoother and therefore more light reflective, hence the lustre.

There are three levels of fibre to an angora fleece. The **kemps**, which are coarse, hollow, stiff and opaque, are often pigmented and undesirable because they are scratchy. The **medulated fibres** are less coarse than the kemps but coarser than the true mohair fibres, and have an interrupted or partially hollow core. They are often as long as the true mohair fibres, but still less desirable. Finally there are the true mohair fibres, from the fine under-down.

Good mohair fleece is made up of locks or ringlets of fibre held in place by their natural curl. It has a light oil-like sheen and a good staple length. The fleece has natural grease called **yolk**, its purpose to protect the fibre from the sun, rain and dust, and help hold the locks in place. Too much grease is difficult to wash out, while too little makes the fleece look dull. Goat grease is not the same as lanolin from sheep.

Kids are usually born in the spring with a coat of kemp hairs, which shed and are replaced with fine mohair ready for the first clip in the autumn. It is this first clipping that produces the finest fibre, although this only represents about 15 per cent of the total yield. The second clipping is in the spring when the kid is about one year old; this also produces a good fibre, ranging between 20 and 24 microns in diameter. Thereafter, each clipping is at six-monthly intervals, with the fibre getting progressively coarser, increasing in diameter as the animal ages. Fibre from older animals tends to be used for carpets and upholstery fabric.

The mohair fleece of a well-nourished angora goat will grow at a rate of 25 mm per month. The fleece of bucks (males) becomes coarser faster, but they produce more fleece than does (females). An average buck will yield approximately 6 kg of **skirted** (stain removed) fibre per annum, while a doe will produce about 2 kg less. Castrated males (wethers) produce excellent fibre; it does not coarsen as fast as that of bucks, but is heavier than that of does.

The ideal fibre is long in staple length with a minimum of kemp. It is durable, resilient and has moisture-wicking properties, as well as being flame- and **crease-resistant**.

Mohair production

Angoras are not as hardy as cashmere goats. They have very exacting demands, require dry climates and can perish from pneumonia if wet or cold. They have high nutritional requirements, which are needed to supplement their fast-growing fleece. They like a variety of shrubs and need an active life. If an angora's social and nutritional needs are well met, then it will yield a good-quality and substantial fleece.

The goats need to be brushed and groomed regularly to ensure the best possible coat at shearing. A clip (shearing) needs to be done in a clean environment to ensure there is no contamination. Goats are separated into age bands and clipping starts with the youngest, to prevent the coarser older hairs being mixed with the more valuable finer ones. Ideally a single cut will produce better results than second cuts. The micron count is based on the age of the animal.

In some climatic conditions, an unshorn strip, called a cape, is left along the spine to protect the goat from catching a chill after shearing.

Mohair fibre is made up of locks or ringlets held in place by natural curl. It has a high tensile strength and moisture-wicking properties.

The coarse kemps need to be removed after shearing, and the fleeces are graded into four categories according to their quality, taking into consideration micron count, colour, lustre, smoothness and general cleanliness.

The fleeces are processed to remove vegetable matter and natural grease. Mohair should be washed before spinning, and it can withstand very hot water without damaging. The use of detergent aids the removal of the grease, and final rinsing in vinegar or denatured alcohol will bring out the natural shine and lustre of the fibre.

Mohair market

South Africa and Lesotho produce over 50 per cent of the total output of mohair, followed by the United States (Texas), where the breeders are subsidized by the government. Turkey and Argentina also produce mohair fibre, as do Australia and New Zealand; their combined yield is about 6 per cent.

Cape (South Africa) mohair is the most sought-after because the animals have been genetically selected to produce minimal amounts of kemp fibres.

France, Italy, Germany, Portugal and Great Britain are all producers of mohair fabric and garments. France and Italy also specialize in mohair yarn for knitting. Japan is considered to be the largest importer of mohair fabric, especially for tailoring, because it makes ideal trans-seasonal clothing.

Total global production of mohair represents only about 1 per cent of the global natural fibre production.

Coloured mohair

The predominant fleece colour is white, while coloured fleeces are rare but becoming more popular. Coloured angoras are a hardier variety with less grease, and their fleece would be described as wavy. There are three colour groups: those that range from brown to black; those that range from tan through apricot to red; and those from silver to blue roan. The diversity of colour is not easily duplicated with artificial dyestuffs. They are, however, sometimes over-dyed to produce a deeper intensity of colour. Naturally coloured mohair fleeces are popular with hand spinners.

New York designers Rodarte playfully reinterpret the iconographic punk mohair sweater for the twenty-first century with this luxury destroyed-chic mohair cobweb-knit dress with matching stockings.

98

Pygora

A **pygora** is a purposeful cross between an angora goat and cashmere-producing pygmy goat, introduced in the late 1980s on a Navajo Indian Reserve in the North American state of Oregon. Pygoras come in a range of colours from light to dark caramel, greys, browns, blacks and cream. They produce three distinct types of fleece.

Type A fleece: Mohair-like fleece with fibres of 16 cm long – or longer – that drape in ringlets. It usually has a single coat or, if with guard hairs, they are very few and silky-fine. The micron count is 28 or under.

Type B fleece: Combination of cashmere and mohair qualities. The fibres are 8 to 16 cm with very few guard hairs and a micron count of approximately 24.

Type C fleece: The most cashmere-like. Very fine with fibres of between 2.5 and 8 cm long and a micron count of less than 18.5.

Although the fibre is used for clothing purposes, it is much favoured by fibre artists for tapestry and other similar work. The harvesting process is similar to that of other goats, although it is preferable that the fleece be washed while it is still on the sheep, as opposed to after harvesting.

Nigora

The **nigora** is a purposeful cross between an angora goat and cashmere-producing Nigerian dwarf goat. Those that are predominantly angora are classified as 'heavy nigora' because of their larger size and larger fleece. Those that are predominantly Nigerian dwarf are classified as 'light nigora' for their smaller size and fleece. Nigoras produce three distinct fibre types.

Type A fibre: Most closely resembles mohair. It is a lustrous fibre, cool to the touch, that hangs in long curly locks of approximately 150 mm. The fleece should be a **single coat** free of guard hairs. The goat needs to be shorn between once and twice a year.

Type B fibre: The most prevalent, referred to as **cashgora**. A good blend between cashmere and mohair, a cross between types A and C. It is a lofty, fluffy fibre between 70 and 150 mm long. Cashgora is a fleece made up of three fibre components: outer coarse guard hairs; fine crimped down, or the 'cash' component; and the intermediate, or the 'gora' component, which is longer, straighter and shiny. It can be shorn once a year or combed or plucked, or allowed to shed naturally.

Type C fibre: Often commercially acceptable as cashmere. The fibres are fine, from 25 to 75 mm long, without lustre but warm to the touch. Harvested similarly to cashgora.

Australian cashmere goat

The **Australian cashmere goat** is a hybrid and a different breed from the 'standard' Himalayan goats that produce the bulk of the world's cashmere.

Goats were introduced to Australia by the Dutch and Portuguese long before it became a British settlement. In the nineteenth century there was a movement to develop cashmere and angora farming and selective breeds were imported from India and China. However, the industry was never developed and the goats were allowed to become feral.

Cashmere was 'rediscovered' in the early 1970s when two researchers identified the down on some feral, or 'bush' goats. With a further 25 years of selective breeding the goat has now evolved into a distinct breed far removed from its bush parentage.

Australian cashmere is hardy with an excellent dense, even fleece and with a good differentiation between guard hairs and down.

A conceptual image for Timothy Everest showing mohair suiting and hair canvas interfacing. Mohair comes in many guises; it is especially favoured for fine tailoring as the structure of the fibre lends itself to enduring form. Any crease in fine mohair tailoring will just drop out when given the lightest amount of steam thus making it perfect for executive travel.

Alternative animal fibres

Luxury fibres are also harvested from **yaks**, **qiviuts** and angora rabbits.

Yak hair

Yaks *(Bos grunniens)* were domesticated in the first millennium BC in what is now Tibet. They inhabit the steppe regions around the Himalayan plateau, living above the snow levels during warmer summer months and descending to lower levels in the colder winter months. The majority of yaks are domesticated, however there is a dwindling number of vulnerable wild yaks remaining.

In the Tibetan language *yak* refers only to the male, but in English it refers to both the male and female animal.

Yaks are an essential aspect of the Himalayan mountain community, being used as beasts of burden and for their meat, milk, fibre and skin. The majority are to be found in China, however all the Himalayan regions have a yak population.

There are several species of yak. The **henduan** from the alpine regions of Tibet produces the best yield, while the **jiulong** from the plateau regions has the best fibre.

Yak-hair fibre
Yak fibre is structurally different to sheep fibre: the angle between the scales and the hair shaft on the external surface of the fibre is smaller than that of wool, so the scales stick to the shaft and feel smoother. It also has greater tensile strength than sheep's wool.

The hair is made up of three components, the coarse outer guard hairs, which are layered in several different lengths, a woolly centre part and the fine down undercoat. The percentage of each varies with age, sex and geographic location, as well as which part of the body the fibre has been taken from. Good animals produce a ratio of about 50 per cent down to 50 per cent hair.

The guard hairs exceed 52 microns in diameter and are only used for making rugs and rope. The mid-hair is between 25 and 50 microns with fewer large crimps. The desirable soft down, which grows before the onset of winter and sheds in the late spring, is under 25 microns in diameter with irregular crimps and a soft lustre. Fibre length after cleaning and de-hairing is between 3 and 4 cm long with a micron count of about 18.5.

Yak fibre tends to be quite even in thickness, has a cashmere-like feel and is very lofty. A one-year-old yak produces fine fibre of between 15 and 17 microns with a length of 4 to 5 cm. Wild yak hair is usually black, while domesticated animals range from black through brown and shades of grey. White underbelly hair is the most rare and thus the most valuable.

Since the 1970s the fibre has been seen as an alternative to fine yarns such as cashmere. However, currently the fibre is of little economic value compared to other yak by-products, and therefore it has not been fully exploited. There are now considerations to develop strains that have a better fibre for production.

Yak-hair production
Yak hair is either combed or pulled in the late spring when the animal sheds its winter coat naturally. On average an animal produces approximately 100 g of fibre annually. The fibre of yaks imported into North America is often spun with silk or lambswool for a unique selling feature. Yak wool is not a commercially viable mass-consumption fibre, but is an interesting alternative favoured by craft spinners, knitters and weavers.

Yaks live on the high steppe regions of the Himalayan plateau and are essential to the local community for their hair, milk, meat, and for carrying loads. Their dung is even burned as fuel.

Qiviut

Qiviut (pronounced kiv-ee-yut) is the under-wool of a musk ox (*Ovibos moschatus*) from the Arctic regions of Canada, Alaska and Greenland. The animals live in the wet riverbeds in the summer and ascend to higher elevations in the winter months. Qiviut, an Inuit word, has long been used to make warm clothing for the local inhabitants; however, since the 1960s cooperatives have been established to encourage the commercial production of qiviut wool from domesticated animals in Alaska and the Arctic regions of Canada, with the revenue used for local communities.

Qiviut fibre

Qiviut is stronger and eight times warmer than wool. It is also softer than cashmere and vicuña, with a micron count of 18. The animals are never shorn, instead the wool is always plucked during the spring moult, which leaves in place the guard hairs, which do not moult.

Qiviut is not a highly commercial fibre, but it does make interestingly fine knitwear.

Qiviut production

An adult musk ox can produce up to seven pounds of qiviut a year. In the spring the qiviut loosens from the animal's skin as it starts to moult. At this stage the undercoat is short but a fairly uniform distance from the skin, and lends itself to being combed from the animal in a single large sheet.

(above) Raw qiviut ready to be processed for spinning. The protective guard hairs and intermediate fibres are first removed before the fine fibre can be spun.

(right) The under-wool, or qiviut, of the musk ox is obtained by hand combing, a process that takes several hours. The animal is never sheared, because it needs its outer hair for protection against the elements.

Tibetan antelope

Although classified in the *Antilopinae* subfamily of the *Bovidae* family, the Tibetan antelope *(Pantholopas hodgsonii)* is now considered to be a closer relative of the *Caprinae* subfamily, or goat. This migratory animal moves around the Tibetan plateau regions of Mongolia, Tibet, India, Nepal and Xìzàng (China), and is traditionally followed by nomads. The animal sheds its down once, nearing the milder regions of the Tibetan plateau, which the nomads would gather and trade with the people of the Kashmir valley. The highly skilled local spinners and weavers made this finest of fibres into shawls called **shatoosh**.

The fibre measures between 9 and 10 microns and is grey to reddish brown in colour, although white from the underbelly is also used. When woven the fabric is so fine that it is almost translucent; it is possible to pull an average-sized shawl through a wedding ring.

The ruling British, during the period of the Raj, were so enamoured with this wonderful product that they exported it to Europe, where its luxury status made it so desirable that the animal became almost extinct. It was hunted down and killed, because this was quicker than waiting for it to moult naturally. Today it is still a rare and endangered species. Through the Convention of International Trade in Endangered Species it has been made illegal to trade or own a shatoosh shawl, but illegal hunting is still a problem in Tibet and the fibre is still traded on the black market.

Angora rabbit

The angora rabbit is believed to be one of the oldest breeds of domesticated rabbit, and is bred for its fine, long silky hair. It was a popular pet with the French nobility in the mid-seventeenth century, from where its popularity spread to other European courts. It first appeared in the United States in the early twentieth century.

Within Europe, France and Germany are important producers, however China dominates global production at over 80 per cent of the total yield. Chile is also important to angora production.

Angora fibre

Angora hair falls into two categories: French type, with more guard hairs and a spikier appearance; and German type, which is almost free of guard hairs and is softer.

The average fibres are between 11 and 13 microns in diameter and 36 mm in length, although the lengths vary. Super-grade angora has a fibre length of 70 mm, although China, the world's largest producer, specifies a minimum of 38 mm.

The principal fibre-producing breeds are:

French: One of the oldest breeds with more guard hairs and a woolly undercoat.

German: This breed tends to produce a higher fibre ratio to weight of animal. They have also been cross-bred with other breeds and produce a variety of colours.

Giant: The largest breed, bred for an abundant yield on small food rations. It has three types of hair, under-wool, awn fluff and awn hair. Awn hairs are the intermediate hairs, which are shorter than guard hairs but longer than the down.

Satin: Cross breed with the softest and finest fibre, said to be the strongest for spinning.

(left) Fine hand-knitted mohair yarn by Habu Textiles.

(above) Angora rabbits thrive on careful grooming and feeding, the reward of which is a fine, soft fibre. Knitted angora garments radiate an almost halo effect.

Angora production

Angora rabbits are albinos and therefore kept in semi-darkness. For a superior, large fibre yield it is important that the animals are well fed and well groomed. Their long hair needs to be combed at least once every two days in order to prevent it from matting and felting.

The fleece can either be shorn or plucked. French Angora production usually involves plucking following a depilatory-inducing injection. This method will produce finer fibres, but does leave the animal in a state of shock. The alternative popular method is to shear. Due to their fast hair growth they are shorn three to four times each year, producing an annual yield of up to 1 kg of fine hair per rabbit. The guard hairs that are then removed represent about 2 per cent of the yield.

After spinning, angora may be used for knitting or weaving. It is however more popular in knitwear, where its **halo effect** is much admired. It is also used to create novelty effects in woven fabrics. As it has no elasticity it should be blended with wool, an 80 per cent angora to 20 per cent merino ratio will still retain the halo effect.

(left) Whisper-light, delicate lacy knit batwing sweater in mohair, wool and polyamide by Finnish art brand IVANAhelsinki. Their design ethos is underpinned by a commitment to traditional handcrafts and their production philosophy is based on ethical and ecological choices.

(above) Jean Paul Gaultier subverts the traditional craft of Aran knit, glamorizing its practical provenance by interpreting it in a fluffy, luxurious yarn and creating open lattices between the traditional cable designs.

(right) Knitted angora hat clearly showing the 'halo' that this ultra-fine fibre has when it traps the light, producing an angelic downy effect.

Silk

Silk is such a seductive, luxurious and desirable fibre that its price has, at times, exceeded that of gold.

Silk possesses a magnificent, shimmering richness that can express a lush, sumptuous personality when woven into precious satins, jacquards and brocades. It is also capable of a sensuous, supple, liquid drape that will be forever associated with the ultimate in luxurious lingerie and glamorous eveningwear.

Silk is widely perceived to be the most beautiful and elegant of all the natural fibres, and even after more than a century of attempting to provide a man-made substitute, no single synthetic fibre has come close to replicating either the magical, myriad properties of silk or the breadth of applications that it can embrace.

Natural fabrics have been the fashion designer's frequent choice, but silk has remained the designer's dream.

The history of silk

Contributing significantly to silk's mystique is its long history, laden with evocative tales of legendary romance and adventure. Silk is one of only a handful of commodities that has shaped world history.

China

The ancient Chinese developed the art of cultivating the delicate **silk moth** and produced threads of incredible quality. The ruling dynasties were acutely aware of their precious commodity, and managed to possessively guard the complex secrets of **sericulture** from the rest of the world, therefore becoming the sole cultivator and producer of silk for many centuries.

An enduring ancient Chinese legend reveres the Lady Hsi-Ling, favoured and chief wife of the Emperor Huang Ti (2677–2597 BC), as the 'lady of the **silkworms**'. Her serendipitous discovery reputedly came when a **cocoon** dropped from a mulberry tree into her cup of hot tea. She then wound the resulting thread around her finger, thus supposedly accidentally discovering the principle of **reeling** silk. Contemporary archaeological excavations, however, suggest that sericulture had long been established in China by this date.

(left) Graphic shift dress in red and black 'changeant' silk, featuring an oriental silkscreen print by Manish Arora.

(opposite page) This beautiful shot-silk pleated scarf by textile artist Karren K Brito uses the traditional Japanese technique of shibori .

The earliest examples of cultivated silk date back to around 3000 BC, and evidence of cocoons goes back to 5000 BC. There is also evidence of small quantities of **wild silk** being produced in the Mediterranean area, India and the Middle East by the time the superior quality and stronger cultivated silk from China began to be exported. The original wild ancestor of the *Bombyx mori* is believed to be *Bombyx mandarina* moore, a silk moth particular to China, and which lived on the white mulberry tree. This uniquely superior moth was the key to China's domination of the cultivation, production and artistry of this natural resource.

Initially, the development of this luxury fibre was seen as frivolous, and sericulture was restricted to women. The allure of the fabric quickly provoked a craze and it rapidly became so completely fundamental to Chinese life that out of the 5,000 most-used characters in Mandarin Chinese, 230 incorporate the symbol for silk. The imperial family decreed strict regulation on its use and for 1,000 years the right to wear silk was restricted to the emperor, the imperial family and the highest dignitaries. Later, other members of society were permitted its use. Peasants did not have the right to wear silk until the time of the Qing Dynasty (1644–1911).

Silk's use was confined to China until the **Silk Road** opened up trade around the second century BC. Silk fabrics and products were exported in large quantities all over the known world, to as far away as Rome. However, the mystery and intricacies of sericulture remained a secret that the Chinese guarded carefully.

China's virtual monopoly on production of silk was maintained for another 1,000 years, enforced by an imperial decree condemning to death anyone attempting to export silkworms or their eggs. Sericulture was eventually taken outside of China in the second century AD. Legend tells of a Chinese princess who was to be married to a prince of Khotan (now Hotan in Xinjiang Province) concealing the silk cocoons in her elaborate coiffure and smuggling them to her adopted country. The introduction of sericulture made Khotan, positioned at the southern end of the Silk Road, very prosperous.

The Silk Road

The Silk Road, or Silk Route, is an interconnected series of ancient trade routes, through various regions of the Asian continent, that connected China with Asia Minor and then the Mediterranean. It extends over 8,000 km across land and sea. The routes linked Antioch and the coasts of the Mediterranean to Beijing, with a journey time of about one year. In the south a second route went via Yemen, Burma and India.

The trade that took place on these routes played a significant role in the development of the great civilizations of China, Egypt, Mesopotamia, Persia, the Indian subcontinent and Rome, and helped establish the foundations of the modern world.

Europe
The earliest record of the cultivation of silk in Europe was made by Greek philosopher Aristotle, who described the metamorphosis of the silkworm, and suggested that the produce of the cocoons was wound onto bobbins for the purpose of being woven. The very origin of the term sericulture is derived from the Greek word *ser*, meaning 'silk'. **Raw silk** was brought from the interior of Asia and manufactured in Cos as early as the fourth century BC. First the Greeks, then the Romans began to speak of the *seres*, or 'people of silk', a term used to describe the inhabitants of the far-off kingdom of China.

Roman poets writing at the time of Augustus allude to the desirability of these remarkably thin, elegantly textured fine textiles. China had jealously guarded the secret of sericulture so

(right) A collaboration between Paul Smith and Gainsborough Silk has produced a collection of sophisticated upholstery fabrics. Gainsborough Silk, founded in 1903, are specialists in jacquard weaving.

(far right) Historically-inspired silk stripe taffeta layered pannier skirt with selvedges, worn with a corseted bodice. By Vivienne Westwood from the Spring/Summer 2009 'Do it Yourself' collection.

effectively, and shrouded its provenance in such mystery, that many Romans mistakenly thought that silk was obtained, like cotton, from a tree, or as Roman philosopher Pliny the Elder wrote 'they weave webs like spiders that become a luxurious clothing material for women called silk'.

Perhaps it was in ancient Rome that silk's associations with decadence and excessive luxury began. The emperor Caligula, notorious for his love of luxury and excess, revelled in wearing it. Rich and powerful Roman men aspired to adorn themselves and their wives with silk. This increased demand provoked consternation among the more severe subsequent rulers who considered silk to be decadent and immoral, and vigorous measures were undertaken to restrict its use: men were forbidden to wear it. The Senate, in vain, issued several edicts to try to prohibit the wearing of silk on economic and moral grounds, attempting to characterize it as an excessively frivolous commodity, since this greed for silk had resulted in a huge outflow of gold, threatening the balance of trade. Demand had reached such a pitch that by the end of the third century the finest silk textiles sold for their weight in gold. To counter this demand, silk woven with a warp of an inferior value began to be much more widely worn by both men and women, with pure silk reserved for the upper echelons of society. Silk woven with gold was kept under the control of the imperial family.

The production of raw silk in Europe was first attempted in the sixth century. It is believed that two monks smuggled silkworm eggs in bamboo rods to Byzantium from Central Asia. As in China, silk weaving was restricted by a strict imperial monopoly. The Byzantine church made fabrics for the emperor and was able to develop a large silk industry in the eastern Roman Empire. The legendary magnificence of Byzantine textile techniques was due to the meticulous attention paid to the execution and embellishment, while actual weaving techniques were derived from Egyptian technology.

The cultivation of the white mulberry, the breeding of silkworms, and the manufacture of silk textiles had been long confined to Greece, but by the twelfth century this expertise was transported to Sicily, from where it was extended to Southern Europe. In the twelfth century the Normans invaded Byzantium, Corinth and Thebes, centres of silk production, and seized the crops and production infrastructure, as well as deporting all the workers to Palermo, thus prompting the flourishing of the Norman silk industry in Sicily. When Constantinople fell, many skilled silk weavers left for Sicily and Italy and contributed to the development of Italy's increasingly large domestic silk industry.

The sudden boom in the silk industry in the Italian city state of Lucca, beginning in the eleventh and twelfth centuries, was due largely to Sicilian, Jewish and Greek immigration, along with many other immigrants from neighbouring cities of southern Italy.

Venetian merchants traded in silk extensively, and encouraged silk growers to settle in Italy. Italian silk was a significant source of trade by the thirteenth century, with silk produced in **Como** becoming the most valuable in the world. In order to satisfy the demands of the rich and powerful, the cities of Lucca, Genoa, Venice and Florence were soon exporting silk

The silk routes, or 'Silk Road' as they are collectively known, are a series of ancient interconnecting trading routes that link China and the West. The map shows the main arterial trading route from East to West, over 4,000 miles long. As well as the luxury of oriental silk, these routes carried other commodities such as tea, spices medicine and were also a conduit for ideas, technical knowledge and cultural exchange, and thus a significant factor in the development of the great civilizations of China, India, Egypt, Persia, Arabia and Rome.

all over Europe. By the late fifteenth century there were over 80 workshops and at least 7,000 craftsmen in Florence alone; its great wealth was built largely on textiles made of wool and silk. Italian silk cloth was very expensive; a result of both the price of the raw material and production costs. Nevertheless, it remained highly prized for its brilliance of colour and elaborate perfection.

Italy's only rival was Spain; however, the expulsion of both the Jews and the Moors in the late 1490s, during the Catholic re-conquest, dealt a blow to the country's silk industry. Some weaving did manage to survive, primarily in Seville, Granada and Valencia, and would be revived again in the 1700s.

In the mid-1400s in France, Louis XI started to develop a national silk industry with the sole objective of reducing France's trade deficit with the Italian city states. In 1535 a royal charter was granted to two merchants to develop a silk industry in **Lyon**. Later a monopoly on silk production was granted exclusively to the city and by the beginning of the sixteenth century Lyon had become the capital of the European silk trade. The oriental style of silk was gradually abandoned for their own Lyonnais textile identity. By the middle of the seventeenth century there were over 14,000 looms in use in Lyon, and the silk industry was so prolific that it fed one-third of the city's population. In the eighteenth and nineteenth centuries Provence experienced a boom in sericulture that would continue until World War I, with much of the silk shipped north to Lyon for production.

In England Henry IV investigated the possibility of developing a domestic silk industry but the lack of expertise did not make it viable. It was not until the 1560s, with the first mass immigration of thousands of French Huguenots fleeing religious persecution, who brought with them their skills in sericulture and weaving, that the silk industry was established. Queen Elizabeth I encouraged them to establish their trades in southwest England. In the north, cities such as Macclesfield saw many high-quality artisan workshops spring up; in London, Spitalfields was the centre of silk expertise. However, the unpredictable British climate prevented England's domestic silk trade from becoming a globally dominant force.

The advent of the Industrial Revolution was marked by a massive boom in the textile industry, and changed much of Europe's silk industry. Remarkable technological innovations galvanized by the cotton industry in England informed the modernization of silk production.

Silk manufacturing benefited from simplification and standardization, as advances followed one another. Bouchon and Falcon invented the punch-card loom in 1775, which was later refined by Jacques de Vaucanson, but ultimately named after Joseph Jacquard, who invented the loom with a string of punch cards that could be processed mechanically in the correct sequence. Skilled workers feared it would rob them of their

livelihoods and immediately denounced the jacquard loom, but it swiftly became vital to the industry. By the mid-eighteenth century the French and English were rivals in design innovation, and, along with the Italians, were producers of the highest quality silks.

In the 1850s the silkworms of Italy and France were virtually wiped out by a ten-year epidemic of the parasitic disease pébrine. Italy was able to rebound from the crisis while France was unable to do so.

Urbanization in the twentieth century prompted many French and Italian agricultural workers to abandon silk growing for more lucrative factory jobs, and raw silk began to be imported from Japan to fill the void. The Asian countries that were once exporters of just the raw material began to develop their own production techniques, enabling them to export higher value finished fabrics and clothing.

Today Italy and France no longer domestically farm silk, however they remain important manufactures of woven and knitted silk fabrics and exceptional clothing. The centres of silk manufacturing remain the regions of Como and Lyon.

The dense satin weave of this structured silk fabric lends a sculptural edge to the waterfall ruffles that cascade from this lacquer-red dress by Pavel Ivancic.

Japan

Silk cultivation is believed to have spread to Japan around 300 AD. The **yamami silk moth** is thought to be an indigenous species, but exactly when Chinese silk technology reached Japan is unclear.

Japan had become the eastern terminus of the Silk Routes during the early Han period (206 BC–220 AD), and took a step forward in the silk trade at the end of this period by establishing its own sericulture. In the third century, following the Japanese invasion of Korea, important expertise in silk technology was brought back into the country. Succeeding emperors encouraged sericulture, and throughout the following centuries the skills and experience of Korean and Chinese weavers were brought to Japan, ensuring progress in technology. Over time Japan increased the domestic silk rearing it had begun. As a result of this expansion Chinese silk imports became less important, although they still maintained their fine, ultra-luxurious status.

The opening of the Suez Canal in 1869 meant that raw silk imported from Japan became more competitive. In the middle of the nineteenth century **Japonisme** joined **Chinoiserie** and **orientalism** as Western trends, and silk export began in earnest. Attention was turned to the possibilities of expanding silk production for home and exports, and in 1876 Japanese weavers were sent to France to study weaving methods and to copy French **brocades**. The Japanese government invested in the most modern equipment and established a model factory to instruct Japanese weavers in power-driven jacquard looms. Enormous strides in silk production were made throughout the nineteenth century, and this drive towards the modernization of sericulture in Japan rapidly made it the world's foremost silk producer. By the 1880s Japan had supplanted China as the largest supplier of raw silk: for a period until World War II it was the major supplier of raw silk to the West.

After the war Japanese silk production was restored, with vastly improved modernized methods for reeling, inspection and classification of raw silks in place. Japan again became the world's foremost exporter of raw silk – a position it held until the 1970s – and remained the biggest producer of raw silk, until broader industrial expansion led to a decline in sericulture and China made a concerted effort to regain her historic position as the world's biggest raw silk producer and exporter.

Today Japan consumes the greatest amount of silk per person in the world, due in part to its inextricable link with the most important Japanese garment, the **kimono**. Despite the adoption of Western clothing, traditional garments are still culturally important, and synthetic materials have never replaced silk in status. Much of Japan's silk is produced in the narrow width necessary for the uncut loom-width construction of the traditional kimono.

Today a combination of a hand-woven aesthetic fused with modern technology can be found in the innovative textiles produced in Japan. Sophisticated technology employs advances in computerized design and manufacture to reproduce the complex and extraordinary weaves of earlier centuries, as well as to develop new ones.

Extravagant chartreuse silk embroidered dress and coat by John Galliano for Dior from the 2007 'Samourai 1947' collection that celebrated the 60th anniversary of the House of Dior. Galliano paid homage to Christian Dior's revolutionary 'New Look' silhouettes from the iconic 1947 collection, and fused this historical aesthetic with inspirational elements from ancient and modern Japanese culture such as Ikebana floral arrangements, Manga art, Samurai martial arts and the rituals of the Geisha.

A contemporary interpretation of the iconic Indian sari by Anand Kabra. The garment usually relies on complex pleating and draping to achieve an elegant dress made from 6 m of uncut fabric. Here the designer infuses the traditional symbol of Indian femininity with contemporary elements of sheer fabric and a hip belt, and features a triangle bra in place of the usual tailored sari blouse.

The Indian subcontinent

Silk – known as *pattu* or *reshmi* – has a long history in India and is widely produced today. Historically, silk was used by the upper castes, while cotton was traditionally for the poorer castes. Elaborate silk **saris** for Hindus and **lehnga, sharara** and **shalwar kameez** for Muslims have a particular significance in celebratory ceremonies such as weddings.

The brocade-weaving centres in India grew in and around the capitals of kingdoms and holy cities in response to the demand for expensive fabrics by the royal families and deities of the temples. The rich merchants of the trading ports further contributed to the development of these fabrics: as well as trading in the finished product, they also advanced money to the weavers to buy the costly raw material. The ancient centres were mainly in Gujarat, Malwa and south India. In the north of the country Delhi, Lahore, Agra, Benares, Mau, Azamgarh and Murshidabad were the main centres for brocade weaving. Ancient traders introduced the complex **jamawar weave** from China, which gained immense popularity among royalty and the aristocracy. Maharajahs and noblemen bought the woven fabric by the yard, wearing it as shawls. Jamawar weaving centres developed in Assam, Gujarat and Malwa.

The region that is now Pakistan has been known for excellent silk weaving since the first millennium. In the Middle Ages the gold and silver silk brocades found eager buyers from Europe, the Middle East and even China.

In 1947 the partition of British India into independent states resulted in mass cross-migration. A large number of Muslim weavers migrated from Delhi and Benares to set up workshops in Lahore, Karachi and Khaiphur, now part of Pakistan. The towns of Orangi and Shershah have emerged as the biggest **khadi hand-loom** markets of Pakistan. The weavers continue to weave brocades in traditional patterns, but have also introduced newer designs deriving inspiration from the old Mughal silks. These weavers mostly fulfil domestic demands using cocoons imported from China and cultivated at Orangi and Shershah.

Islamic teachings forbid Muslim men to wear silk, because it is perceived as feminine and unnecessarily extravagant. The devout were advised 'he who dresses in silks in his lifetime forfeits luxury in the next'. Despite injunctions against silk for men, its popularity for women was retained. A cotton and silk mixture called **mashru** (meaning 'permitted') was developed in this part of the world to allow men access to the luxury of silk. Mashru has silk warps and cotton wefts. The construction is usually of a satin weave, which gives it a smooth silken face and a cotton underside. This satisfies the Muslim edict that silk must not be worn next to the skin.

Today, India and Pakistan produce very competitively priced silk fabrics in traditional and contemporary designs, and are an important source for international designer labels and mass-market high-street retail chains.

Thailand

Silk production in Thailand can be traced back over 3,000 years, to the region of Ban Chiang in the northeast province of Udon Thani. Archaeological discoveries in this area suggest that Thailand's sericulture and weaving history may be as old as that of China.

After the fifteenth century the importance of the Silk Road began to decline as less hazardous sea routes were discovered. This promoted trade between China, Southeast Asia, India and the West. Sea traders reached the Dvaravati Kingdom which controlled the settlements along the Gulf of Siam, and silk was one of the commodities traded.

The Thai silk industry began in the Khorat plateau in the northeast region. Elsewhere, the prevailing Theravada Buddhists' religious belief system forbade the killing of the silkworm inside the cocoon, but the northeast had more relaxed religious views, allowing silk production to flourish. Cultivation is still centred in the Khorat region, and production is mainly in Chiang Mai, the northern captital.

The area known as **Isan** is traditionally famed for its ikat weaves (or mudmee) which use a painstaking **space dyeing** (dyeing sections of continuous yarn in different colours along its length) technique passed down through the generations. Complex weaves and arresting colour combinations typify Thai handloom silks. Elaborate and sophisticated brocades have, over recent centuries, attracted the patronage of the royal families and ensured that the unique variety of local silk weaving techniques has not completely died out.

In the nineteenth century, King Rama V introduced advanced techniques in weaving and created the foundation of the country's expanding silk industry.

In 1901 King Chulalongkorn invited a team of Japanese experts to advise on the modernization of silk production. This marked the beginning of a rapid sericulture development and technological advancement in Thailand. By 1910 more than 35 tons of Thai silk were exported annually. Then in 1948, American entrepreneur Jim Thompson founded the Thai Silk Company, producing distinctive and beautiful hand-woven fabrics that inspired many copies. The artisan appeal of the fabrics was due to their uneven surface, caused by the inconsistencies in the hand-reeled silk from which they were woven. Thompson was a master of public relations, who managed to get his products introduced to fashion luminaries including the influential fashion editor Diana Vreeland, costume designer Irene Sharaff and Parisian designer Pierre Balmain. Custom-made weaves produced for Hollywood epics such as *The King and I* and *Ben-Hur* inspired a craze for his distinctive look in fabrics.

Sustaining growth on a long-term basis, however, proved a problem in the face of cheaper factory-produced fabrics from China and Japan. In 1994 the European Union provided funding for a five-year project to sustain and upgrade sericulture in Thailand. An initiative designed by Prime Minister Thaksin Shinawatra, based upon the Japanese 'one village, one product' model, was launched in 2001. The project has given small villages the opportunity to make a good living keeping traditional Thai arts alive. Queen Sirikit has effectively promoted this initiative and, to this day, silk production in Thailand is still primarily a hand-loom cottage industry, with some larger factories in Bangkok producing cheaper silks.

111

(left) Menswear by Etro from the Spring/Summer 2009 collection. The glowing Asian-inspired saffron tones exemplify the exotic appeal of silk shantung.

(above) This Thai fabric is a typical Jim Thompson design where a traditional fabric has been rescaled and treated with contrasting random raised weft ikat stripes.

The silk market today

By the middle of the 1990s world silk production reached 81,000 tons.

All of the countries with a historical link to the silk trade – China, Japan, India, Thailand, Italy, Spain and France – continue to produce magnificent silks to this day. China, with its recent economic reforms, has once again become the world's largest silk producer, with over 50 per cent of global production. India produces around 15 per cent and Japan a little over 10 per cent.

Other countries producing silk include Bangladesh, Bolivia, Bulgaria, Colombia, Indonesia, Iran, Israel, Kenya, Nepal, Nigeria, Pakistan, Peru, the Philippines, Sri Lanka, Turkey, Uganda, Zambia and Zimbabwe. Brazil, North Korea, Uzbekistan and Vietnam together produce about 4 per cent of the world's raw silk.

The advent of cheaper substitute fibres such as rayon and nylon initially reduced the domination of silk. However, world silk production has more than doubled over the last 30 years, and the total number of people dependent on silk rearing and processing worldwide is rapidly approaching 35 million.

Silk and synthetics

Silk is desirable, but not affordable to all levels of the market. It was therefore inevitable that synthetic copies — artificial or **art silks** – would be developed to satisfy the needs of the less affluent customer.

Nylon was developed in the United States and used as a replacement for Japanese silk during World War II. Its properties and tensile strength when wet were far superior to those of silk and **rayon** – the other major synthetic substitute – making it ideal for military applications, such as parachutes. The use of nylon for stockings revolutionized the hosiery industry. It was not seen as inferior to silk, but rather a modern, more wearable and accessible new product, with its historical connotations of glamour assured by associations with American GIs bearing seductive gifts during World War II.

After World War II, silk, as a commodity, was unable to regain many of the markets lost to the more accessible 'new-age' man-made fibres, which were greeted with great enthusiasm by postwar consumers. The new fibres were not only much cheaper, but far easier to care for. They seemed to represent a future where desirable fashion products were within the grasp of all members of society.

The future for silk

The invention of substitute fibres initially reduced the domination of silk but its status as a premium luxury fibre has endured; despite innovations in man-made fibres it has remained a desirable and luxurious commodity. None of the new fibres has managed to duplicate the breadth of applications that silk can embrace.

Designer Julian McDonald says: 'As far as I'm concerned nothing will ever replace silk. It can look tenderly feminine or high-tech, timeless or cutting edge.'

New York entrepreneurs developed the process of **fibrillation**, or 'sueding' silk in 1982 as a response to the emerging lifestyle trend epitomized by the casual low-key elegance of the 'dress-down Friday' culture. The goal was to achieve a **pre-shrunk**, crease-resistant and machine-washable silk to compete with the easy-care fibres that the consumer was already familiar with.

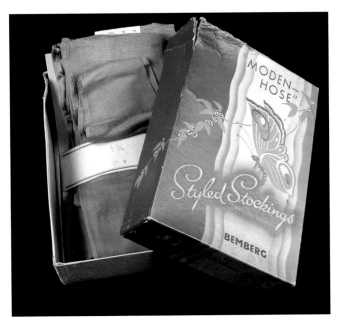

'The demand for silk garments continues to rise due to growing concern for protecting the environment, particularly among industrial countries which are prohibiting the use of certain dyes and chemicals, and prefer natural to chemical fibres. Thus natural textiles, in particular cotton and silk, are witnessing a new era of global demand.'
Rajatvaty K. Datta and Mahesh Nanavaty, *Global Silk Industry*, Universal Publishers, 2005.

Vintage stockings from the Deutsches Strumpf Museum. Before the advent of nylon, silk was used for stockings. Gifts of nylon stockings helped to endear the American GIs to European women during World War II.

The impact of sand-washed silk

The 1990s witnessed an explosion of sales in **sand-washed silk**, thanks to the consumer's renewed interest in natural fibres. Produced in China, the silk was washed in machines containing sand, pebbles or even tennis balls, resulting in an ultra-soft, peach-skin surface with a familiarly comforting, aged effect. The fabric was perfectly in tune with the dressed-down, luxe sportswear effortlessly interpreted by designers Calvin Klein and Donna Karan.

Shamash and Sons, a New York based converter, and one of the largest importers of silk into the US, launched its own range of washed silks for the 1988 season, using a process developed in Germany. Perfection of the technique for volume (and therefore lower price) was achieved in South Korea. Washed silk products were, at the height of the boom, available at every level of the market, including mail-order and supermarkets. To satisfy the seemingly insatiable demand for sand-washed silk of the late 1980s and early 1990s, the world silk supply doubled to over 1,000,000 tons. Many of these products, promoted as easy-care, proved to be of low quality, pushed onto the market hastily in order to satisfy the demand. The association with low-quality products damaged the noble and precious heritage of silk, and its reputation was in danger of being jeopardized.

The future of worldwide trade in 'the queen of fibres' looks positive. Although silk accounts for less than 10 per cent of the world's fibre market by volume, its importance in monetary value is several times higher, with the US alone importing $2 billion-worth of silk textiles and garments at the end of the twentieth century.

113

(left) Silk stripe top and silk panne velvet pants by Vivienne Westwood from the Spring/Summer 2009 'Do it Yourself' collection.

(above) Sand-washing silk gives the fabric a scuffed and tactile 'peach bloom' surface. The treatment lends this languid full-length crêpe de chine slip dress by Narciso Rodriguez a relaxed elegance.

Silk fibre

Silk fabric has a soft, smooth texture, but depending on the weave can express an almost sculptural structure, a weightless delicacy or a sensuous liquid drape.

Silk is categorized as a **natural protein fibre**, and is naturally produced by the *Bombyx mori* moth **pupa**. Insects that metamorphose primarily secrete silks, but substances categorized by the term silk can also be produced by web spinners, such as spiders. There are over 200 varieties of wild silk moths found in locations all over the world, however most of these produce silk filaments that are generally irregular or flattened in form. Flatter threads tangle more easily and therefore break easily if unwound. It is only the *Bombyx mori* moth that is capable of producing the much-prized filament, which is smooth, fine and rounder than that of other silk moths.

Properties of silk

Silk is extraordinarily strong in relation to both fibre dimension and the perception of its delicate nature. It is stronger than wool or cotton and weight for weight is actually stronger than steel. It is resistant to mineral acids, but can be dissolved in sulphuric acid. Its high level of absorption lends it superior ability to accept dye. A pure silk textile survives longer than a silk fabric mixed with other fibres.

Silk is a poor conductor of electricity and it is this that makes it comfortable to wear in cool weather. This low conductivity also means it is susceptible to static cling. Its isothermal properties make it feel cool in summer and warm in winter, and its insulative properties have led to fine silk knit undergarments traditionally providing unequalled warmth as skiwear layers. Silk floss or kapok is the lightest and warmest of all quilting materials.

Brilliant fibre

Silk is highly prized for its lustre and shimmering appearance, a result of the fibre's unique triangular, prism-like structure that allows the cloth produced from it to refract incoming light at different angles. When light plays upon a piece of silk fabric the surface appears to glisten, tremble and graduate in colour. For this reason silk can be described as a 'bright fibre', meaning it has a natural lustrous reflectiveness and therefore appears to shimmer. Before the gossamer threads become fabric, complex processing ensures that the brilliance and luminous qualities of the filament are preserved.

Wild silks

A wide variety of wild silks have been known throughout China, India and Europe from the earliest civilizations, however the scale of production has always been smaller than that of cultivated silk. Wild silk cannot be replicated using farmed caterpillars.

Wild silks differ greatly in colour gradation and texture depending on the species, climate and food source, but are generally characterized by an uneven appearance and rough feel, because the single thread that makes up the cocoon has been torn or shredded into shorter lengths by the emerging moth, lending wild silks a characteristic slubby, bark-like effect and dry textured handle. (See also peace silk on page 121.)

(above) Flowing citrus-yellow sheer silk-chiffon kaftan by Etro.

Billowing extreme-proportioned djellaba-style silk chiffon dip-dyed tunic by Antoine Peters.

Raw silk

The term raw silk is often applied erroneously to **silk noil**, or noils, which are the short fibres left over from spinning silk. The fibres are relatively short, weaker and considered far less valuable than spun silk.

A noil is the fibre that remains after the fibres are separated by combing in preparation for spinning. These shorter staple fibres can be used for spinning in the same way as cotton or linen would be spun. Noil fabric is characterized by a dry handle, nubby texture and low sheen. It often has occasional slubs and specks.

Spider silk

Web spinners, such as spiders, produce silks that have been used for medical applications and telescope sights. In the future, genetic modifications may see spider silk being developed as a fibre in its own right.

(left) Hand-spun silk yarn recycled from shredded Nepalese saris. The resulting yarn has an intense colour vibrancy that is informed by the random nature of the raw material. The natural inconsistencies lend it a textured feel, similar to tussah or raw silk. The hand spinning is carried out by women's cooperatives that provide fair wages and generate funds for educational programmes.

(below) Hand-spun silk yarn, also recycled from shredded Nepalese saris, and then over-dyed to a uniform colour.

(above) Heavyweight hand-loom raw tussah silk shawl by Indian designer Rohit Khosla. Made from the silk of cocoons gathered in the wild, it features the characteristic natural 'flaws' and heavily textured 'tree-bark' appearance and colour palette associated with this type of silk.

Silk production

The best-known of all the natural fibres is produced using the substance secreted by the larvae of the silk moth as a shroud to protect itself while in the cocoon, during the transformation into a pupa and eventually a moth. Several other insects produce silks, but only the silk derived from moth caterpillars has been used extensively for textiles. Silk production today is a combination of both modern technology and ancient techniques first developed and perfected by the Chinese many centuries ago.

Cultivation

Silkworm breeding depends on a highly developed agricultural system capable of sustaining the large-scale cultivation of mulberry trees. One hectare of mulberry trees yields 11 tons of leaves, which will in turn sustain 200 kg of cocoons, which produce 40 kg of raw silk. Specially reared *Bombyx mori* moths are so inbred that they can no longer survive in the wild, and are blind and flightless. They must be raised under careful, temperature-controlled conditions in well-ventilated, closed rooms, because they are unable to live in the open air. The moths lay their eggs on specially treated paper placed on bamboo trays. When the eggs hatch, the caterpillars are fed on the leaves of the white mulberry tree, *Morus alba*.

After about 35 days and four moultings, the silkworms are 10,000 times heavier than when they first hatched, and a little over 7.5 cm in length. The silkworms are removed from the trays and covered with straw, to which they can attach their cocoons. The insect spins a cocoon by secreting a continuous filament of fibroin protein (liquid silk), which protects it while in the cocoon. This liquid silk is coated in **sericin**, a water-soluble protective gum, which is produced in two of the silkworm's glands. Liquid silk is forced through **spinnerets**, openings in the silkworm's head, and as the substance comes into contact with the air it solidifies. Within two or three days the silkworm will have spun approximately 1,600 m of **filament**, and be completely encased in its protective cocoon.

After this entire process the silkworm metamorphoses into a moth. However, in sericulture it is necessary to kill the **chrysalis**, either by steaming, baking in the sun or hot air or by soaking in salt water, before it reaches the moth stage. To obtain the filament, silk cocoons are sorted by fibre size and fibre quality. Defective cocoons are carded and immediately spun, while a certain number of perfect cocoons are set aside for breeding the next generation of silkworms. Approximately 5.5 kg of cocoons will generate 0.5 kg weight of raw silk.

(above) This haunting design from John Galliano for Dior, Autumn 2000, beautifully expresses the crisp sculptural properties of tightly woven silk.

(left) The caterpillars of the *Bombyx mori* moth feasting on their diet of white mulberry leaves. Over a month of intensive feeding later, the moths are 10,000 times larger and ready to spin their precious cocoons.

(above) The highly cultivated *Bombyx mori* moth is unique among the moth species in that it produces cocoons that are uniformly pure white in colour and texture. Centuries of in-breeding and controlled cultivation have resulted in colour consistency and a reliably fine filament.

(left) The delicate spectral appearance of the *Bombyx mori* moth highlights its fragility and the expertise required to cultivate it. Centuries of selective breeding have resulted in a creature that is blind, flightless and dependent on a highly regulated environment in order to survive.

Cooking

The cocoons are first thrown into a cauldron of boiling water, a process called **cooking** or **maceration**, which softens the sericin gum that binds the filaments together. Traditional pan cooking is carried out in open vats, and the cocoons are immersed for several minutes. Cooking is a crucial stage for subsequent reeling; a high proportion of waste can be produced if it is not carried out with sensitivity. Overcooked cocoons increase the number of breaks during reeling, while undercooked cocoons do not unravel easily, thus reducing the efficiency of the reeling process.

The brushing process, by which the reelable end of the filament is located, also produces a considerable amount of filature waste.

Reeling

Reeling, or winding, the cocoons extracts the silk filament, and is a specialist job. Once the reelable ends of the filaments have been secured, known as clearing, the prepared cocoons are transferred to reeling basins and a number of cocoons are unwound simultaneously. Several filaments are grouped together and taken by the **threader**, the machine-feeding device, to the reelers, where they are reeled onto a bobbin to produce one long, smooth thread.

The finest fabrics are woven from threads made by reeling together the filaments from only four cocoons.

Thrown threads

Applying a twist to silk filaments to hold them together is known as **throwing**, and the variety of silk threads throwing produces is extensive.

Leonardo da Vinci (1452–1519) had an avid interest in the mechanics of the silk throwing process, and in 1500 he invented a highly innovative winged, or fly spindle, machine, which performed stretching, twisting and winding operations on three consecutive stretches of thread. With no further major important modifications, his device became the basis for later development of the continuous spinning machine that is still employed in contemporary systems for throwing or silk thread making.

The five general categorizations of **thrown threads** are defined primarily by their intended final use: embroidery; knitting; sewing; wefts; and warps. Within each category a large spectrum of different yarns can be obtained by altering the number of threads, turns and direction of the twist. Common examples include:

Thrown singles: Individual raw silk threads twisted in one direction.

Tram: Weft threads produced by twisting two or more raw silk threads together in only one direction; usually this is a light twist, just sufficient to hold them together.

Organzine: The raw silk is given a preliminary twist in one direction, then two or more of these threads are twisted together in the opposite direction. Generally, **organzine** demands the best quality raw silk and is used for the warp threads, which bear the tension of the loom.

Crêpe: Thrown in a similar way to organzine, but twisted to a much greater degree, resulting in a crinkle effect.

Mommes

Silk is traditionally measured by weight. The **momme** (pronounced mommy) is the unit system used in the silk industry, and quantifies the density of silk as opposed to the thread count, as used for cotton fabrics. It originates from the Japanese cultured pearl industry.

1 momme is equal to 3.6 g of silk fabric per yard.
A 17-momme fabric would weigh 61.2 g per yard.

The usual range of momme weight for different weaves of silk are:
Habotai: 5 mommes to 16 mm.
Chiffon: 6 mommes to 8 mm.
Crêpe de chine: 12 mommes to 16 mm.
Gauze: 3 mommes to 5 mm.
Raw silk: 35 mommes to 40 mm.
Organza: 4 mommes to 6 mm.

Isabella Whitworth domestically de-gums silk cocoons in soda and ash solution.

Once the silk yarn has been de-gummed and bleached white, it is wound into skeins and laced up ready for dyeing.

Primary finishing processes

Primary finishing involves several processes that prepare the silk for dyeing. First the silk must be **de-gummed** to remove the sericin, a process that is usually carried out by the dyer and involves boiling the silk in soap, detergent or enzymes. This process has a great effect on the quality of subsequent dyeing. Defects in dyeing can be due to inadequate de-gumming, or fibre damage by overly harsh processing. Bleaching may also be required if a pure white colour is desired.

Fabric weighting

Silk is purchased by weight, and the amount of weight that silk loses in the process of de-gumming (20–25 per cent) is a major consideration. Common practice in the silk industry is that of **weighting** the fabric by loading it with a finishing substance, in order to compensate for the weight lost in the de-gumming process. The loading process increases the volume of the thread and gives the silk a characteristic heavy and supple handle, lending the fabric crispness, lustre and a firm feel. Taffeta is the most common heavily-weighted fabric. Weighting may also lend the cloth better flame-retardant and crease-resistance properties. Weighted silk is generally less compactly woven than unweighted silk, so less silk is used in the manufacture of the cloth.

Weighting is usually done during the dyeing stage. In order to weight a coloured silk, stannic chloride is used, followed by treatment with sodium phosphate. Black silks may be weighted with metallic mordants such as iron salt. Due to the complexity of processes and problems related to chemical pollutants, mineral loading is now almost obsolete. Today weighting is almost exclusively achieved by grafting **acrylic monomers** (usually methacrylic amide) using ammonium persulphate as an initiator.

Weighting can have a remarkably positive effect on the ability of the fibre to take dye, because the types of salts used have been traditionally used as dye mordants. The term **pure dye silk** indicates that weighting was not added at the dyeing stage.

Weaving

Silk weaving follows a similar process to other fibres and yarns.
Warping This prepares the warp by rolling all the warp yarns on to a beam under the same tension, and strictly parallel to each other.
Pirning The weft, or cross-wise yarns are put on to a pirn, which is placed inside the **shuttle** in order to lay the weft yarn between the warp yarns.
Non-stop high-speed weaving has been made possible by the introduction of automatic pirn-changing and shuttleless looms that employ compressed air to shoot the weft yarn between the warp yarns.

Despite technological advances, certain types of silk cannot be made on high-speed machinery, particularly complex novelty fabrics, or those that reproduce the traditional effects that were developed on the original punch-card jacquard looms.

Dyeing

There are two main ways of dyeing silk fabrics. The first method is to dye the yarns before they are woven into fabrics – these are known as yarn-dyed or dyed-woven (eg taffeta, duchesse satin and many pattern-woven fabrics). Multiple colours can be woven together in one cloth. Up until the early nineteenth century, this was the only method of dyeing silk, and today the same basic techniques are used for this process, skeins of raw silk being soaked in tanks full of dyestuff.

The second method is to dye after weaving; fabrics dyed in this way are referred to as piece-dyed fabrics (eg, crêpes, twills, etc). Industrial scale piece-dyeing was introduced in Lyon, France, in the mid-nineteenth century. The fabric is fed into the dye bath through two cylinders, or fixed to a round jig, which is then immersed in the bath. The fabric is then fixed, rinsed and dried.

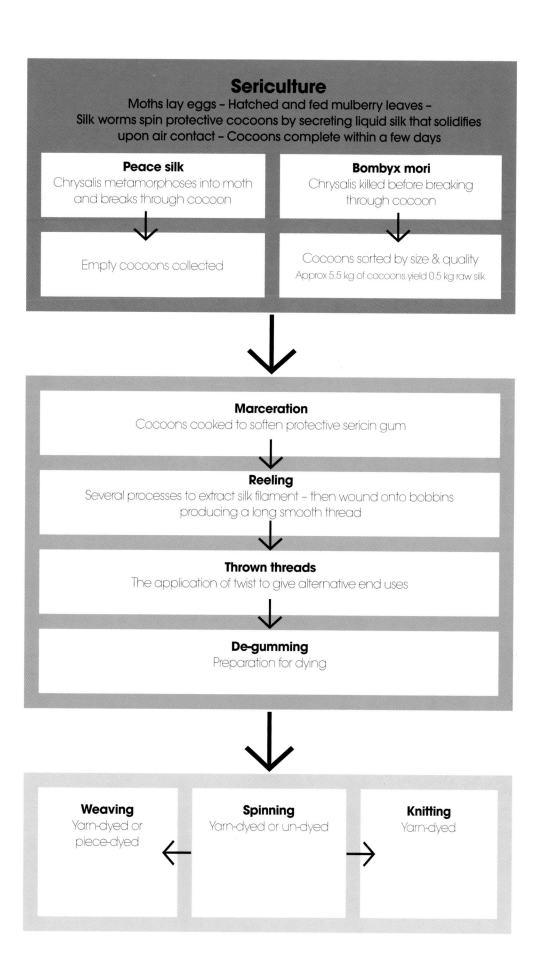

Sericulture
Moths lay eggs – Hatched and fed mulberry leaves –
Silk worms spin protective cocoons by secreting liquid silk that solidifies
upon air contact – Cocoons complete within a few days

Peace silk
Chrysalis metamorphoses into moth
and breaks through cocoon

Bombyx mori
Chrysalis killed before breaking
through cocoon

Empty cocoons collected

Cocoons sorted by size & quality
Approx 5.5 kg of cocoons yield 0.5 kg raw silk

Marceration
Cocoons cooked to soften protective sericin gum

Reeling
Several processes to extract silk filament – then wound onto bobbins
producing a long smooth thread

Thrown threads
The application of twist to give alternative end uses

De-gumming
Preparation for dying

Weaving
Yarn-dyed or
piece-dyed

Spinning
Yarn-dyed or un-dyed

Knitting
Yarn-dyed

Additional finishing processes

The purpose of these processes is to restore the fabric's natural brilliance, softness and characteristic handle, counteracting the drying effects of previous treatments.

Calendering: Steel rotary cylinders press the fabric as it passes in between them. By varying the speed of rotation and the heat or pressure, various degrees of glossiness and softness can be achieved.

Tamponing: A very fine, even film of oil is applied to the fabric by machine, to smooth out irregularities and correct any chaffing that has occurred during previous processes.

Breaking: A breaking machine, or breaker, is used to lend a particularly soft handle and brilliance to the surface of the fabric. Two types of machine can be used. The first is known as the 'button', because the fabric is passed rapidly back and forth over small rollers with brass buttons. The alternative machine has slanted knives, and the fabric is similarly passed rapidly back and forth over them.

Steaming: This is applied to pile weaves to encourage them to fluff out and appear more voluminous.

Pressing and lustering: The fabric is passed through heated rollers and then soaked in dilute acid to bring out the lustre. This process removes wrinkles from the finished fabric.

120

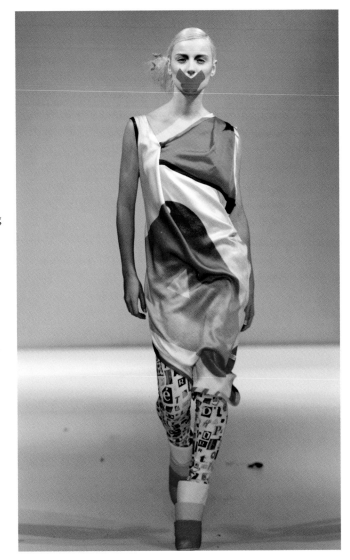

(above) Asymmetric hand-painted dress in fluid silk by Antoine Peters.

(above) This close-up of a butterfly's wing illustrates the visual 'morphing' of colour that creates this shimmering array of colours. The effect is created by light refracting on the structure of the wing. The unique triangular structure of silk fibre responds in a similar way.

Special care

Deterioration of silk is accelerated by exposure to dust and dirt (which will, over time, cut the fibres), and light and grease, so it should always be cleaned and stored in a dark environment. Insects may also attack it, especially if it is left dirty. Silk has a moderate to poor elasticity and can lose up to 20 per cent of its strength when saturated.

Optimum humidity of 50–55 per cent is desirable for silk to retain a supple handle. Dryness makes the fibres brittle, and they break.

Ethical considerations

The process of harvesting silk from a cultivated cocoon kills the larvae, therefore sericulture has been criticized on the grounds that traditional silk production kills silkworms, preventing them from living out their life cycle.

The provenance of silk has not been without controversy to religious practitioners worldwide, dating back many centuries. Chinese Buddhists initially forbade the wearing of cultivated silk because its use violated the prohibition against the taking of life. However, the use of silk in the robes of Chinese and Indian monks is acceptable if the moth has emerged from the cocoon. Similarly, Mahatma **Gandhi**'s criticism of silk production was based on the **ahimsa philosophy** of not hurting any living thing.

In addition to the controversy regarding animal welfare issues, some of the manufacturing procedures, particularly in hand-reeling silk factories, have health and safety implications.

Wild silk and peace silk

Peace silk, also known as vegetarian silk, refers to silk harvested from cocoons from which the silk moths have emerged naturally. Their silk is de-gummed and spun like other fibres. Peace silk moths can be wild, semi-wild or even farmed. The term peace silk is a perfect marketing tool for consumers with ethical concerns who do not want to forego experiencing the beauty of silk.

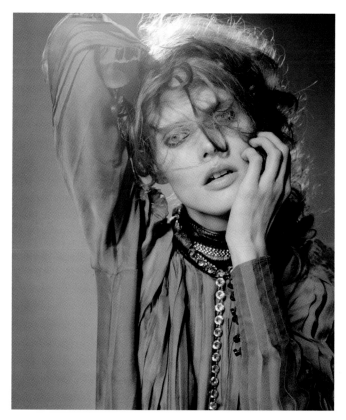

Thai silk moth

The Thai silk moth is adapted to tropical conditions and is **multivoltine**, producing at least ten batches of eggs per year. The silk is reeled by hand from green cocoons, and traditionally the pupa is not killed prior to reeling. The natural colour spectrum of the silk filament spans a range of shades from light gold to light green. Thai raw silk is characterized by an irregular and bumpy appearance. Although it is soft, it has a relatively coarse texture with knotty threads.

Ahimsa peace silk

Ahimsa peace silk is made from the cocoons of wild and semi-wild silk moths and is promoted in parts of southern India for those who prefer to wear ethical silk. There are several species of silk moth used for ahimsa silk, in addition to the conventional mulberry-feeding silk moth.

Eri silk
The **eri silk moth**, *Philosamia ricini*, is a type of wild moth that feeds on the castor plant. The cocoons are roughly the same size as those of cultivated silk moths, and are characterized by a very light colour, almost as white as the cultivated *Bombyx mori* cocoons. They are gathered from across a large area, then cut to allow the moths to emerge and escape.

The cocoons are made up of several layers of silk. The outer layers are relatively soft and fluffy. The inner layers are glued together like paper. Most cocoons have a hole at one end, where the moth has naturally emerged.

Eri cocoons are raised in a natural situation with minimal interference from man, and are considered to be equivalent to organically grown.

Muga silk
The **muga silk moth**, *Antheraea assamensis*, is a wild and semi-wild species that lives only in a restricted area in Assam, India, and produces a special type of wild silk. The villagers in this forested region gather the cocoons in the wild and then semi-cultivate them from the eggs of the wild moths that emerge.

Tussah silk
Tassah or tassar moths, *Antheraea mylitta* and *Antheraea proylei*, are wild and semi-wild silk moths respectively. Tussah is the most commonly used of all the wild varieties, and lends its name to a particular type of silk.

Grey silk blouse by Danish eco-brand Noir. The fabric used conforms to the stringent 'Oeko–Tex Standard 100' regulation that certifies that the product is free from more than 100 substances known to be detrimental to human health. This initiative reflects the latest in textile chemistry and governmental regulations from around the world. The accreditation does not indicate however that the textiles are necessarily organic.

Silk fabrics

The fabrics listed represent the most popular silks in use and would give any designer or merchandiser an extensive selection for designing a range or building a collection. The list, however is not exhaustive.

The fabrics are all primarily made from silk yarns, though some names are shared with other natural and/or synthetic yarns.

(above) Emerald green jacquard outfit by Markus Lupfer for Armand Basi. The simple silhouette and enlarged proportions of this skirt and top are enhanced by the richly figured raised design of the fabric.

(right) This oversized silk cloqué drop-waisted dress by Markus Lupfer for Armand Basi challenges preconceptions of scale and proportion. The nature of the cloqué weave emphasizes the 'blown' effect of the style.

Sumptuous

These dense, three-dimensionally expressive silks feature complex textures.

Brocade An elaborate and richly figured jacquard, often with metallic threads.

Jacquard Refers to both the loom and the resulting patterned fabric.

Damask A reversible self-patterned fabric woven on a jacquard loom. The design is distinguished from the background by contrasting lustre and matt textures.

Velvet A cut warp pile fabric. 100 per cent silk velvet is rare and extremely costly. Silk is usually combined with rayon viscose to achieve a beautiful drape.

Cloqué A woven double cloth where the two sets of warp and weft yarns have a different shrinkage potential that produces a three-dimensional 'blister' effect.

(above) The languid drape and lush sheen of viscose silk velvet is apparent in the relaxed glamour of this 'bathrobe' style wrap coat by Kostas Murkudis.

(above) Roksanda Ilincic black satin column evening dress with fluted emerald overskirt that highlights the sumptuous, sculptural properties of the densely woven silk satin duchesse.

Crisply sculptural

Mouldable and architectural, these fabrics are lush or papery to the touch.

Shantung A crisp, slubbed and sheeny silk woven from wild silk originating from the Shantung province of China.

Tussah The name is associated with the wild *Antheraea* caterpillar that produces a very textured, naturally brown silk.

Dupion A crisp, lustrous silk with a slubby texture that is woven from an irregular silk reeled from the twin filaments of double cocoons.

Taffeta A tightly plain-woven, crisp fabric. Often produced with warp and weft of different colours.

Moiré A structured fabric with a pronounced rib is embossed with rollers in the finishing process, creating a 'watermark' effect.

Satin A weave with the maximum amount of warp showing on the face. The sheen is enhanced by the use of a continuous filament yarn.

Duchesse or Peau de Soie A rich, satiny, medium-weight fabric with fine cross ribs and a moderately stiff drape.

(left) The lush optical qualities of silk moiré are showcased in this late-nineteenth-century corseted evening dress by Mae Primrose, from the Victoria and Albert Museum collection. The distinctive 'watermark' effect that characterizes this fabric is achieved by pressing the ribbed construction of the silk weave with heated rollers. The bow on the bustle of the gown highlights the exceptionally crisp and sculptural quality of the fabric.

(above) A refined woven check tussah silk provides the structure and drape for this beautifully cut all-in-one by SANS.

Sheer

Ethereal and whisper-fine or stiff, transparent and gauzy in structure.

Chiffon A very light, diaphanous fabric made with a tightly twisted single yarn in a loose plain weave.

Georgette Made in the same way as chiffon, but with a two- or three-ply yarn.

Tulle A fine, transparent net or mesh construction.

Habotai A smooth and light semi-sheer plain-weave silk with a good drape.

Gauze A thin open-weave fabric with a floppy handle.

Organza An extremely crisp, plain-woven fabric.

Gazar A structured plain-weave, highly twisted double-yarn with a crisp handle and flat, smooth texture.

(above) Alexander McQueen manipulates the tenderness of sheer silk tulle in graduated shades of mauve by draping and wrapping this delicate fabric over a structured taffeta base to create an ethereal form.

(left) Extravagant boned silk organza dress by Rachel Cassar, composed of layers of pre-worn and antique textiles, such as shot silk chiffon, wool, nylon and velvet with synthetic tulle and metallic rope. The designer's ethos is underpinned by a commitment to sustainable design.

(below) Ethereal hand-woven gossamer silk textile by Sallie Temple.

(above) 'Peony', multi-layered silk organza evening dress by Maurizio Galante. The expertly cut 'petals' of the dress perfectly showcase the esoteric properties of the finest silk organza. When worn, movement indicates the weightless delicacy of this weave, which belies its firm structure.

Liquid drape

Sensuous weight and tactile, like a second skin.

Jersey A lightweight knit in silk yarn with a particular drape and handle.

Crêpe A pebbly textured silk woven from high-twist yarns.

Crêpe de Chine A lightweight plain-weave crêpe silk made with alternating S- and Z-twist yarns.

Charmeuse A light satin-faced crêpe-backed fabric with a tactile drape.

(above) Designer Markus Lupfer glamorizes a super sized T-shirt silhouette by cutting it in a heavyweight silk satin trimmed with a chunky cashmere rib.

(left) The liquid drape of sheer silk jersey transforms the oversized silhouette of this sweater dress into a more sensual form. From Antoine Peters' collection entitled 'I will never wear a sweater'.

(far left) Conceptual 'extreme fit' jacket by Ada Zanditon made from 100 per cent silk jersey dyed with AzO-free dyes, ruched over hemp canvas reinforced with steel and boning. The lining is digitally printed silk, printed in England by the Silk Bureau. The ruching and finishing were hand-stitched.

Section 2
Plant
fibres

Linen

Linen reflects a heritage and aspirational lifestyle that speaks of refinement and quality.

Linen has been highly valued for many centuries for its incomparable handle and unique visual appeal. It embodies a desirable, authentic, low-key luxury that continues to transcend the vagaries of fast fashion.

Linen fibre possesses unique practical properties, which, coupled with a subtle and refined touch, have assured its fashion longevity. It has become synonymous with a classic, relaxed elegance and is the supreme choice for comfort in hot weather. Its cool, absorbent properties are well recognized the world over and are unparalleled by any other natural fibre.

Linen has a very specific tactile appeal; smooth and lustrous to both the eye and hand, the fibre is almost silky in texture, yet embodies a springy freshness. It can also express a robust personality in heavier weaves that may lend it a satisfying drape. Conversely, lighter weights can have an almost featherlight aspect evocative of the draperies of Ancient Egyptian and Greek cultures.

Pure linen will always endure in contemporary fashion. Its natural creasing lends clothing made from it an unmistakable character, while its inherent anti-static properties make it fall away from the body, flutter and undulate in response to movement.

The development of new blends and finishes for linen ensures that this ancient fibre remains relevant to the demands of the modern consumer. Synthetic blends can improve crease recovery, create exciting new textures and offer aspects that appeal to both premium brands and price-competitive markets seeking to experience previously unattainable luxury products.

The history of linen

Linen is the oldest textile in the world, predating cotton and possibly even wool, and is known to have been in use during the Stone Age. Since then its popularity as a clothing textile has risen and fallen with the changing times, but it is thankfully once again being appreciated for all it has to offer the contemporary consumer.

(opposite page) Blended linen by Donghia.

Gudrun Sjödén 100 per cent linen trousers and dress. The classic pieces reference the easy layering of traditional costumes from hot and humid climates devised to provide maximum comfort. Linen is the optimum choice of fibre in hot weather.

Early history

Linen is believed to have first been systematically cultivated in Mesopotamia, in the Middle East region known as the 'cradle of civilization', around 5000 to 6000 BC. The ancient Egyptians and Babylonians cultivated flax, which was then traded with other societies of the region by the Phoenicians. The ancient Egyptians developed a sophisticated linen 'industry'; so valuable was the commodity that it was sometimes used as a form of currency. Linen was seen as a symbol of light and purity, as much as it was a display of wealth for the afterlife. A shroud for an important Pharaoh would often consist of 1,000 m (over half a mile) of fine linen. Some of these shrouds were so finely spun and woven that they still cannot be replicated by modern methods. The linen curtains that shielded the tomb of Tutankhamun were found intact after over 3,000 years, while parts of the shroud of Rameses II were microscopically examined by the British Museum and found to be structurally perfect after almost 3,500 years.

Among the earliest records documenting the manufacturing of linen are the ancient Greek tablets of Pylos. Concurrently, ancient Roman blueprints show that their manufacturing methods closely resembled current manufacturing processes.

Range of uses

Linen is ostensibly a tough fabric. Ancient Greek infantrymen wore protective clothing made of linen, and jackets of padded linen were worn under the chain-mail of medieval knights for additional protection against arrows. Symbolic of purity, Jewish and Christian religious vestments were and are still made from linen.

The structure of woven linen made it a perfect medium for all types of embroidery and drawn thread work. It was also the yarn of choice for fine **needle-** and **bobbin-lace** work. Sixteenth-century **ruffs** were made of heavily starched linen, the best of which was from Flanders (see page 134).

Linen was also used for making paper and bindings for books. The *Liberlinteus of Zagreb* is an intact Etruscan textbook made of linen. It is still today the material of choice for archival quality book-binding, and many artists choose to paint on linen canvas.

130

The meaning of linen

The word linen is derived from the Latin word for the flax plant, *Linum usitatissimum*, which literally translates as 'useful linen', and recognizes the inherent value of this humble plant. Today there are several words in the English language that owe their etymon to the importance of linen. The word 'line' is derived from linen thread, which was used to determine a straight line. Similarly, the word 'lining' developed from the same source, because linen was often used to line woollen and leather clothing. Lingerie, originally a French word, also has its origins in linen, because it was once the fabric of choice for intimate apparel.

(above) Florentine linen. The structure of woven linen makes it a perfect medium for all types of embroidery and drawn thread work.

(left) Linen is lint-free, making it the fibre of choice for household textiles.

Sophistication and practicalities

Throughout Renaissance and Baroque Europe, linen was associated with wealth. In various European courts, periodically, sumptuary laws were passed to curtail the inordinate expenditure on dress, which often referred to the use of linen lace. This was also a useful method of enforcing strict social hierarchy through dress, an early form of dress code.

In the eighteenth and nineteenth centuries the appearance of linen was more restrained, perhaps echoing the new age of enlightenment, but it was still considered an almost obligatory sign of refinement. A gentleman's wardrobe and status was judged by the quantity and quality of his linen. Beau Brummell (1778–1840), the famous Regency dandy and arbiter of taste, had the maxim: 'fine linen and plenty of it, all perfectly starched and freshly laundered'. He considered this to be 'the maximum of luxury in the service of minimal ostentation'. In 1805, at his most fashionable, he ordered 75 yards of fine Irish linen for his shirts and bed sheets, as well as a quantity of Irish linen **damask** for his nightshirts.

In nineteenth-century Europe the status of a gentleman was judged by the quality and quantity of his linens, however flax was also part of the fabric of everyday village life. Prior to the Industrial Revolution and mass urbanization, flax (see 'Linen fibre', page 136) was cultivated, spun and woven by peasant farmers for their own consumption, producing a cloth that was coarser and less refined than the flax that was commercially traded and valued.

(above) Extravagantly proportioned crisp white shirt with boned collar by Nabil El Nayal. The designer explores historical references and plays with the idea of the social importance of well-laundered linen as the foundation of a genteel wardrobe.

(left) Menswear by Rui Leonardes featuring a deconstructed modernized gothic frayed linen ruff.

Linen continued to be the fabric of choice until the end of the nineteenth century, used for all intimate apparel, gentlemen's shirts, women's chemises and dresses, as well as for general household textiles. So omnipresent was linen as a household textile that today, in English-speaking countries, the term is generically used to describe bed, bathroom, table and kitchen textiles, even though the majority are now no longer made of linen. Linen cupboards are still in use and retail stores still refer to 'linen' departments.

The last vestige of linen as an essential symbol of a well-dressed gentleman was a neatly folded, well-laundered pocket handkerchief worn in the out-breast top pocket of a suit, a styling detail that was to become a fashion anachronism with the new wave of social changes of the mid-1960s.

The First World War

Until the twentieth century flax cultivation was very much a cottage industry; however, with increased mechanization the demand for factory-scale production became inevitable. Flax was a vital supply during World War I, for both sides. It was used for tents, ropes and canvas for aeroplanes. The scale of production was insufficient to meet the voracious appetite of the war machine, so the supply was supplemented with cotton, which was more readily available due to its faster manufacturing methods. During the interwar years this less expensive, and perhaps more manageable, fabric eventually usurped linen's position as the fabric of choice.

Postwar demands

In the industrialized world, linen, in common with other natural fibres, fell out of fashion after World War II. The new preference was for synthetics, which were more in tune with the contemporary preoccupation for modernity and expectations of an easy-care lifestyle, which better suited women's new role in the workplace. High-maintenance fabrics, together with many other domestic chores, were replaced by anything and everything that could simplify life.

By the 1960s, in Great Britain and North America, linen had developed something of an esoteric status, appealing to only a certain type of consumer. However, in the Mediterranean and South America linen continued to enjoy popularity, because synthetics were not able to offer the same level of coolness and comfort in hot climates.

By the mid-1970s linen as a clothing fabric was at an all-time low, with less than 10 per cent of linen produced being used for fashion textiles. Investment in the industry during the 1980s and into the 1990s resulted in technological developments that eliminated many of the traditional characteristics of linen that were not liked by the average **high-street** retail customer. Mechanical pre-treatments, **enzymes** and ammonia have made linen into a totally modern fabric that can be wrinkle-free, shrink-resistant and sometimes even non-iron.

By the mid-1990s linen's unique appeal was once more appreciated, with around 70 per cent of linen production being again used for fashion fabrics. Today there are special linen and cotton blends being developed for use in denim production, with the aim of improving the feel of this fashion staple in hot and humid climates.

The development of European linen

The countries that more aptly developed the growing of flax, together with more sophisticated spinning, weaving and manufacturing techniques, are those that today are still recognized as producing the best product. Until the 1950s, Belgium, France, the Netherlands and Ireland were considered the best producers and manufacturers of linen. Italy, alongside other Mediterranean countries, was valued for producing good, handmade linen products.

Irish linen

It is believed that the Phoenicians first traded Egyptian linen fabric and flax seeds with Ireland long before the advent of Christianity, although evidence of an organized industry was not apparent until the twelfth century. Fifteenth-century English travellers remarked on how 'the wild Irish wore chemises of 30 to 40 **ells** of linen, dyed with saffron'.

Huguenots

In 1685 Louis XIV revoked the Edict of Nantes resulting in religious persecution against the Protestant Huguenots. The majority of Huguenots lived in northeast France and Flanders and were predominantly skilled silk and linen weavers. Many of the silk weavers fled to London, settled and set up their looms in Spitalfields. By contrast, the linen weavers migrated to Ulster (Northern Ireland). The British government knew that their skills in weaving fine linen would benefit the existing industry, so encouraged the Huguenots to the province with privileges and financial incentives. Louis Crommelin (1652–1727) was invited by the government of King William (of Orange) to join fellow Huguenots and further develop the industry. He introduced new industry methods, such as mass bleaching, and developed the commercial export trade. His lasting legacy was the foundation of today's modern linen industry.

Linen has been so fundamental to the region that it was often described as the 'fabric of Ireland'.

The classic pea coat is reinterpreted here in a textured Irish linen with deconstructed multi-fabric decoration by John Rocha.

(left) Fluid Irish linen jacquard dress with swerving seams by John Rocha expresses the natural ease and relaxed wearability of this luxury fabric.

Irish Linen Guild logo, an assurance of quality. Yarn or fabric must be either spun or woven in Ireland to carry the logo of authenticity.

133

Linen industry

In 1711 the Board of Trustees of the Linen Manufacturers of Ireland, also referred to as the **Linen Board**, was established. This, together with the introduction of tariff protection, further encouraged the development of the industry. By the mid-eighteenth century around 500 Huguenot families had the controlling influence in the Irish linen trade, by now firmly established in the northern provinces between the rivers Bann and Lagan, collectively known as the 'linen homelands'. Flax needs well-prepared ground and was therefore usually planted after a potato crop. This rotation of crops saved the region from the potato blight and famine that adversely affected the rest of Ireland.

The region further profited from the American Civil War, because the resulting shortage of cotton increased the demand and price of linen. At its height almost two-thirds of the linen produced was destined for export, of which nearly 90 per cent was to England. By this point Belfast was known as **Linenopolis**.

The Industrial Revolution came late to Ireland. Labour was cheaper here than in mainland England, so the linen industry developed more slowly than that of cotton, giving cotton the competitive edge. However, when the Revolution did reach Linenopolis, the province's engineering developed quickly around the requirements of its most important industry.

Up to and during World War I, Ulster was the largest linen producer in the world, and strategically very important to the war effort. By the early 1920s almost every town or village had a mill or factory, and 70,000 people, which represented about 40 per cent of the workforce of Northern Ireland, were directly involved in the linen industry. Today there are only about ten significant companies, and fewer than 4,000 people directly employed in producing linen. Very little flax is now grown in Ireland; the majority is imported from Eastern Europe. The expertise that was once the backbone of the linen industry is now the driving force behind design and technology in spinning, dyeing and weaving.

Luxury linen

Irish linen is a valuable and desirable commodity and if spun or woven in Ireland can carry the Irish Linen Guild's logo of authenticity. This assures it is a luxurious product worthy of global recognition.

In the mid-1990s the **Living Linen Project** was set up to record first-hand information about the linen industry in the twentieth century, since it is considered integral to the country's cultural identity.

(Notes from a lecture by Mr Daniel McCrea to students of the Irish Linen Guild, 1971)

Flemish (Flanders) linen

Historically Flanders is the geographic region that now overlaps parts of northeast France, Belgium and the adjoining Netherlands. Today Flanders designates the Flemish community of these regions. The cities of Ghent and Bruges in Belgium and Lille in France were all once part of Flanders.

The climate and geography of the region make it ideal for the cultivation of flax, which was originally an ancillary crop grown to be woven during the long winter months, while the farmers waited for the next crop-growing cycle to begin.

During the fourteenth and fifteenth centuries – the golden age of Flemish fabrics – the linen trade flourished. Linen fabric and yarn for lace was especially valued, bringing prosperity to the region, which became one of the most urbanized parts of Europe. Tielt in West Flanders was the centre of the linen industry. Around the 1790s nearly 20 per cent of households were involved in linen production, a figure that grew to over 70 per cent by the 1840s.

Flax was cultivated in the region around Ypres using seeds from both Holland and Riga, which produced better crops.

Spain and its South American colonies formed the primary export market, however trade barriers were later imposed that dramatically affected the industry – as did the mechanization of cotton production – which fell into decline.

Today, through design, technology and the merging of several companies, Belgian linen is once again a desirable commodity and a competitive product equalling that of Irish linen.

CELC (Confédération Européenne du Lin et du Chanvre) is a non-profit-making trade organization for linen (flax) and hemp in Europe. Masters of Linen, based in Paris, is a subsidiary of CELC, providing information and promoting European quality linen.

Italian linen

While not important in the cultivation of flax, Italy is very important within the linen industry as a whole. It is singularly the largest converter of flax fibre into yarn and fabric for both the export and domestic markets. Although linen represents approximately 5 per cent of Italy's textile production, it is an important percentage because it represents high value, export-led merchandise.

As with other Mediterranean countries, Italy has a long heritage in working fine linen for both clothing and household textiles. These were once cottage industries, where designs and techniques were passed down from mother to daughter. Today, Italy's preoccupation with design-led technology has resulted in the development of sophisticated machinery that can produce competitively priced fine linen products. Although much of the lace work, embroidery and pulled thread work is now machine made, the results continue to echo the handcrafted linen work of previous generations.

Linen market

Approximately 70 per cent of linen is used for the clothing industry, while approximately 30 per cent is used for household textiles.

The principal countries that process flax into high-quality yarn and fabric are Italy, France, Belgium, Northern Ireland, Germany and Japan. Eastern Europe and the Baltic countries are now important producers of flax, as is China. However, the most desirable linen, whether yarn, fabric or manufactured goods, still remains in the domain of Belgium, France, Ireland and Italy. The European Community's agricultural policies department sets European flax prices, which are prevented from falling below a certain level.

The major consumers of linen clothing and household textiles are the United States, Italy, Germany, Japan, France and Great Britain. Italy is the single largest consumer of flax. The country produces yarn and woven fabrics and has one of the most sophisticated linen knitting industries producing fully-fashioned knitwear.

A relaxed modern luxury is conveyed in this extra-fine Russian linen knitwear by designer Marina Shlosberg. The cardigan combines a fine knit with the vintage appeal of handmade lace panels, incorporating traditional craft skills into contemporary design.

Linen fibre

Grades of flax differ, with flax cultivated in Western Europe usually of a better quality.

Linen is the yarn and fabric made from the fibres of the stem of the flax plant, the only cellulosic plant indigenous to Western Europe. Flax, also referred to as linseed, is a commercial field crop plant grown for its fibres, which are used to manufacture cloth, rope or paper. Flax grows in many parts of the world but prefers temperate maritime climates and good soil to flourish well.

Flax stems vary from 60 to 120 cm in height, and the individual **bast** fibres are held together in 'bundles' by **pectin**. It takes about 100 days for planted flax seed to grow to maturity and be ready for harvesting. The plant has small, five-petal flowers that are either blue or white and that blossom for only one day: the plants with blue flowers tend to yield better crops. The fruit capsules contain the seeds, which are converted to linseed oil.

Properties of linen

Flax fibres are the strongest of all the vegetable fibres, two to three times stronger than cotton. They vary in length from approximately 20 to 130 cm, with a micron count (diameter) of 12 to 16. The cross section of the fibre is made up of irregular polygon shapes, which give it a coarse and crisp appearance.

Natural flax colours range from shades of ivory, tan and grey. White or pure white is only achieved through various bleaching processes.

After the impurities have been removed the fibre becomes hygroscopic, absorbing up to 20 per cent of its weight in moisture or perspiration, which it quickly releases into the atmosphere, making it dry to the touch. The fibre does not lock in or trap air or have any insulative properties, allowing the linen wearer to feel cool. It is thermo-regulating, encouraging the body to acclimatize in hot environments. For this reason it is believed that in hot climates linen bed sheets give you a far more restful sleep than cotton sheets. Flax is also believed to have therapeutic properties that promote sleep.

The slight stiffness of the fabric stops linen from clinging to the body, instead it tends to billow away, thus drying more quickly and eliminating perspiration. Linen can be blended with more insulative fibres, such as cashmere or wool, to become trans-seasonal.

Linen has a longer staple relative to cotton, is **lint**-free and does not **pill**. It is resistant to stains, which can be washed out at lower temperatures than cotton due to the smoother surface of the fibre. Although good-quality linen carries a premium price tag, products made from this precious fibre are regarded as investments because they can endure regular use by many generations. Durable and practical, the more often it is worn and laundered, the softer, smoother and more beautiful it becomes. The surface of linen fabric responds well to steaming and pressing, acquiring an almost polished finish. It is believed to be unharmed by germs and resists humidity.

Linen does not have any natural give or stretch, but is resistant to damage from abrasion, however it can 'break' if constantly folded in the same place.

The natural absorption properties within linen mean that it is able to absorb a good depth of colour in the dyeing process, and remains colourfast for a long period.

The slubs along the length of the yarn are sometimes considered a characteristic of linen, but are technically a defect that denotes a lesser quality of fabric.

Flax flowers are either blue or white and bloom for one day; plants with blue flowers tend to yield better crops.

Ecological considerations

Linen is a more expensive fibre than cotton, with much more of a niche market, making it an ideal vehicle for organic cultivation and ecological production methods.

Flax is or can be an ecologically pertinent and sustainable crop. It grows best when crops are rotated annually, a sound method of crop production that does not strip the soil of all its nutrients. Flax is environmentally friendly, requiring little irrigation and energy to process, and is fully biodegradable. With crop rotation it is not necessary to use chemical fertilizers and pesticides, and even when these are used flax requires only one-fifth of the pesticides and artificial fertilizers required for commercially grown cotton. Additionally, linen is up to 12 times stronger than the equivalent cotton product, which dramatically increases its life span, which means it does not need to be replaced so often.

Linen absorbs dye well, especially natural dyes, and does not require chemical treatments. It can be sun bleached to avoid the use of artificial agents.

A paper bag neckline 'Galaxy' dress by Icona Vera in coral-pink linen showcases the crisp weave structure, desirable natural irregularities and natural sheen of the fibre.

Linen production

The fundamental principles of producing linen yarn from the flax plant have changed little since early Roman times. However, modern technology has revolutionized the efficiency and flexibility of the yarn, and the speed at which it can now be produced.

Flax processing is labour-intensive, requiring skilled workers; however several by-products are also produced – including linseed oil for linoleum, soap, fuel and cattle feed – meaning there is minimum wastage.

Today's technology

Until recently linen production was in the domain of specialist manufacturers, however today's advanced technology has allowed it to be more widely produced. Technological advances have also improved the quality of the crops at both the growing and finishing stages, so fungal attacks are now averted in the field. The shuttleless loom means that smaller weaving sheds can be used, while mechanical pre-treatments have made linen into a modern fabric that maintains its age-old advantages. Enzymes smooth out the fibres making them softer and ideally suited for knitting single jersey fabric with less propensity to shrinkage. The use of liquid ammonia makes linen into a wrinkle-free and non-iron fabric, while pre-washing stops it shrinking.

Cultivation

Flax is one of the few crops still produced in Europe. Russia, alongside other countries of the Federation, is currently turning much of its land over to flax production. The majority of the production is **tow**, the lower-grade shorter fibres. France sows about 60 per cent less but produces a much greater quantity of **long-line fibres**. Flax production in Northern France, Belgium and the Netherlands is relatively small by global production standards but it is considered to be by far the best quality. Of the three countries France is the largest producer.

Canada and China are two of the principal flax producing countries, between them producing just over 50 per cent of total global production. India and the United States are also important producers. In Africa both Egypt and Ethiopia produce flax while in Eastern Europe, Russia, the Ukraine, Belarus and the Baltic countries of Latvia and Lithuania are expanding their flax production.

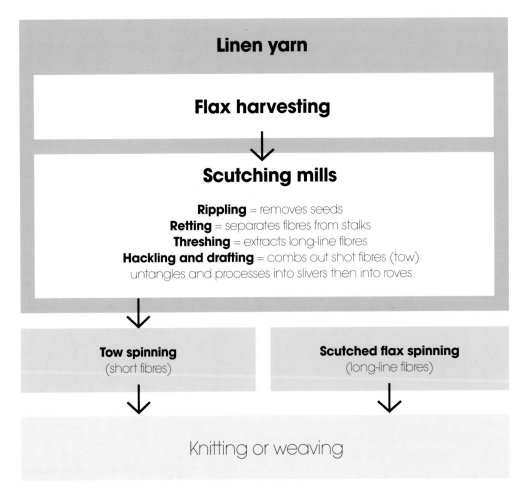

Linen yarn

Flax harvesting

Scutching mills

Rippling = removes seeds
Retting = separates fibres from stalks
Threshing = extracts long-line fibres
Hackling and drafting = combs out shot fibres (tow)
untangles and processes into slivers then into roves

Tow spinning
(short fibres)

Scutched flax spinning
(long-line fibres)

Knitting or weaving

Harvesting

The quality of the final linen yarn and fabric is dependent on flax's growing conditions and harvesting methods. Flax needs well-prepared ground and is sensitive to weeds. It is a renewable resource needing little fertilization in the form of chemicals or pesticides, and is harvestable after a single growing season.

The shoots are ready for harvesting approximately 100 days after planting. This is about four weeks after the plant has flowered and two weeks after the seed capsules have formed. The shoots are 80–120 cm (31–47 in.) long and start to yellow at the base. If they are allowed to go brown the fibre will be degraded.

Harvesting can be mechanized using combines, or it can be carried out manually which maximizes the fibre length and thus the quality of the eventual yarn.

Mechanized harvesting involves cutting the plant and raking it into windrows. When sufficiently dry, a combine harvests the seeds.

Hand harvesting involves pulling the complete plant with root from the ground – this gives the longest and most desirable fibres, since the fibres go all the way to the root. The second-best option is cutting the plant stalks very close to ground level.

Scutching

This process extracts and cleans the fibres contained within the stalks, with the objective of producing long-line fibres. The entire process involves up to ten successive operations that fall into two principal categories. The first is separating the different elements that make up the plant to enable the extraction of the fibres, and the second is the cleaning processes that eliminate all the other materials. **Scutching** mills represent an important part of the manufacturing process. The short tow fibres are used for coarser fabrics and household textiles, while the long-line fibres are used for fine clothing and bed linen.

Rippling

Rippling as part of the scutching process is the removal of the seeds, which is done by metal-toothed comb machine. The process also aligns all the stalks parallel to each other for easier separation. The seeds are then kept for the next season's sowing. After rippling, the flax is passed through a further series of speeding toothed rollers that reduces the thickness. The next process, referred to as breaking, crushes the woody fibres into small particles known as shive.

Cottonizing

Traditional cotton machinery is sometimes used to process linen fibres in a similar way to cotton, an alternative and faster production process that requires less equipment. However, the fibres tend to lose their linen characteristics.

Long fibres (linen flax) processed through a turbine after scutching.

Retting

Retting is a process used for all bast vegetable fibres, to separate the fibre from the stalk. This can be achieved through the use of chemicals, although these are harmful to both the fibres and the environment. Alternatively, and ecologically more prudent, the stalks can be immersed in warm water tanks. Through sufficient soaking and the introduction of enzymes, bacteria will form and decompose the pectin that binds the fibres together.

Historically, the stalks were left in the fields in the autumn where nature would naturally decompose the binding agent. This process was known as 'wind retting'. In some areas the stalks were left to soak in shallow river areas, however this may contaminate the water.

The flax is then collected and pressed into large bales and stored until it is time to extract the fibres.

Threshing

The process consists of beating or threshing the material in turbines, which extract the long flax fibres from the epidermis, shive and short fibres known as tow. The resulting long fibres of scutched flax are also referred to as long-line flax; this is then hand-sorted and classified according to colour and cleanliness.

Hackling and drafting

Hackling combs out the short broken fibres or tows as well as untangling the bundles, rollers then process and divide the bundles to form continuous **slivers** which are further processed by means of doubling and drafting; this evens out the weight and produces **roves** which are ready for the final spinning process.

(above) Sliver of flax obtained during drafting and preparation, after combing and before spinning.

(above right) Weaving linen yarn.

(right) Three stages in the process of converting flax into linen thread: (left to right) broken flax stems; finally hackled flax line; hand-spun and bleached linen thread, all produced by Alverna Messersmith-Learn using the traditional processes performed at her Pennsylvania family farm in the early years of the twentieth century.

Spinning

There are two methods of spinning flax. One involves spinning the long fibres and is known as scutched-flax spinning. The other is tow spinning and is used for the shorter fibres or tows. Spinning is the final process that turns the roves into yarn. Both the long fibres and the tow can be spun using wet, dry or semi-wet techniques. Wet spinning long-line fibres will achieve a very fine-quality yarn used for fine clothing and the best bed linen. Dry spinning will result in a coarser, less regular yarn with some naps, and is mainly used in household textiles. A final process eliminates defects and impurities and then joins the yarn by means of knotting and splicing.

Finished linen fabric can range from rough and stiff to fine and smooth.

Units of measurement

Using a **yarn count** is a way of grading linen according to the fineness of the fibre.

In the United States linen yarn is measured in **LEA**. The finer the yarn the higher the LEA number.

**1 LEA = 1 x 300 yards (yarn) to the pound weight,
40 LEA = 40 x 300 yards to the pound weight
(i.e.12,000 yards)**

In Europe the metric system is used, represented by the letters **Nm**, indicating the number of 1,000-metre lengths per kilogram.

In China the English **cotton-count** system is used, indicating the number of 840-yard lengths or hanks per pound weight.

(above left) Linen damask of sateen-weave construction. Here the design is reversed out, showing the satin-weave construction.

(above) The almost rustic texture of this natural linen fabric with a pronounced slubby weave provides a supple and luxurious feel to this men's suit by Yohji Yamamoto.

(above) Linen chambray shirt echoing the appeal of jeans styling with indigo-dyed warp and un-dyed natural weft.

Cotton

Cotton is the most egalitarian and practical of all natural fibres.

The democratic appeal of cotton allows it the scope to be relevant to myriad marketing possibilities, from the most value-driven price categories through to cutting-edge designer fashion. It may be woven or knitted, superfine and as gossamer light as voile, lending it a luxurious personality. Conversely, its perennial appeal can be expressed by hardwearing canvas-type weaves or drill constructions, which provide the ultimate democratic classic fashion fabric: denim.

Cotton possesses the qualities of comfort and natural absorbency, and can embody, depending on processing, either cool or warm aspects that make it truly trans-seasonal. The raw fibre in its natural state is visually evocative of its potential usefulness to man, the small cloud-like formations of the cotton **bolls** suggestive of a comforting end product.

The history of cotton

Cotton cultivation is said to have started almost simultaneously in India and South America. The Harappans, living along the banks of the Indus river valley (now Pakistan), first produced cotton fabric 6,000 years ago, and exported it to Mesopotamia (now Iraq) during the third millennium BC, from where it was introduced to the Egyptians of the Nile valley. Dating back over 7,000 years, fragments of fabric found in Mexican caves prove that cotton was also indigenous to early South and Central American people. It was important to the Moche and Nazca cultures of pre-Spanish Peru, who grew it upriver then made it into nets that they traded with the fishing villages along the coast.

The usefulness of cotton spread, and in late medieval Europe it was acknowledged as an important fibre. It was initially used in its relatively raw state as wadding for padded protection, before being developed as a yarn.

(above) Freshly picked raw cotton.

(right) Organic jeans by Dutch brand Kuyichi. Cotton denim is the ultimate democratic fashion fabric, eternally desirable to all consumers.

(opposite page) Cotton is the most commonly used natural fibre. The production and export of cotton extends to more than 100 countries, with an estimated 350 million people involved in its production, farming, transportation and manufacturing.

143

The Spanish conquistadors in Mexico noted the wearing of clothes made from cotton by the indigenous peoples of the region. By the 1500s cotton was well known around the globe, and by the close of the sixteenth century it was being fully cultivated throughout the warmer regions of Asia and the Americas.

It is an ironic tragedy that India's once important cotton-processing industry was actively sabotaged during the period of British Raj and colonial rule in the eighteenth and nineteenth centuries. The British East India Company had a policy of de-industrialization in order to force the closure of cotton processing and manufacturing workshops throughout India. This was purposefully done to ensure that the Indian markets supplied only the less valuable raw material and in turn were then obliged to buy more expensive manufactured textiles from Britain.

(above) Cotton weaving on a traditional hand loom. Cotton was actively farmed and used for clothing by the indigenous peoples of South and Central America long before the arrival of the Spanish conquistadors in the early sixteenth century.

144

Tree wool

Greek historian Herodotus (c. 484–425 BC), observing Indian cotton, wrote: 'there are trees which grow wild there, the fruit of which is a wool exceeding in beauty and goodness that of sheep'. These early poetic observations endured, as cotton was popularly believed to be some form of 'tree wool'. This concept continues today: in the Germanic languages the word for cotton, *Baumwolle*, literally translates as 'tree wool'.

Industry

The Industrial Revolution boosted cotton manufacturing and made textile production Britain's leading export. New machines were invented, such as the roller spinning machine and the flyer-bobbin system that were used to draw cotton to a more even thickness. The **spinning jenny** was invented in 1764, followed by the **spinning frame** in 1769. Both machines enabled the spinning of multiple yarns at one time, and revolutionized the Lancashire cotton industry. In North America, Eli Whitney (1765–1825) was credited with the invention of the **cotton gin** (1794), which was fundamental to the mass production of cotton fibre. Small gins were hand powered, while larger ones were powered by horse or water. The cotton gin facilitated much larger-scale harvesting and only required an unskilled labour force, which in the southern United States consisted of slaves. The gin is credited for vastly increasing the financial assets of the economy of the United States. An Indian machine called a **charkha** or churka predated the American cotton gin but was unsuitable for shorter-staple cotton.

English weavers were now able to produce cotton yarn and fabric to higher and more consistent standards, at faster speeds with increased productivity. A contemporary slogan of the time read, 'Britain's bread hangs by Lancashire threads'. Manchester's wealth was founded and further prospered on the manufacture and export of cotton; as the undisputed capital of the global cotton trade it acquired the nickname of **cottonopolis**.

(above) John Smedley Mill in Matlock, Derbyshire. While the area was important for knitting cotton hosiery it was Manchester (Lancashire) that enjoyed the sobriquet of 'cottonopolis' as the undisputed capital of the nineteenth-century global cotton trade.

American cotton

Improved technology and the increased control of world markets allowed British traders to develop a commercial chain where raw cotton fibres were purchased cheaply from colonial plantations, then processed in the Lancashire mills and re-exported on British ships to captive colonial markets in West Africa, India and China via Shanghai and Hong Kong, all at a considerable profit. Such vast quantities of raw cotton fibre were required that by the 1840s India, the then principal supplier, was no longer able to meet the insatiable appetite of the Lancashire mills. Shipping low-cost bulky raw cotton was both expensive and time-consuming, so British merchants turned to the emerging cotton plantations of the southern states of America. The advantage of American cotton was threefold: the two varieties of domesticated Native American species produced a longer-staple fibre of superior quality; the cotton production was far less expensive because it was picked and grown by a slave labour force; and finally, it incurred a shorter shipping time, because the sea route did not entail the lengthy and arduous Cape of Good Hope. By the mid-nineteenth century the commodity known as '**King Cotton**' had become the backbone of the Confederate States of America.

Egyptian cotton

When the southern US ports were blockaded by the northern Union during the American Civil War (1861–1865), Britain and France, the main buyers of Confederate cotton, had to find an alternative source. They found it in Egypt but at the end of the Civil War they turned their allegiances back to the cheaper American cotton. Through the British, the Egyptians made heavy economic investments in their cotton industry, and the sudden departure of their two primary buyers sent their economy into spiralling deficit and eventual bankruptcy. To protect its investment, Britain seized control of the government and later made Egypt a British protectorate. Cotton remained an important commodity and was one of the reasons Britain held on to Egypt, until it seized full independence in 1956.

Indian cotton

In 1869 the Suez Canal opened to shipping, connecting the Red Sea to the Mediterranean and halving the journey time from India to Britain. This renewed an interest in Indian cotton, and cultivation in turn increased. However, the British government imposed heavy tariffs to discourage the production of cotton yarn or fabric in favour of the less valuable raw fibre.

Mahatma Gandhi (Mohandas Karamchand Gandhi 1869–1948) was the political and spiritual leader of India during its struggle for independence from colonial rule. He pioneered non-violent resistance by means of mass civil disobedience, non-cooperation and the boycotting of British goods, especially fabrics. He symbolically wore a cotton **dhoti** and shawl, woven with yarn he hand spun on a charkha. He recommended that all Indians spend time each day spinning khadi (homespun and woven cloth) in support of the independence movement. The charkha is fundamental to India's cultural heritage and is symbolic of its long struggle for independence – its symbol was incorporated into the Indian flag, which should, in principle, be made of cotton khadi.

Mahatma Ghandi wearing a dhoti and spinning khadi cloth on a charkha. The term khadi can be applied to any fibre that is hand-spun and hand-woven.

145

American cotton after the Civil War

The emancipation of slaves at the end of the American Civil War did not diminish the importance of southern cotton as a key crop. Black farmers continued to work on the white-owned plantations in return for a share of the profits, known as **sharecropping**. Vast labour forces were required for cotton picking, which was all done by hand. In the 1920s some basic machinery was introduced, however it was not until the 1950s that mechanisms reached any level of sophistication as to not damage the fibre (see page 148).

The United States is still a major exporter of cotton, the majority of which is of the long-staple variety.

The 1950s and early 1960s in North America, and to a lesser extent in Northern Europe, were periods enamoured with synthetic materials, which were seen as desirable, sophisticated and worldly. Cotton production plateaued sharply, and by the mid-1960s the American cotton producers had initiated a self-help programme to research and promote the use of cotton, a proactive policy intended to counteract the rapid decline in cotton consumption. In 1966 The Cotton Research and Promotion Act was passed, aimed at combatting the rise in popularity of synthetic fabrics and re-establishing the market for cotton. Concurrently, the socio-political undercurrent of the time, in the guise of the flower-power movement, helped create a 'new' interest in natural produce, from which cotton benefited substantially, reborn as a seminal fabric.

Modern material

Today, technology works harmoniously with cotton's natural characteristics, giving us a product that surpasses expectations. Oiling and waxing were early 'low-tech' applications to weatherproof cotton, and today, **bonding**, lamination and chemical treatments can turn a basic fabric into a performance fabric.

Summer or winter, cotton is now a fashion perennial at all levels of the market, from designer to high street. Its pan-global appeal has seen its demand increase at an average of about 2 per cent per year over the last 50 years, and by approximately 4 per cent over the last decade. Cotton is the best-selling fibre in the United States, and one of the best worldwide.

Cotton market

The production and export of cotton extends to more than 100 countries; it is believed to employ an estimated 350 million people in its production, farming, transportation and manufacturing.

The largest producer and consumer of raw cotton is China. It consumes around 40 per cent of the world's raw cotton output, for both domestic consumption and export of its manufactured goods. Although the largest producer, China has to supplement its domestic production with additional imported raw material, in order to feed the insatiable appetite of its garment manufacturing industry and the demand for Chinese-made clothing. India, Pakistan and Turkey also supplement their domestic raw cotton production with imported raw material to, similarly, fulfil their export production orders.

The southern United States, known as the **cotton belt**, is the second largest producer of raw cotton. California has the largest global yield per acre, while Texas leads in production. After China and the US, other primary global cotton producers are India, Pakistan, southern Brazil, Burkina, Uzbekistan, Australia, Greece and Syria.

Israel and the USA are the two highest-cost cotton producers in the world. Australia, China, Brazil and Pakistan are among the world's lowest-cost cotton producers.

One-third of all global raw cotton production is traded internationally, the majority of which will go to countries that do not have domestic crop production to supply their spinning, knitting and weaving industries. These manufacturing hubs include: Bangladesh, Indonesia, Thailand, Taiwan and Russia.

146

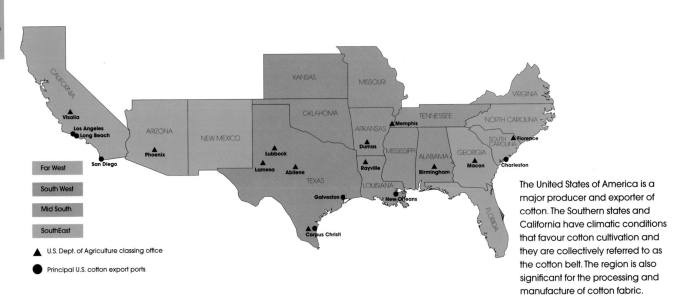

The United States of America is a major producer and exporter of cotton. The Southern states and California have climatic conditions that favour cotton cultivation and they are collectively referred to as the cotton belt. The region is also significant for the processing and manufacture of cotton fabric.

▲ U.S. Dept. of Agriculture classing office

● Principal U.S. cotton export ports

Far West

South West

Mid South

SouthEast

Cotton fibre

Cotton is the most commonly used natural fibre.

Cotton is a soft fibre that grows around the seeds of the cotton plant, which is grown between latitudes 45 degrees north and 35 degrees south. In tropical climates cotton is a perennial crop.

The cotton plant is a small shrub with greyish green tri-lobed leaves. The flower is cup-shaped with creamy white to yellow petals that have purplish to red spots near the base. The cotton fibres are the white hairs that cover the seeds in the 'fruit' capsules (the bolls).

As a native of tropical and subtropical regions, the cotton plant produces flowers and 'fruit' throughout the year. It takes approximately two months after the seeds have been planted for the flower buds to appear, which then blossom after a further three weeks. These last about three days before they start to fall, leaving the remaining pods or 'cotton bolls'.

Cotton's aesthetics vary depending on the applied treatments and the grade of the fibre. A typical untreated cotton fabric has a matt lustre, soft drape and a smooth touch, making the fabric comfortable to wear. Cotton garments have a good level of moisture absorption and can typically be machine washed and dried. Dyed cotton retains its colour longer if washed in warm or cool water.

Cotton is susceptible to acids such as lemon juice and should be rinsed quickly. Sunlight causes oxidization, turning it yellow. If the fabric has not been pre-treated with shrink resistant finish then it is liable to shrink.

Cotton plant

There are 43 species of cotton plant, including four primary domesticated species.

Although cotton is native to many regions, the vast majority of the cotton grown today is from one of two principal varieties of the American species *Gossypium hirsutum* and *Gossypium barbadense*.

Cultivation

Cotton cultivation requires long, frost-free periods, plenty of sunshine and a moderate rainfall. The soil needs to be fairly heavy and does not require high levels of nutrients. These conditions tend to be best met within the seasonally dry tropics and subtropics, in both the southern and northern hemispheres. However, today cotton is also cultivated in areas with far less rainfall, the water being obtained by means of irrigation.

Production of the crop starts soon after the autumn harvesting of the previous season's crop. Planting time in the northern hemisphere varies from the beginning of February to the beginning of June.

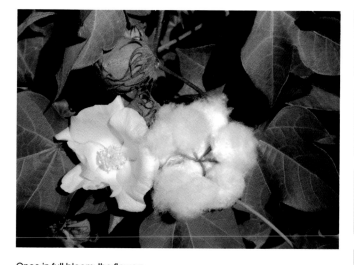

Once in full bloom, the flowers (left) last approximately three days before dropping, leaving the remaining pods, or cotton bolls (right). The white hairs that cover the seeds are the cotton fibre.

The four principal cotton varieties

Gossypium hirsutum
Maya civilization, Central America

Gossypium barbadensa
Inca civilization, South America

Gossypium herbaceum
Harappan civilization, South Asia

Gossypium aboreum
Egyptian civilization, North Africa
Indo Pakistan subcontinent

147

Cotton production

The production of cotton is generally efficient, with less than 10 per cent of the picked weight lost in the subsequent processes of converting the raw cotton bolls (seed cases) into pure fibre.

Harvesting

One hundred million rural households around the world are involved in cotton production, the majority of which happens within the developing world where cotton continues to be picked by hand. In Europe, Australia and the United States, on the other hand, it is mechanically harvested by one of two types of harvesting machine, depending on the cotton variety grown. A **cotton picker** removes the cotton from the boll without damaging the plant, while a **cotton stripper** machine strips the entire boll from the plant. Strippers are used in climatic regions that are too windy to grow the 'picker' varieties of cotton.

In some cases a chemical defoliant is first used to remove the leaves; alternatively natural defoliation would occur after a temperature freeze.

After harvesting the land is tilled. The conventional method is to cut down the reaming stalks and turn the soil ready for the next round of seed planting. The alternative method, known as the 'conservation method', leaves the stalks and the plant residue standing on the surface of the soil, and the new seeds are planted through the 'litter' that remains.

After harvesting a machine known as a **module builder** compresses the cotton into large modular blocks that are covered and temporarily stored in the fields. These are collected by specially designed trucks and transported to the **gin**.

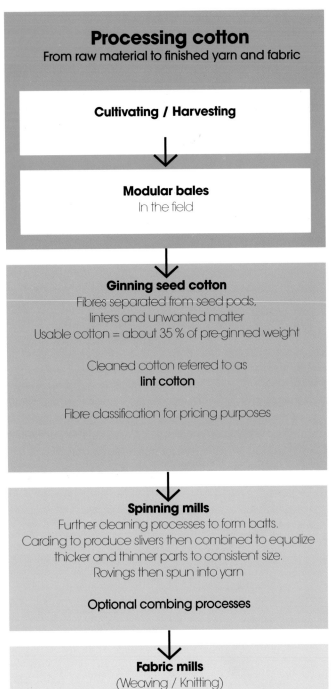

Processing cotton
From raw material to finished yarn and fabric

Cultivating / Harvesting

↓

Modular bales
In the field

↓

Ginning seed cotton
Fibres separated from seed pods,
linters and unwanted matter
Usable cotton = about 35 % of pre-ginned weight

Cleaned cotton referred to as
lint cotton

Fibre classification for pricing purposes

↓

Spinning mills
Further cleaning processes to form batts.
Carding to produce slivers then combined to equalize
thicker and thinner parts to consistent size.
Rovings then spun into yarn

Optional combing processes

↓

Fabric mills
(Weaving / Knitting)

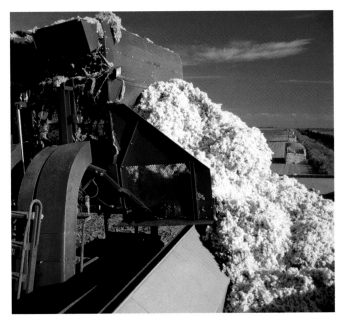

Ginning

Ginning is the generic term used for the complete process of turning the cotton bolls into fibre, and the building in which these processes occur is referred to as the gin. The name was originally used as an abbreviation of the word 'engine', and is now part of cotton vocabulary. At this stage, and until the ginning process has been completed, the cotton is referred to as **seed cotton**.

Once the cotton blocks have been delivered to the gin they are broken apart and fed into the ginning machine, which efficiently separates the cotton fibres from the seedpods, removing leaves, burs, dirt, stems and the fuzzy down known as **linters**. Usable cotton fibres will make up about 35 per cent of the pre-ginned cotton weight. The balance of the pre-ginned weight is made up from 55 per cent removed seeds and 10 per cent waste. The seeds are refined and made into cottonseed oil for human consumption. The linters are used in the manufacture of paper, as well as within the plastics industry.

The ginning machine also cleans the cotton, which is now referred to as lint instead of seed cotton.

Classification

The next stage is the classification of the cotton for the purpose of pricing. The lint is formed into bales from which samples are taken to establish fibre quality. Staple length, colour, cleanliness and **micronaire** are the four principal aspects by which the ginned cotton is judged. Micronaire represents fibre fineness and maturity, which is influenced by the climate during the growing period. A poor micronaire count affects the processing and therefore the value of the cotton. After pricing the bales are sold to cotton merchants who in turn sell them on to textile mills or spinners.

Processing and spinning

Once processed to remove traces of wax, protein and seeds, cotton fibre consists of nearly pure **cellulose**, which is a **natural polymer**. The arrangement of the cellulose is such that it gives cotton fibres a high degree of strength, absorbency and durability. Each fibre is made up of between 20 to 30 layers of cellulose coiled in a neat series of natural springs. The fibres of the open boll dry into flat, twisted, ribbon-like shapes that become kinked and interlock together. It is this interlocked form that is ideal for spinning into fine yarn.

Spinning is a generic term for all the processes the fibres will pass through to become yarn, ready for eventual weaving or knitting.

Once at the spinning mill, which may also be referred to as the 'spinners', the bales are opened and further cleaned to remove any residue vegetable matter and short lint. A machine called a **picker** beats, loosens and mixes the fibres, which are then passed through toothed rollers of varying sizes to remove the residue vegetable matter. The fibres finally come off the machine in batts, large bundles of multiple strands of fibres, which are then ready to be carded. The short lint is sold on for other processes and end uses.

The **carding machine** lines up the fibres evenly to make them easier to spin. This is done by passing the batts through different-sized rollers that produce what is termed slivers (pronounced sly-vers), or untwisted ropes of fibres. Several slivers are then combined to equalize the thicker and thinner parts of the slivers, thus making a more consistent size. These are now too thick, so are separated into **rovings**, long, narrow bundles of fibre with twist to hold them together.

In addition to carding, fibres can also go through an optional combing process to make them smoother (see page 13). Finally, the rovings are spun into yarns.

(opposite page) Mechanized cotton harvesting in the United States.

(above) Seed cotton ready for the ginning process.

Naturally pigmented Peruvian Pakucho™ cotton from Ecoyarns.

Luxury cotton

Luxury cotton is defined as cotton with characteristics far superior to those of the standard varieties and finishes.

A longer-staple fibre tends to be more desirable, because it can withstand additional combing processes that in turn will make it smoother and finer to the touch. Long-staple cotton may be obtained from many different countries or regions.

Egyptian, **Sea Island** and **Pima** are all names that denote a traditionally luxurious and fine-quality product. The pedigree of their heritage assures the consumer that the product they are buying has an added value. They also provide a USP (unique selling point) for brands targeting a more discerning customer.

Egyptian cotton

Egyptian cotton is used for clothing and household linens alike; however, it is possibly for bed and bath linen that the name most evokes a product of luxury and quality. The term is applied to all cotton grown in Egypt; however, less than half of Egyptian cotton has the desirable extra-long staple length.

Ironically, the cotton species that best produces this extra-long staple is an indigenous American plant, *Gossypium barbadense*. The French and English introduced Native American cotton into Egypt at the time of the American Civil War, when the northern Union ships were blockading southern ports to stop the export of Confederate cotton. Egyptian cotton became a realistic alternative, with the advantage of shorter shipping times to that of cotton from India. Today the term Egyptian cotton is also applied to another indigenous American species, *Gossypium hirsutum*.

In summary, the term 'Egyptian cotton' can be applied to either of the two long-staple varieties. Most importantly the term Egyptian used as a prefix implies luxury and refinement and is considered the ultimate in cotton.

Grey cotton jersey-dress featuring undulating three-dimensional 'landscaping' detailing by Ria Thomas. The easy and comfortable drape expresses one of cotton's many versatile characteristics.

Sea Island cotton

The term 'Sea Island' is applied only to extra-long-staple cotton. However, unlike Egyptian cotton, it is not applied to the *Gossypium hirsutum* species but only to *Gossypium barbadense,* also known as Pima and **Creole** cotton. This species grows as a smaller bush requiring full sun and high humidity and rainfall; it is also sensitive to frost. The plant has a natural anti-fungal property that contains the chemical gossypol, making it naturally insect-repellent and therefore an ideal candidate for organic cotton. The cotton fibres are particularly long and silky.

The species is now cultivated widely across many countries, although its pedigree can be traced back originally to pre-Spanish conquest Peru, then subsequently to the West Indies. Barbados was the first British colony to export cotton and is possibly the original source of the name.

Whereas Egyptian cotton conjures up the idea of luxurious woven fabric, Sea Island cotton is associated with luxurious fine-gauge knitwear.

Luxury cotton types

Egyptian cotton

Gossypium hirsutum
and
Gossypium barbadense

Two long-staple cotton varieties grown in Egypt

Sea Island cotton

Gossypium barbadense

A long-staple cotton that is widely grown in several geographic regions. (Caribbean origins)

Pima cotton

Gossypium barbadense

A long-staple cotton grown by Pima Indians in southwest United States

Pima cotton

Pima cotton is silky smooth and is the popular name for *Gossypium barbadense,* which is the same species marketed under the Sea Island prefix, and also one of the two species of the extra-long-staple Egyptian cotton. The progenitors of American Pima cotton were indigenous Egyptian plants interbred with earlier South American varieties that became known as Yuma cotton in the early 1900s and then finally named after the Pima Indians that helped to first grow it. In the United States Pima cotton is grown in the southwestern states of Texas, New Mexico, Arizona and parts of southern California where the climate is dry and hot. Many plantations are run or owned by Native American Pima Indians. Supima® (superior Pima) cotton is a registered trademark of the Supima Association of America and is exclusively 100 per cent American-grown Pima cotton. It is often considered better than Egyptian cotton because it has a guaranteed staple length of between 2.5 and 3.7 cm. Only a very small percentage of the world's cotton is Supima. The Calvin Klein brand is an active exponent of Pima cotton for its products.

Pima cotton is also grown in Peru, together with a similar variety called **Tangüis cotton.** Both are grown organically. Some species of Tangüis cotton are naturally pigmented and can create natural mélange effects when mixed with white.

Today thousands of Indian peasant farmers are benefitting from the revival of native organic cotton.

Mercerized cotton

Mercerized cotton is not a type or variety of cotton but a treatment applied to the cotton to give it a more lustrous and smoother appearance. Named after John Mercer, who invented the technique in the mid-nineteenth century, it was not popularized until the 1890s, when the processing technique was improved.

Mercerizing can be applied either to the yarn or to the fabric, or for ultimate luxury it may be applied to both, when it is then referred to as double mercerized.

Mercerizing is a series of processes that exposes the yarn or fabric to caustic soda while under tension. The caustic soda 'burns' off superfluous surface fibres or lint to create a 'rounder', smoother yarn, resulting in a lustrous effect achieved by light reflection on the improved yarn. Long-staple cotton is an ideal candidate for mercerization. The end product results in a finer fabric that is also cooler and more comfortable to wear, sometimes with an almost silk-like appearance.

(left) Fine-knit cotton longjohns by John Smedley.

(above) Mercerized cotton vest by Zimmerli of Switzerland. Mercerizing is a process that 'burns' off superfluous surface fibres resulting in a luxurious and lustrous silk-like effect that is cooler and more comfortable to wear.

151

Cotton lisle

Cotton lisle is similar to mercerized cotton in that all the lint and threads are burnt off to give a smoother touch. It is used for expensive cotton underwear and socks.

Filo di Scozia

Filo di Scozia® is a registered trademark that represents the highest grade of cotton fabric or yarn. It is two-ply, combed, long-staple, double-mercerized cotton. It has the unique characteristics of brilliance, softness and a silky touch and, above all, the ability to maintain these characteristics over time. Filo di Scozia® is used for the very best cotton knitwear and hosiery.

Cotton cupro

Cupro is pure organic cellulose fibres reborn from the discarded linters that are part of processing cotton. Although a by-product of cotton, the fuzzy down, or linters, when processed are perfectly round and smooth in cross-section, with a naturally silky smooth finish, and possessing many of the attributes of cotton, such as moisture management. Cupro makes a perfect lightweight lining; it is far cooler to wear than both silk and man-made linings, provides the gentleness of a natural fibre with the functionality of a man-made one and is also biodegradable. Bemberg produce excellent cupro linings, which are favoured by many of the prestigious Italian tailoring houses.

Relaxed men's suit and tunic by Kostas Murkudis in a silk and cupro mix. Cupro is a pure cellulose fibre made from cotton linters, a by-product of cotton processing.

Ecological and ethical considerations

The increasing demand for cotton at competitive prices has resulted in what may be considered mass-exploitation of poor cotton farmers and the land upon which cotton is cultivated. However, there are alternatives that allow the consumer to choose a product from an ethically and environmentally sound source.

Approximately 30 per cent of the cotton harvested and knitted for T-shirt production is shipped to a second country for manufacturing, impacting on cotton's carbon footprint.

Some cotton cultivation is known to make use of a variety of pesticides and insecticides. These are especially prevalent in the developing world and some sources attribute deaths within the cotton industry to their use. Cotton Incorporated is a company with offices worldwide that offers extensive information regarding all aspects of cotton, from farming and 'green issues' to design and manufacturing. It also has an extensive list of fabric resources.

The American and Australian cotton industries have invested in **biotechnology** to try to combat the excessive use of insecticides associated with standard commercial cotton production. However, this has resulted in much of the cotton grown today being **GM cotton**.

There are two types of GM, or transgenic, cotton in use. **Bollgard**® is obtained from a naturally occurring soil bacterium, *Bacillus thuringiensis*, referred to as **Bt cotton**. This naturally occurring soil organism is used as a spray, which reduces the use of insecticides by up to 85 per cent compared to conventionally grown cotton. It gives the plant an in-built tolerance to its main pest, the *Heliothis* caterpillar, and in North America the boll weevil. The alternative product is **Roundup Ready**®, which is obtained from the soil bacterium *Agrobacterium tumefaciens*. This herbicide-tolerant cotton reduces the amount of soil cultivation and herbicides needed to control weeds. It also promotes healthier soil through less disruption and a reduction in herbicide residues.

Organic cotton

GM cotton shares with **organic cotton** the same issue of chemical usage in the growing cycle, however the similarities stop there as organic cotton has a completely different ethos.

Slowly but steadily there are now a growing number of farmers moving towards a more organic, ecologically sound and socially sustainable method of production. Organic agricultural methods rely upon crop rotation and the use of natural enemies, such as ladybirds, to suppress harmful insects, rather than the use of agrochemicals, artificial fertilizers and other toxic-persistent chemicals. Organic cotton does not use genetically modified organisms but seeks to build a biologically diverse agricultural system, replenishing and maintaining the soil's fertility.

Organic cotton is far more expensive to produce; however it does not pollute and there is no over-production. Unfortunately, currently it only represents a small percentage of global cotton production.

Organic cotton is grown in around 20 countries, with Turkey the primary producer. The United States, India, Peru, Uganda, Egypt, Senegal, Tanzania, China and Israel also produce organic cotton.

Men's organic cotton seersucker suit by San Francisco based eco-brand Oda. The company is founded upon an ethos of socially-responsible manufacturing practice and only uses environmentally-sound materials to make its clothing.

153

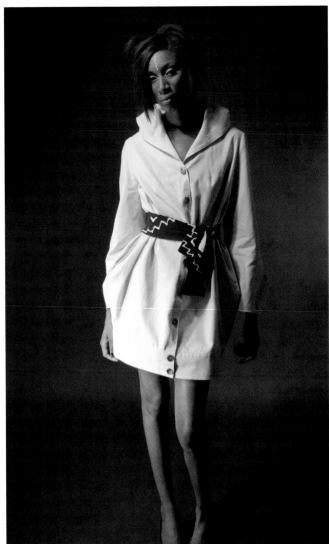

Citrus 'Loisangine' coat dress in an organic cotton and hemp blend by Céline Faizant.

Water

Cotton is a thirsty crop, a fact that is fast presenting problems to countries whose economic growth overly relies upon the cotton industry but whose geographical position suffers from water shortages. Uzbekistan and Kazakhstan, both once part of the former Soviet Union, have in parts been turned into a desert through the excessive cultivation of cotton, which in turn has also led to the shrinking of the Aral Sea.

Developments are now being made in the cultivation of new plant varieties that include drought-resistant, flame-resistant and wrinkle-free genetically modified cotton.

Striking organic cotton 'little black dress' by visionary Danish fashion brand Noir, whose visual identity and uncompromising aesthetic belie the brand's sustainable eco-credentials upon which the company was founded.

Naturally coloured cotton

Peruvian Pima and Tangüis cotton is naturally coloured and grown organically.

Five millennia before the advent of European settlers, Native American peoples of the Peruvian coastal valleys cultivated **naturally coloured cotton**, the principal colours being (then as now) cream, beige, brown, chocolate and mauve. Many varieties and landraces of New World cotton plants were identified and named in the following two centuries, describing the wide range of both fibre lengths and natural pigmentation.

Europe's Industrial Revolution saw an explosion in commercial cotton manufacturing, where the contemporary concern was with printing and dyeing, processes for which white cotton was preferred. Furthermore, the shorter fibres of the coloured plant species were more difficult to spin commercially. This lack of financial incentive meant naturally coloured cotton remained commercially dormant until the early 1980s.

Algodón pais, as the traditional farmers call the naturally coloured cotton plants, continues to be farmed for domestic use, artisan textile crafts, traditional medicinal cures and religious rituals. In traditional communities infants wear pads of naturally coloured brown cotton, as it is believed to protect their fragile skulls. It has recently been discovered that cotton seeds contain modest amounts of natural antibiotic substances.

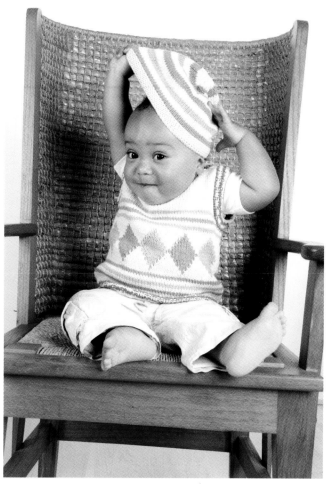

(above) Children's knitwear by Stella James. The range of cotton colours featured in this outfit is naturally occurring. Naturally coloured cotton offers an extra benefit in that it has inherent flame-retardant properties.

(left) Picking naturally coloured cotton in Peru.

Naturally coloured cotton rovings.

Naturally coloured cotton requires minimal maintenance after sowing: compared to other varieties, it is far more resistant to insects and diseases, does not require fertilizers and pesticides, needs far less water during its growing cycle and so can grow successfully in desert soils. Brown cotton does not require chemical treatment because it has natural fire-retardant properties and is ideal for children's clothing.

In Peru, Peru Naturtex Partners offers local farmers a lucrative cash crop – organic **Fairtrade**-certified Pakucho, naturally pigmented cotton – as an alternative to growing coca, the natural ingredient of synthesized cocaine. The company is the first in Latin America to develop naturally coloured organically grown cotton on an industrial scale.

In the US, Fox Fibre produces naturally coloured cotton in a range of colours that include browns, greens and rusts. Most of the cotton is organically grown and has been engineered to have a longer fibre that can be commercially spun. It is grown in Texas, New Mexico and Arizona.

(Source: James M. Vreeland Jr., www.perunaturtex.com)

(opposite page) Unlined hooded coat in lightweight, naturally-coloured cotton muslin by Rohit Khosla. The coat features hemp-rope tied sections that reflect the technique used to create the pleated crinkle cloth.

Ecological and ethical considerations

Fairly traded cotton

Cotton is one of a number of cash crops. A cash crop, in agricultural terms, is grown for money as opposed to domestic subsistence. In the United States cotton is the leading cash crop and is the number one **added value crop** – a crop grown under a written contract with the intent of receiving a premium because of its special attributes. Cotton is a very important global commodity; however many farmers in the developing world are paid very little for their produce. They find it difficult to compete with the developed countries, especially when government subsidies artificially depress the global price of cotton; it is estimated that the price would be at least 15 per cent higher if the market was not manipulated. In 2004 West African cotton farmers were paid approximately 30 per cent of the true market price for their cotton. By contrast, US producers (who currently receive subsidies equal to their total crop value) were paid 70 per cent above the market price. In 2003/4 60 per cent of US cotton was dumped on the global market, this figure rising to 76 per cent in 2003/4.

Fairtrade cotton is defined as cotton which has met the international Fairtrade standard for production of seed cotton (harvested with seed and fibre attached) and is therefore eligible to carry the FAIRTRADE mark. It is an independent product certification label that means the farmers receive a fair and stable market price, as well as benefiting from longer term and more direct trading relationships. Cotton farmers are at the bottom of the supply chain and therefore susceptible to price exploitation within the trading system. The Fairtrade certification helps to redress the situation by basing the Fairtrade price on the actual cost of sustainable production. If the market price is higher than the minimum price then the market price applies.

Fairtrade food products were first launched internationally in 1994. Cotton carrying the certified FAIRTRADE mark was launched in the United Kingdom in November 2005 and cotton farming groups currently selling into the UK market include India, Mali, Egypt, Cameroon, Burkina Faso and Senegal. There are plans to extend certification to include Peru and East Africa.

53 per cent of global cotton is government subsidized. Unsubsidized countries find it difficult to trade at a fair price.

Tackling subsidies

In 2002 Brazil was the first country to make a formal complaint to the United States under the world trade disputes process of the World Trade Organization (WTO) regarding the issue of government subsidies and their ethical implications. Australia acted as a third party mediator. The resulting recommendation was to withdraw export credit guarantees and payments to domestic users and exporters, and to remove the adverse effects of mandatory price subsidies. Although little has been done to redress the situation it has led to a fair trade in cotton clothing. Fairly traded footwear was added to the rapidly growing market for organic clothing.

Hand-dyed jersey top with organic cotton eyelet gored skirt by San Francisco based eco-brand Oda. A strong commitment to socially and environmentally sound materials and practices underpins the company's ethos.

Ethical trading

Fairtrade clothing is not to be confused with ethical trading. Ethical trading or sourcing is a business model that aims to ensure that acceptable minimum labour standards are met in the **supply chain** for the whole company and their range of products.

Fairtrade

There is now an international Fairtrade fortnight in the UK, and schools are encouraged to join the Fairtrade schools scheme.

For a cotton product to be eligible to carry the FAIRTRADE mark, the cotton must be sourced wholly from a certified Fairtrade source, while a blended product (cotton plus other fibre) must be at least 50 per cent Fairtrade certified cotton.

Fairtrade certified cotton farmers receive a stable and fair price for their cotton and better access to the cotton market.

Fairtrade standards encourage a greater respect for the environment.

Fairtrade encourages closer links between shoppers and producers.

White organic cotton jacket by Danish brand Noir. The brand was founded upon ethical and ecological principles by Peter Ingwersen in connection with textile company Illuminati II, which was created 'to prove that organic and ethical fabrics can be used in luxurious and sexy designs'.

159

The Australian cotton industry is a leader in sustainable production, and growers do not receive any government subsidies. As a body it self-funds environmental audits.

Organic Fairtrade cotton

Clothing made with Fairtrade cotton is not to be confused with ethically traded clothing, as they are quite different things. Fairtrade specifically aims to improve the position of marginalized producers in the developing world by empowering them to invest in sustainable development projects that have a wider community benefit.

Not all Fairtrade certified cotton is organic. At present only about 20 per cent of the Fairtrade cotton producers are farming organically, although those that are not organic producers must implement a system of integrated crop management to establish a balance between environmental protection and business results. Organic fertilizers and biological disease control methods are used to replace industrialized methods of farming. The Fairtrade standards prohibit the use of genetically modified seeds as well as encouraging appropriate water management. (Source ICAC 2004)

Peru Naturtex is the first company of its kind in the Americas to deal in organic cotton on a Fairtrade basis.

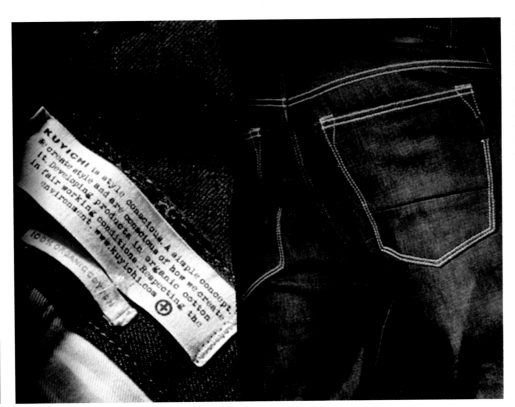

(left) Organic jeans by Dutch design brand Kuyichi. Cotton denim is the ultimate democratic fashion fabric, eternally desirable to all consumers.

(below) Hand-printed cotton boots by Como No. The products are handmade in Argentina from transitional cotton, which will be fully certified as organic in 2009. This transitional cotton comes from small producers from northern Argentina. All processes, from the growing of the cotton to the finished product, are manufactured under Fairtrade. The exclusive prints are eco-friendly and heavy-metal free.

160

Designer Antoine Peters up-cycles strips of cotton sweaters knotted and knitted together to form this multi-coloured 'mega sweater' dress.

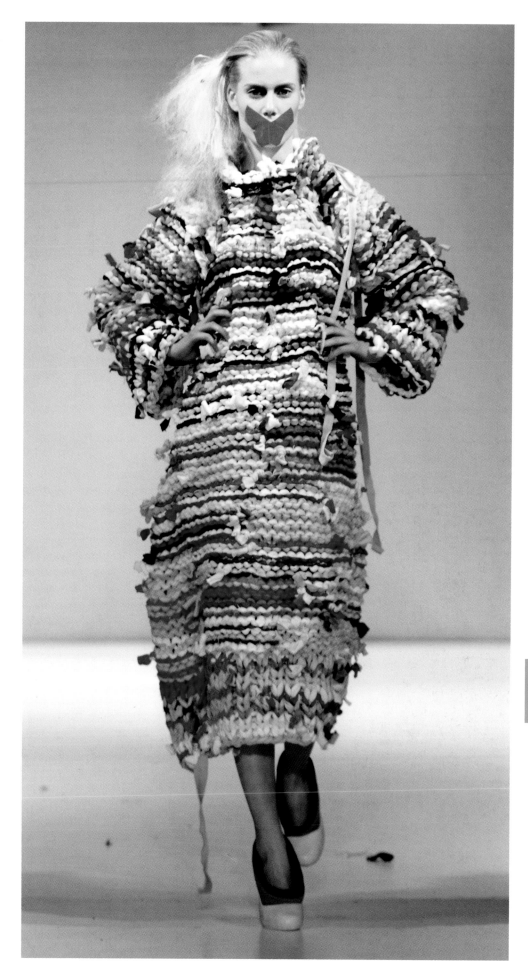

Cotton fabrics

The fabrics listed represent the most popular cottons in use and would give a designer or merchandiser an extensive selection for a collection. It is not, however, exhaustive.

    The fabrics are primarily made from cotton yarns, though some names are shared with other natural and synthetic yarns.

Furry

These cotton fabrics have three-dimensional, tactile, rough textures.

Chenille French for 'caterpillar', which it closely resembles, this fabric has a fur-like texture.

Corduroy Cut-pile fabric, usually cotton. The original French name, corde du roi meant 'cloth of kings'. Corduroy is described by the size of its wales (ribs).

Flannelette A soft-brushed surface on a basic cloth.

Moleskin Medium-weight firm fabric with a fine-brushed nap to one side.

Towelling Woven fabric with uncut loops to one or both sides. Knitted towelling is usually referred to as terry towelling.

Velvet Straight or diagonally woven fabric with a cut pile. The choice of yarn to make velvet will greatly influence its visual appearance, more so than with many other fabrics.

Velveteen A lighter and often finer version of velvet.

Velour May be woven or knitted fabric with a close-cropped velvet effect.

Textured

Raised surface effects.

Aertex A cellular fabric constructed with tiny 'air holes' for warmth.

Bedford cord A flattened warp ribbed effect without the usual raised surface of a classic corduroy.

Cloqué A double-cloth weave where different shrinking factors achieve a figured or blistered effect. Also known as 'blister fabric'.

Crêpon The yarn has been heat crêped before weaving, creating an uneven crêpe effect.

Crinkle All-over heat-pleated or crinkled fabric.

Seersucker Yarns with differential shrinkages are woven then washed to create a crinkle effect. May be plain, check or stripe.

Piqué or piquette Has a bird's-eye raised effect. May be woven or knitted.

(right) This 100 per cent cotton washed denim (Italian) with darker blue weft and whitish warp has been washed with chemicals to achieve a smooth finish. The different shades were achieved by twice hand over-dyeing the original denim, achieving three shades of the same colour. The long shirt worn underneath is made of a 100 per cent worsted wool (Italian), usually used for men's suits with a shiny finishing.

(left) Denim modernizes the traditional shape of this oriental tunic, inspired by the exploration of clothing and textiles from other cultures by surface textiles designer Gabrielle Miller. The tunic features an original screen print and embroidered borders.

Sheer

These are more fragile fabrics.

Batiste Very finely woven and almost sheer.

Gauze A very light, straight weave that is semi-translucent.

Muslin Very lightweight, plain-weave fabric that is almost transparent.

Voile Fine, sheer and semi-transparent plain weave using tightly twisted yarns.

(above) Crisp cotton poplin shirt and skirt by Kris Van Assche.

(above) Inspired by Elizabethan costume, designer Nabil El Nayal has cut this voluminous 'six-sleeve' dress from 16 metres (52 ft) of cotton shirting.

(left) Menswear by Kris Van Assche. This outfit exploits the crisp and airy qualities of pure white cotton and lends them a fresh, contemporary edge.

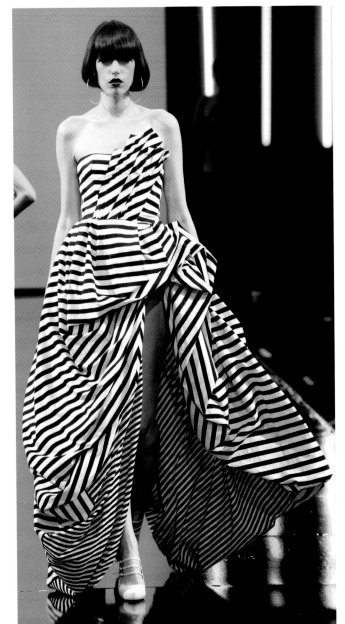

Smooth

These fabrics have a polished effect.

Chintz A Hindi word for printed cloth with a **glazed** surface, originating in India in the seventeenth century and made popular during the Raj. Now generically used to imply flower-printed fabric.

Ciré French in origin. A high-gloss look is achieved by impregnating the fabric with wax and heating and pressing it.

Lawn Very fine, lightweight plain-weave fabric with a crisp finish originating in Laon, France.

Sateen Satin-weave fabric with a polished sheen to the face side.

164

The versatility of cotton is expressed in the graphic appeal of this crisp corseted and draped gown by Elaine Kinney from her black and white 'monochrome' collection.

Functional

These fabrics are grouped by weave and construction rather than weight. For example, twills, drills and denims come in many different weights and finishes, ranging from pristine to aged and from smooth to **brushed**.

Chambray Light- to medium-weight plain weave using alternate **indigo** and white yarns.

Denim Usually a twill weave using both white and indigo dyed yarns.

Drill Heavier-weight twill weaves with a workwear feel.

Gabardine Diagonal weave with clearly defined diagonal rib effect to surface.

Gingham Lightweight plain weave with yarn-dyed stripes or checks of an even size.

Madras Originally a vegetable-dyed hand-woven fabric from Madras, India. Today it is suggestive of any bold check or stripe.

Poplin A strong plain-weave fabric with a very light cross-rib effect. The fabric was originally made for the pope and referred to as 'Papalino'.

Twill Diagonal weave.

Authentic

Utility cottons.

Calico Generic name for lighter-weight plain-weave, coarse-yarn fabric, often used for making a toile.

Canvas Generic name for plain-weave coarse fabric, often un-dyed, in many different weights.

Cheesecloth Thin, loosely woven, plain-weave Indian cloth originally used in the food trade but made into an iconic 1960s hippy fabric.

Duck Plain weave with a canvas-like feel.

Hopsack Straight-weave construction using roughish yarns, often with a slub.

Repp Has a pronounced weft rib effect.

Ticking A heavy diagonal-weave fabric striped with a coloured yarn.

Toile Generic name for a straight-weave fabric, as well as implying a prototype/sample made in a workroom.

(above left) Gary Harvey challenges preconceptions of used clothing by reforming and glamorizing reclaimed garments. This reconstructed crinoline-shaped dress is made from aged and gradated colour indigo-dyed jeans.

165

Supple cotton jersey all-in-one, influenced by traditional men's underwear by Adam Kimmel.

Sustainable plant fibres

Renewable and sustainable fibre sources that can thrive without chemical intervention are the way forward if we are to use our resources wisely.

A steadily growing awareness of the impact of our actions upon global resources means that educated consumers are beginning to respond to information regarding sustainability and ethics, and are electing to make choices to consciously support brands that assert a sustainable profile. In the future, brands that operate without accountability and transparency risk losing market share. The challenge for the future is to think beyond the immediate creative and technical processes that bring a product to life, and to be aware of the wider context in which the product exists.

The fashion and textile industries are substantial employers and contribute significantly to economic systems globally. More than ever it is crucial that the designer or product developer makes informed choices, based not only on aesthetic and tactile properties of a fabric but also on the provenance of the raw material and how it impacts upon the environment and the communities that generate the fabrics.

The variety of sustainable plants now being commercially grown is encouraging to both the designer and consumer. This section considers a variety of fibre types obtained from the stems or leaves of plants. Some of these fibres have been in use for thousands of years, while others are modern-day developments of indigenous plants that are being cultivated for their strong eco-credentials and sustainability.

Today stylish and sustainable are no longer mutually exclusive.

Oil

During much of the twentieth century the focus of fabric development and manufacturing centred on a traditional group of natural fibres, some synthetics regenerated from cellulose and a large number of synthetic **polymers** based, predominantly, on oil. The issue with petroleum-based man-made fabrics is their reliance on a diminishing, non-renewable natural resource. The price of polyester is inextricably linked to the price of oil. Reducing our dependency on polyester will in turn reduce our dependency on oil.

(opposite page) Consideration of the whole life cycle of a product must become second nature to future industry professionals. Awareness of the provenance of raw materials and their impact upon the environment and the communities that generate the products will impact on future supply chain issues.

'"It is a question of discipline" the little prince said to me later on. "When you've finished your own toilet in the morning, then it is time to attend to the toilet of your planet, just so, with the greatest care."' Antoine de Saint Exupéry, *Le Petit Prince.* Lingerie made from discarded pine branches by French brand g=9.8.

Ecology and sustainability

Fashion reflects the zeitgeist of contemporary living, and ecology and sustainability are key issues in today's society. Concerns that were once relevant to a few committed activists have now become an urgent set of criteria that affects how we view everything we consume. What started as a trend will very soon be a real part of the market that affects designers, retailers and the buying public.

Students and graduates of fashion courses, as the next generation of industry players, have a critical role to play, and hold the potential to exert a real influence over the way the fashion business is managed in the future.

Informed choices

At the end of a product's life issues of quality and durability are implicated: will it be recycled or does it need to be **biodegradable**? Informed choices need to be made with these criteria in mind. We have a responsibility to understand what is most appropriate for our products and be informed about the impact our decisions can have, as well as the implications on the ecology and prosperity of the countries that specialize in processing certain fibres.

The way forward

New waves of eco-textiles are providing new solutions and benefits. Designers and brands with sustainability and corporate responsibility woven into their philosophy and operations can offer the consumer real sartorial choice.

Companies such as Patagonia, manufacturers of outdoor performance clothing, accept their old products back for recycling; while a company called Potential Fashions uses recycled clothing to create new clothing by making 'additions' to the old pieces to create new styles. Traid is a registered charity that recycles, through retail outlets, approximately 80 per cent of the discarded clothing it receives, in addition it has a division called Traidremade, which adapts and redesigns, or 'up-cycles', old pieces into new, one-off designs. The brand From Some Where goes through a similar creative process with their recycled clothing.

Linda Loudermilk's silk and cotton treescape printed cape dress exemplifies the designer's approach to cutting-edge design coupled with proactive research and development of sustainable fabrics to create a luxury-eco brand that targets the most demanding luxury consumers.

168 Textile diversion

Textile re-use is not classified as recycling, but as textile diversion. Soiled or wet old clothes are not always usable and may end up in landfill sites, because washing and drying facilities are not always present at sorting units.

Damaged textiles are sorted to make industrial wiping rugs.

Green chemistry

There are 12 principles that explain what the definitions of **green chemistry** should mean in practice, as set out by Paul Anastas and John Warner. They help to define the true ecological, ethical and sustainable credentials of a raw material or product. These should be considered seriously by anybody looking to source or work with green fabrics for ethical reasons rather than pure marketing potential.

Prevention Preventing waste is better than treating or cleaning it after it is formed. This is self-explanatory. Currently there is a whole industry built on cleaning waste. It is very expensive to treat waste and contain it. The waste has to be monitored even after it has been contained.

Atom economy When creating materials it is important to maximize the incorporation of all the materials used into the final product. In other words, waste as little material as possible. For example, if the process has 50 per cent atom economy, then half of the materials that are used turn out to be waste. Only half of the materials actually end up as product.

Less hazardous synthesis Processes should be designed to use and generate substances that have little to no toxicity. Plan the process of creating the materials to use substances that are not toxic and to produce substances that are not toxic. This is often easier said than done!

Designing safer chemicals Chemical products should be designed to function well while reducing toxicity. Reducing toxicity of the products reduces hazards to people and to the environment.

Safer solvents Whenever possible avoid the use of additional substances such as solvents and separating agents. When these substances are needed they should be non-toxic.

Energy efficiency Energy efficiency should be considered when designing and producing a product. The energy requirements should be minimized since they impact the environment and raise cost. When possible, processes should be conducted at room temperature and pressure.

Use renewable resources When possible the feedstock (or material used to make the product) should come from renewable resources. For example, there is research being done to make chemicals out of products such as corn instead of coal or oil. Also, when choosing a feedstock look at waste from other reactions being made in the lab.

Reduce derivatives Derivatives are chemicals that are used to cause a temporary effect in the process. This could be a chemical that protects a certain part of the substance that is later removed, or it could be a chemical that causes a temporary change in a property so that a reaction can take place. Using derivatives should be avoided when possible. They do not end up in the final product and only increase waste.

Catalysis Use selective catalytic reagents over stoichiometric reagents. A catalyst helps a reaction occur with less energy, plus it speeds the reaction.

Consider the end Design for the proper disposal of the item. The product that is made should break down into non-toxic substances after it has been used. This way the product will not remain and build up in the environment.

Use real-time pollution prevention Methods need to be further developed to allow real-time monitoring of chemical processes. This includes monitoring while the process is happening, detection and control of the formation of hazardous substances and monitoring after the substance has been disposed of.

Accident prevention The substance and the form of the substance (liquid, gas, etc) should be carefully chosen to minimize accidents during the chemical process. Accidents include fire, explosion and accidental release.

Source: *Green Chemistry: Theory and Practice*, Paul T. Anastas and John D. Warner, Oxford University Press, 2000

'Green we go', a conversation piece by Myka Baum. While the scourge of environmentalists, the much-maligned plastic bottle can today be recycled into fleece fabric.

Bast fibres

A bast fibre, also described as a soft fibre, is obtained from the **phloem** or inner skin of a plant. The fibre needs to be separated from the xylem or woody core and sometimes also from the epidermis, the outermost layer of cells carrying nutrients to the leaves. Bast fibres tend to have good tensile strength.

Jute

Jute, or **hessian** as the fabric is better known, is one of the cheapest natural fibres to produce and is the second most important vegetable fibre after cotton in terms of usage, global consumption, production and availability.

Jute is native to the monsoon regions of the world, growing during the monsoon season. The most important region for jute has always been Bengal in the Ganges delta, where it was an integral part of the local culture.

The history of jute

During British rule of India in the nineteenth and early twentieth centuries jute was shipped to Dundee in Scotland to be processed and woven, and was an important part of their economy until the 1970s, when it was usurped by synthetics. In Bangladesh it was once referred to as the 'golden fibre', because it represented the largest foreign currency into the country. Demand dropped and local farmers burnt their crops rather than sell at unsustainable prices; however, recently there has been an increase in demand and prices have risen steadily. Bangladesh and West Bengal, in India, are still the principal producers of jute, while China and Thailand also have a strong jute production.

Today jute is an important component in the automotive industry because it is high in both **tensile** and **ductile strength**: its strength and lightness of weight make vehicles more fuel-efficient and thus a better ecological proposition. The fibre is also used for paper, film, **composite materials** and **geo textiles** in environmental engineering.

In North America it is referred to as **burlap**.

Jute fibre

Jute is a long, soft, shiny vegetable fibre that is coarse and strong. Jute fibres are composed of mainly cellulose but also **lignin,** a wood fibre. It could therefore be described as a fibre that is part textile and part wood.

The plant is of the *Corchorus* genus and is native to tropical and subtropical regions. The two varieties are white, or Indian, jute (*Corchorus capsularis*), and tossa jute (*Corchorus olitorius*), an Afro-Arabic jute. Tossa jute is also now grown in India. Tossa jute is softer and silkier than white jute; the more lustrous the fibre the higher the quality of the product.

Jute fibres have a high tensile strength and blend well with other natural and synthetic fibres. When dyed they retain colour well, being both colour and light **fast**. Jute is anti-static, has low thermal conduction and a high level of UV protection. It is mostly used in the furnishing textile industries; however, due to its many advantageous properties, it is also now being developed for high-performance technical textiles.

Jute production

The fibre is produced from the outer skin or stem of the plant. The first process is retting, which involves immersion in running water. Stripping follows, usually done by women and children, and involves removing the non-fibrous matter to reach the fibres on the stem.

Ecological sustainability

Jute has very strong environmental credentials, because it does not require excessive watering, fertilizers or pesticides. It is a fast-growing plant with a good yield ratio of fibre to weight and acreage. It can be recycled several times within its life cycle and also has important biodegradable properties.

Tussah silk shoe with hemp rope ties by Indian designer Rohit Khosla. The shoe shape reflects a French rococo influence reinterpreted in hand-loom, raw and humble materials. The natural colours and texture of the hemp and raw silk complement each other.

Ramie

Ramie is a very old fibre crop used for textiles and believed to date back over 7,000 years. In Ancient Egypt mummies were sometimes wrapped in inner layers of linen with outer layers of ramie, while in China the fibre was mainly used for farm workers' clothing. In English-speaking countries it is pronounced either as RAY-mee or rah-mee.

China is the largest ramie producer, and it is also produced in Taiwan, the Philippines, Indonesia, Thailand, South Korea and India. In the western hemisphere, Brazil is the only important producer, the majority produced for domestic consumption with little being traded internationally. The principal consumers of the fibre are Japan, France, Germany and the United Kingdom. Ramie is also an important woven and knitted fabric for the North American market, where it is seen as a cheap 'linen-look' alternative.

Ramie fibre

Ramie is a strong fibre with a tensile strength between three and five times tougher than cotton and at least twice that of linen (flax), although it is brittle and will break if consistently folded in the same place. It holds its shape well but does tend to wrinkle easily, and is often **blended** with cotton and wool.

Fabric woven from ramie has a thick and thin horizontal appearance, giving it many of the visual characteristics of linen, and has often been used as a linen alternative because it costs far less to produce.

Ramie production

Ramie (*Boehmeria nivea*) is a flowering plant of the **nettle** family, native to Eastern Asia. It flourishes best in warm, humid temperatures, but is also able to withstand droughts. The two types of ramie are **China grass**, also known as true ramie or **white ramie**, and **green ramie**, believed to have originated in Malaysia. The fibres are produced from the bark or stalks of the plant, which are harvested on average two to three times each year, although under some growing conditions may be harvested up to six times in a year.

The plant is harvested soon after flowering, when it will produce the maximum amount of fibre. It is either cut just above the root, or bent at ground level where it can be stripped while still in the field, a process called **de-cortication** that removes the hard outer bark. Further scraping reveals the fibrous parts while also removing some of the gums and pectin. The third stage involves washing, drying and de-gumming, ready to extract the fibre for spinning. The de-gumming process requires chemical processing, which will eventually reduce the original dry weight by about 25 per cent. Ramie is a very absorbent fibre that also dries quickly, making spinning and weaving difficult due to the brittle characteristics of the fibre; good utilization depends on improved processing techniques.

Ecological sustainability

Ramie is a sustainable plant that has a long fibre-producing lifespan of up to 20 years and can be harvested up to six times a year.

Hemp

Hemp is the generic name for the entire *Cannabis* family of plants. There are several cultivated varieties and subspecies, as well as wild and feral cannabis. *Cannabis sativa* L. subsp. *sativa*, commonly known as **industrial hemp**, is the variety grown for fibre and other non-drug related purposes. Conversely, *Cannabis sativa* L. subsp. *indica* is the variety grown for both recreational and medical drug use. By contrast to its 'industrial' relative, this variety has poor fibre qualities. The principal difference between the two varieties is the level of THC (tetrahydrocannabinol) that each secretes.

The production of hemp in Western countries is growing steadily to meet the growing eco-demands of contemporary society. In Canada the export of hemp seeds increased by over 300 per cent during 2007–2009.

The history of hemp

China has the oldest tradition for hemp cultivation, where it was used for rope, clothing, shoes and early forms of paper. Hemp remains have been found in ancient Chinese pottery dating back 10,000 years. In Japan many traditional kimonos were decorated with images of hemp because it was considered a beautiful plant. In medieval Europe hemp was first cultivated on a small-scale domestic basis, and most communities would have had access to a hemp field for domestic cloth and rope production: hemp was easier to produce than flax for linen. In Germany and Italy, hemp was also used for culinary purposes, in soups and as fillings in pies. Under the reign of Elizabeth I of England (1558–1603) all landowners were obliged to grow hemp for sails and rope for naval use. Commercial hemp production in Europe vastly expanded in the eighteenth century with colonial and naval expansion, and it was popularly said that the British Empire was built on hemp. It was an essential element of shipbuilding, being used for sails, ropes and oakum (tarred fibre preparation used to pack joints of timber ships). During the Napoleonic Wars many military uniforms were made of hemp, favoured for its strength and low cost. Hemp was considered a commercially viable plant because it produced a high volume of fibre to the ratio of land used for its cultivation.

The term 'money for old rope' was coined after old hemp rope was recycled to make early bank notes.

In North America, hemp was primarily grown in Kentucky and the Midwest. The American Declaration of Independence was drafted on hemp paper, and Betty Ross made the first American flag from hemp canvas. America's first president, George Washington, was a hemp farmer and recommended 'that it be planted everywhere'. The early republic became an important Western producer, inventing and developing machinery to better produce the fibre and its importance in nineteenth-century America was second only to King Cotton.

In the nineteenth century 80 per cent of the world's fabric was made from hemp.

The advent of steam-driven iron ships using steel cables rendered hemp almost redundant for naval purposes. In addition, the development of synthetic fibres in the twentieth century further reduced its reign. **DuPont** and William Randolph Hearst, industrialists who had financial interests in the petrochemical and timber industries respectively, were major adversaries of hemp cultivation, viewing it as a financial threat and lobbying the government until The Marijuana Tax Act was passed in 1937, which caused prices to plummet. The fibre fell out of

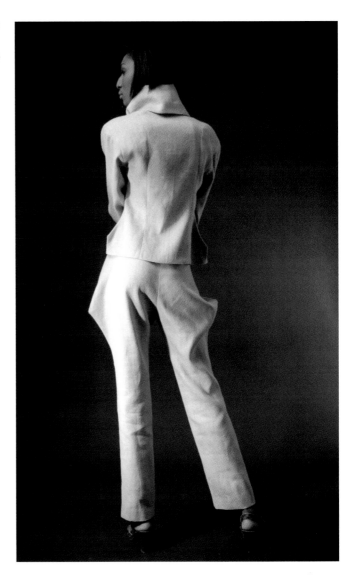

Oatmeal 'Mong' trouser suit by Céline Faizant in 55 per cent organic hemp and 45 per cent organic cotton.

service, in part due to the paranoia linked with its association with marijuana and illicit drug use, although the fibre-producing species and drug-producing species are quite different.

The Japanese invasion of much of the South Pacific during World War II meant that **Manila hemp**, or **abacá**, which the US navy used for ropes and canvas for uniforms, was unobtainable, and American domestic hemp was once again essential. Advertising propaganda of the time read 'Hemp for victory'.

Hemp's importance is now back in ascendance because it is seen as a viable and sustainable alternative crop for mass-cultivation for a variety of uses, including textiles.

Hemp fibre

Industrial hemp is an efficient crop that has multiple uses. The most valuable part of the plant is its fibres for production for the fabric industry, and it is also extensively used for biodegradable plastics and biofuels. It contributes to the construction and automotive industries as well as the health-food and cosmetics industries. It is second only to soy in its nutritional value, is highly digestible and an effective unsaturated oil. Hemp has good thermal values and resists decay and infestation.

Colours range from creamy white, shades of brown and grey as well as green and black. The fibres are strong and durable, resist mould, have good absorbency and offer protection against ultraviolet light.

Hemp production

Years of selective breeding have produced many different-looking varieties of hemp plant. Since the 1930s the focus has been on the production of strains that offer poor sources of drug material. The plants are long and slender with fibres that are between 1 and 5 m (3–16 ft) long running the full length of the plant. If the plant is harvested before it flowers it will produce finer fibres and be less effective as a potential drug source, although the THC is already much lower in industrial hemp. Male and female plants need to be planted together because it is the female plants that produce seeds for the next crop. Good seeds are integral to successful hemp production.

In some parts of the world hemp is still harvested by hand, otherwise the greater majority is now machine harvested. It is cut 2–3 cm (about 1 inch) above ground level and left to dry. Traditional methods of separating the fibres included dew and water retting. One involved floating the bundles of harvested hemp in water, while the other made use of natural ground dew and bacterial action. Modern retting involves mechanical thermo-pulping. Hemp can also be **cottonized** by a process similar to that used for flax.

Hemp is not easy to spin but does make for a very good blend when used together with cotton in a 50:50 ratio.

Hemp can be made into fabrics as diverse as the finest lace through to heavyweight industrial canvas.

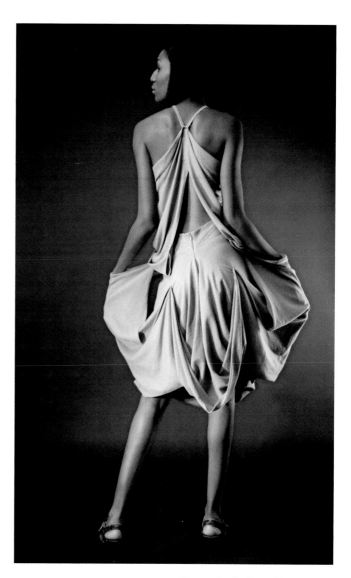

'Touareg' softly draped lilac skirt and top in a 45 per cent organic cotton 55 per cent organic hemp blend by designer Céline Faizant, whose mission statement is to 'Realize creations in ecological, organic or Fairtrade fabrics, and to allow a responsible consumption by offering transparency of manufacturing networks. To work towards defining a new luxury, and to participate in controlled channels in terms of ecology and human rights. Then elegance will not only be plastic ...'

173

Hemp market

Hemp is cultivated all over the world, although in the United States it is still illegal to grow hemp; however some states have granted licences for industrial hemp. Canada, the United Kingdom and Germany lifted the ban in the 1990s but within the European Union and Canada a licence has to be issued for its cultivation, described as 'industrial hemp for non-drug purposes'. Japan, under American influence, restricted the growth of hemp in 1948 and is one of the few Eastern countries to have prohibited its cultivation.

Up until the mid-1980s the old Soviet Union was the largest hemp producer, much of it being cultivated in Ukraine and the parts of Russia close to Poland. The world's premier institute for the development of hemp is still situated in Ukraine, where it develops new varieties with improved fibre content, increased yield and low THC.

Other important producers of hemp include China, North Korea, Romania and Hungary.

India produces a variety of hemp known as **Sunn** or **Bombay hemp**.

Ecological sustainability

Hemp is ecologically and sustainably important, and is often referred to as the world's most useful plant. It is non-toxic in use, renewable and non-polluting during its life cycle. It needs few if any pesticides, crops grow quickly, and around 100 days after harvesting the soil is left in better condition as it has been replenished with nutrients and nitrogen. In addition hemp controls topsoil erosion and produces a great amount of oxygen.

The seeds and stalks, as well as the general fermentation of the plant, produce an oil that may be used as biodiesel: as a low-energy fuel it is better than other similar crops. It can also be used for biodegradable plastics.

Hemp paper is eco-friendly because it does not require the bleaching processes of wood pulp. About 1 acre of hemp will produce the same paper quantity as around 4 acres of trees.

Kenaf

Kenaf is a species of hibiscus with visual similarities to jute. The word kenaf has Persian etymology, however in different parts of the world it is known by several other names, including **bimli, ambary, ambari hemp, deccan hemp** and **bimlipatum jute**.

Kenaf has a long history of cultivation in parts of Africa, India and Thailand. Today the major producers are China and India. The traditional uses for kenaf have been rope, twine and coarse cloth, as well as fuel and nutrition. It is an ideal candidate for sustainable ecological cultivation because it requires the minimum use of pesticides and fertilizers. The emerging uses for it today span engineering applications, insulation paper and clothing-grade cloth, as well as providing vegetable oil from the seeds. The fibres are naturally white and do not need to undergo any bleaching processes for either paper or cloth uses.

Kenaf is not produced in vast quantities and may not become commercially viable without financial investment and enthusiasm.

Nettle

The common stinging nettle has potential for fibre crop production; it is far stronger than cotton and finer than other bast fibres. It is an ecologically sustainable plant requiring far less water and no chemical pesticides or fertilization. It also sustains many varieties of invertebrate species.

Nettle is being investigated for possible use as an alternative eco-fibre, however its use is currently limited to a specialist clothing market.

Nettle yarn from Habu Textiles.

Bamboo

In China, bamboo is often referred to as the plant of a thousand uses.

Bamboo is a stem fibre that has been used for thousands of years, and is part of the cultural identity of several Asian countries. Today, through technology, perseverance and a will to find sustainable organic alternatives, textiles can be added to its list of traditional uses. Bamboo fibre has unique beneficial characteristics and qualities, with the added bonus that it helps to reduce greenhouse-gas emissions and enriches land that may have been drained of its nutrients through non-sustainable methods of cultivation.

Bamboo is a perennial evergreen of the grass family. It is of great cultural significance in many East Asian countries where it has been used for thousands of years as a building material, for ornamental garden design and also as a source of nutrition. In addition to its many historic and contemporary uses it has been developed as a fibre for the textile industry by Beijing University.

Bamboo fibre
Bamboo fibre is strong and durable with a good stability and tensile strength. The regenerated fibre has visual similarities to cotton but is far softer, while the fineness and whiteness of bamboo fibre make it comparable to rayon, which undergoes similar processing being derived from wood pulp.

Bamboo fibres naturally block out over 90 per cent of both UVA and UVB rays. Bamboo textiles are soft and have a natural sheen.

At a microscopic level bamboo has a round cross section, making it smooth to wear next to the skin. In the US its softness has earned it the description of 'cashmere from plants'.

The surface of the cross section is covered with micro-gaps and micro-holes, which make it moisture-absorbing and a good source of ventilation. This microstructure allows fast absorption and evaporation, and bamboo fabric outperforms cotton's absorbency rate by more than threefold. It will wick away and evaporate perspiration instantly, keeping the wearer drier and cooler. It is also believed that the fibre will keep the wearer one or two degrees cooler in a summer climate than other natural fibres which is, perhaps, why it is marketed in some Asian countries as 'air-conditioning dress'. The fibres also naturally block out over 90 per cent of UVA and UVB rays.

Bamboo kun is a natural substance within bamboo that protects the plant from pests and pathogens (biological agents causing disease to a host plant), and it is this substance that prevents bacteria from cultivating in processed bamboo fabric, thus making it naturally anti-microbial, making it less likely to cause skin irritations than fibres enhanced with chemical antibacterial additives. Japanese laboratory tests have shown that even after 50 washing cycles bamboo fibres continue to maintain the same level of antibacterial properties. Bamboo also has anti-static characteristics that make it sit well next to the skin and not cling. These qualities are used to promote bamboo as an ideal fabric for active sportswear clothing, especially for sports that generate a high degree of perspiration. It is for these same reasons that it is described as the perfect eco-performance fabric.

Bamboo production

Natural bamboo is one of the world's most prolific and fastest-growing plants; it can reach maturity in about four years, compared to the typical 20 to 70 years of many commercial tree species. There are around 90 genera and 1,000 species of bamboo spread across its extensive native habitat, ranging from the high altitudes of Asia down through to the north of Australia and west to India and parts of Africa and the Americas. Bamboo for commercial use is plantation grown and not harvested from tropical forests. The variety grown for conversion into textile fibre is **moso bamboo** or *phyllostachys*, which was and is still used in the construction and food industries.

Bamboo fibres are stem fibres, so, unlike bast fibres, the entire stems or culms are used. The stems can either be naturally converted into cellulose for processing into fibre, or chemically processed into bamboo **viscose**. Raw bamboo is crushed and pulped, then the process of hydro-alkalization extracts the natural cellulose that contains the bamboo kun (also spelt kunh), which is made into fibre. Bleaching processes may also be required.

Bamboo fibre can be spun finer than hair and is often blended with cotton to a 70:30 ratio of bamboo to cotton. Bamboo textiles are much softer than the softest cotton, and the fabrics have a natural sheen to the surface that is sometimes compared to silk and cashmere.

Ecological sustainability

Bamboo is a naturally grown and sustainable resource that does not require the use of pesticides or chemicals, partly due to the anti-microbial and anti-fungal bamboo kun. Bamboo biodegrades naturally through exposure to soil and sun. It is a naturally regenerative tropical grass with an extensive root system that self-replenishes, and some species can grow as much as 140 cm (55 ins.) a day. It also has the ability to improve and replenish soil in degraded or eroded areas, as well as generating more oxygen than the same acreage of trees. Bamboo offers a far greater greenhouse-gas conversion to oxygen rate than any other plant, as well as regenerating itself almost immediately after each harvesting. The more bamboo that is planted the greater the **photosynthesis**, resulting in a reduction in greenhouse gasses.

Processed bamboo fibre, referred to as tops, ready for the final spinning process. The fibre's natural smooth sheen is evident in the image and will remain apparent in the finished fabric. Bamboo wicks away and evaporates moisture efficiently, keeping the wearer drier and cool in hot humid climates.

For bamboo to be truly ecologically friendly it must also be processed in an environmentally appropriate manner and adhere to the 12 principles of green chemistry. Unfortunately, many Chinese producers process the bamboo cellulose into bamboo viscose fibre by the use of sodium hydroxide, caustic chemicals and further bleaching agents, defeating the purpose and ethos of a truly green alternative. The more environmentally appropriate high-tech processing methods include refining the stem fibre through engineered enzyme processes with no chemical additives. If the bamboo culms are young they may also be steamed or boiled to soften before being processed into cellulose for fibre. Litrax, a Swiss company, has pioneered 100 per cent eco-friendly processing of bio-bamboo fibre, yarn and textiles.

This exercise in extreme corsetry by Ada Zanditon uses bamboo fabric and organic linen canvas padded with material sourced from secondhand furniture and toys. The trousers are silk and the trimmings make use of reclaimed materials.

A structured jacket silhouette made from bamboo-fibre fabric teamed with organic cotton jersey Zouave pants by Ada Zanditon.

Leaf fibres

Leaf fibres can be produced from the strands of fibres that run through the leaf and hold it in place, and are classified as 'hard' fibres, as opposed to bast or 'soft' fibres. The classification is quite fluid, because some may actually be softer than bast fibres.

Fibres such as raffia and **piña** may never make commercial sense on a global scale, however they do represent interesting alternatives as well as, in the case of piña, being inherently linked to cultural identity.

Abacá

Abacá, also spelt abaká and pronounced ah buh KAH, is the plant from which Manila hemp, also known as **daveo** and **cebu hemp**, is produced. The fibre has been produced in the Philippines since the 1800s; however commercial plantations were started by Britain and the Netherlands in the early 1920s in Borneo and Sumatra. It is also cultivated in Central America, where it has been sponsored by the United States Department of Agriculture.

It is not commercially used as a clothing fibre but there are developments underway hoping to unearth its viability as a sustainable alternative.

Abacá production

The abacá leaves form a sheath that grows from the trunk of the plant. The fibres range in length from 1.5 to 3.5 m and are extracted from the sheaths in a three-stage process. The first, **tuxing**, is the separation of the outer and inner sheaths of the leaves, followed by stripping the fibres then sun drying. Once the fibres have been separated they are sold as Manila hemp, named after the country's capital.

Piña

Piña is obtained from the leaves of the pineapple plant. Although native to several parts of the world, it is in the Philippines that it is used as a fibre for clothing purposes. Strands are hand scraped from the leaves of the plant then hand knotted, one by one, to form a continuous filament. The fibre is soft and lightweight, easy to care for and has a good translucent lustre. It is usually white or ivory in colour.

The filaments are traditionally woven on a hand loom into **piña cloth** and made into the **barong Tagalog**, an embroidered shirt worn for formal occasions and wedding ceremonies by Filipino men, and sometimes women.

Raffia

Raffia palms (*Raphia*) are native to the tropical regions of Africa, Madagascar and Central and South America. The fibres are long and thin and absorb dye well. Raffia is used for shoe, hat and bag production, as well as for decorative textiles.

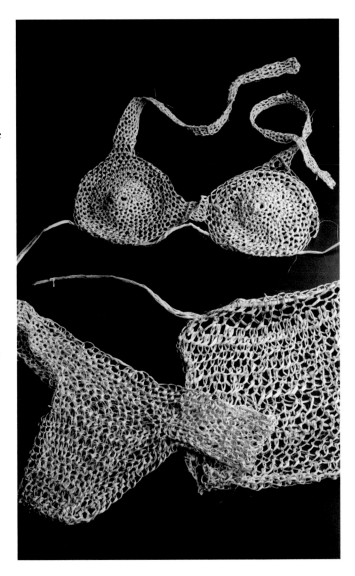

Hand-crafted 'underwear' by Brazilian cooperative Creollus, whose mission is, 'To create a sustainable resource for commonly discarded but highly recyclable materials. The entire company product inventory is born from techniques that equally value and respect a cleaner and healthier natural environment through the recycling of common commercial and household materials. We are enabling a unique group of sorely underserved artists to form a business cooperative that will significantly improve their standard of living, and give them an appreciative, worldwide audience for their craft.'

(above) This whimsical sculptured cape by Rachel Caulfield is formed from a cane basket weave. The aesthetic for the collection of which this piece forms a part was influenced by Scandinavia, furniture design and also an interest in combining different elements: the wearable and unwearable, natural and artificial, to produce challenging clothing concepts.

(left) Traditional Balkan backless shoes, woven from pliable raffia. Materials used by communities for centuries have often been abandoned in favour of man-made developments. Contemporary concerns for our resources may mean that some raw materials and methods of manufacture will be revisited and examined with a fresh approach for future uses.

Biopolymers and protein fibres

This section considers a few alternative plant sources that have not traditionally been used for fibre production. However, by applying current technological and scientific developments involving either naturally occurring processes or chemical intervention, most of these sources can now be turned into fibres for the textile trade. If processing into fibre can be achieved through the engineering of natural enzymes, then these staple plants could be truly labelled eco-friendly. If, however, they require chemical intervention for conversion into fibre then consideration must be given to how exactly this impacts upon the environment.

This section is not exhaustive of all the current developments; it is purely illustrative of how science and technology combined with a desire for ecologically sustainable materials are currently being developed.

Corn

Plentiful supplies of corn (also known as maize) grown in the heartlands of the United States are now a possible source of commercially viable man-made fibres obtained from 100 per cent annually renewable resources.

Corn fibre

The **Ingeo™** fibre is high in strength and stability, has low flammability, is more resistant to UV light and is more hydrophilic (attracting water) than common synthetics. Once blended with cotton or wool the resulting fabric is light and wicks moisture away from the skin.

Diesel is one of several fashion companies using Ingeo yarns.

Why Ingeo? Diesel likes challenges! Creating and transforming something natural is, for sure, a bet, especially if the final result is 'Diesel Style.' The company's strength is the courage to transform a crazy idea into something real, despite trends and thoughts. Diesel at ingeofibres.com

Corn-fibre production

By means of photosynthesis, the starch naturally stored in corn is broken down and converted into dextrose sugar. The carbon and other elements of these natural sugars are used to make a **biopolymer** by means of fermentation and separation to produce the lactic acid. The water is then removed and the resulting resin, branded NatureWorks® PLA (polylactic acid), when extruded into high-performance fibre is branded Ingeo™. Originally an American development, producing Ingeo is now a joint venture with a Japanese company. The fibre is spun into yarn for woven or knitted textiles. DuPont has also developed a new polymer from corn called Sorona®.

Ecological sustainability

Producing fibre from corn is a low-cost process that uses little fossil fuel, and there is a great quantity of available raw material. The garments, once discarded, can be returned to the earth, degrading into natural compost with the passage of time.

There is, however, the concern that an increasing amount of the corn cultivated in the United States is genetically modified.

Processed cellulose fibre.

Soybean fibre.

Processed soy fibre referred to as tops ready for the final spinning process.

100% soy T-shirt, print by Miguel Arias worn with organic cotton and crochet panelled funnel neck cropped top with silk and tulle trims by eco-brand Oda.

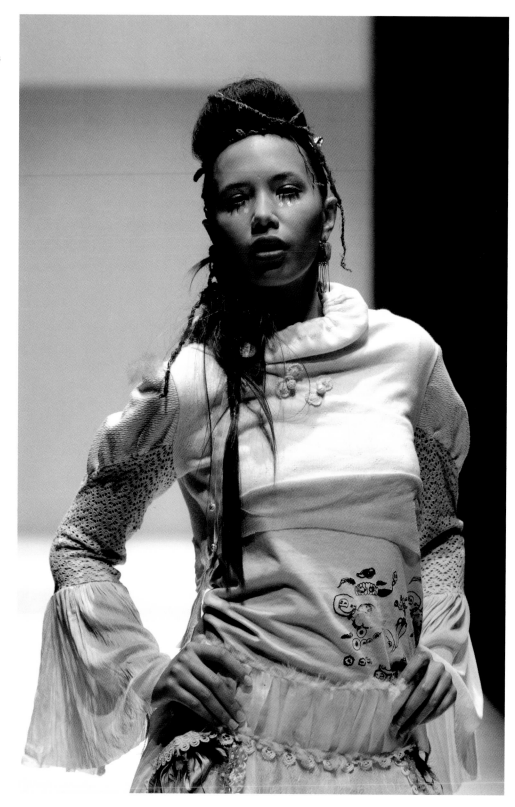

Soya

It is believed that soy (or soya) was first harvested in China over 5,000 years ago. It was introduced into the United States almost by accident in the early 1800s when Yankee clippers, trading with China, often used soybeans as inexpensive ballast. Today the United States is the largest producer of soybeans.

Soya fibre

Soya is a renewable botanic **protein fibre** consisting of 16 amino acids that are considered beneficial when worn next to the skin. Clothing made of soy is moisture-absorbing, and the structure allows for good ventilation. The fabric drapes well and is often considered to be as smooth as cashmere. It is also believed to synthesize the qualities of natural fibres with the physical properties of synthetics.

Currently garments made of soy fibre tend to be targeted at a mid-market consumer, however with more demand it should be inexpensive to produce.

Soya production

Soya-bean protein fibre is an advanced textile fibre produced by bioengineering technology from soybean 'cake'; the protein is distilled from the cake and refined. Through various processes, and by the use of auxiliary agents and biological enzymes, the structure of the protein changes into a confected substance that can then be extruded into fibre by means of a wet-spinning process. Finally, the fibre is stabilized and cut into short staples.

Ecological sustainability

Soy fibre is often marketed as the green fibre of the twenty-first century that is completely biodegradable. The manufacturing process does not pollute, because the auxiliary agents used in producing the fibre are non-poisonous. The residue that remains after the protein has been extracted may be used as animal feed. However, in many countries soy production is non-organic and genetically modified. This means that crops may be treated with chemicals to enhance production and deter weeds, and this is believed to affect the welfare of neighbouring livestock.

Sustainable wood cellulose

Lyocell is a cellulose fibre made from eucalyptus, an evergreen plant that grows to a height of up to 40 m (131 ft). The aromatic raw material is extracted from eucalyptus wood. Eucalyptus is an interesting raw material since it grows very quickly and without any artificial irrigation or gene manipulation. The wood pulp is dissolved in a solution of amine oxide, then is placed the material in a spinneret. The spinneret produces long fibres, which are then dried and woven into cloth. The solvent is extracted as the fibres pass through a washing process. The manufacturing process recycles 99.5 per cent of the solvent, which is reused. It is non-toxic, non-corrosive and non-hazardous. Lyocell is fully biodegradable within six weeks in an aerated compost heap.

Lyocell is better known by the brand name TENCEL®, and is produced exclusively from forest plantations that practice sustainability. The success of earlier cellulose fabrics made from wood pulp (such as rayon as a replacement for silk) was the inspiration for its development. Branded as the new-age fibre, it is manufactured by Lenzing AG, one of the world leaders in cellulose-fibre technology. TENCEL® is most suitable for sportswear and also for garments and bedding for people with sensitive skin.

Lenzing Modal® is similar to TENCEL, but is extracted from beech wood. The beech tree is thought to be unbeatable when it comes to improving the soil; it is often referred to as the mother of the forest. It is extremely resistant to pests and environmental damages. Beech groves are a completely sustainable source and need no artificial irrigation.

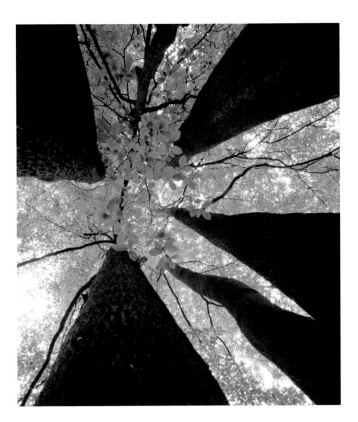

Towering beech groves supply the raw material for Lenzing Modal®.

(below) The top of this outfit by Ada Zanditon is organic cotton, while the trousers are made from crustacean fibre. This new development is a mix of TENCEL® and processed waste from the food industry, which when combined produces a strong and durable jersey that has natural antibacterial, hypoallergenic and anti-static properties. These properties are inherent within the crustacean fibre, and are usually applied as a finishing treatment to other fabrics. Mario Boselli produces this naturally dyed and woven fabric in Italy. It is also completely biodegradable.

(above) Outfit by Ada Zanditon. This extreme silhouette employs the tactile drape of this finely gathered TENCEL® jersey by Lenzing to form a 'skin' over the underlying boned structure of the outfit.

(left) 'Origami' skirt and top by Céline Faizant in 55 per cent TENCEL® and 45 per cent hemp. The transparent fabric of the 'Ori' shirt is 100 per cent organic cotton.

183

Useful

informati

on

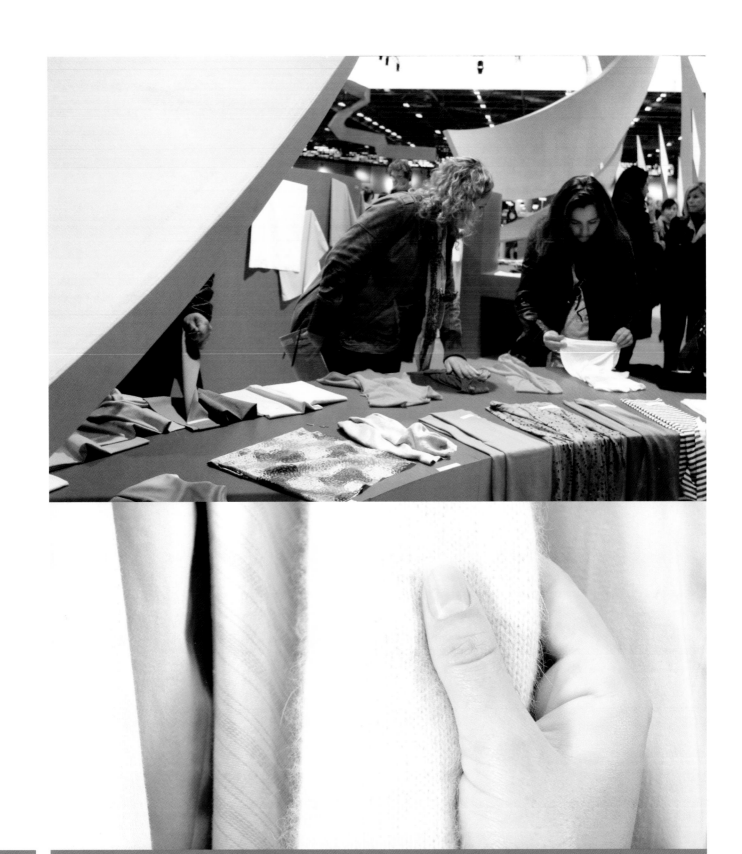

Fabric and the fashion industry

Working with fabrics

The selection of fabric is fundamental to the creative and commercial viability of a collection and should realistically precede any design development work. Fabric is the medium that expresses two of the essential ingredients of fashion design – colour and tactile appeal. Both are key considerations at the conceptual stage of designing and planning a collection.

A mood board is usually compiled at this stage to consolidate a variety of inspirational sources, and to communicate a concept or theme; it helps to focus direction and to make objective and strategic design decisions. This is especially important when working as part of a team.

Sourcing fabrics

Trade fairs

These are shows or fairs where international fabric mills come together to showcase all their new fabric designs and developments for the forthcoming season. Generally designers and buyers will request samples, which are then forwarded for sampling, prior to ordering bulk fabric for production.

Mills

Fabric is woven or knitted in a textile mill. Mills often tend to specialize in specific types of fabric, or are known for their expertise with certain processes. Popular fabrics and colours are usually held in stock, while others are made to order and will need to meet production minimums. These vary depending on fibre type, fabric construction and finish. For example, screen-printed silk from a mill in Como, Italy, may only require a 50m (164-ft) minimum while a yarn-dyed cotton from a mill in China may require a 1,000m (3,280-ft) minimum.

Agents

An **agent** is a 'middle' person or company that represents the interests of a fabric mill or mills. Agencies enable mills to show their fabric collections to designers and buyers internationally.

The fabrics are shown on **header cards** which consist of a large swatch of fabric used as a feeler for touch and drape, a range of colour options and all the information regarding construction and composition. Agents do not carry stock but help organize the ordering and delivery of sample lengths and eventual production.

Importers and stock houses

These are fabric wholesale companies that buy fabrics from domestic and foreign mills in large quantities and then sell the fabric on, usually without any minimum requirements.

Converters

Converters buy large volumes of greige piece goods (unfinished fabrics) directly from the mills, then dye, print and finish the fabric into smaller quantities, according to market trends. They work closely with designers and manufacturers to allow a quick response to trends in colour and print, without the commitment required from large fabric minimums.

Jobbers

Jobbers specialize in buying stock fabrics from mills or garment manufacturers that are in excess of their requirements. They sell these fabrics at competitive prices; it is unlikely that, once sold, the fabric can be repeated.

(left) The prestigious fabric fair Première Vision is held in Paris twice a year, showcasing textile collections from the most important mills in the world. Punctuating the spaces between the exhibitors' stands are small trend-focused 'tendance' exhibitions of the most directional colours, fabrics, knits and textile treatments emerging in different product categories.

Sourcing considerations

Fabric type

Sourcing fabrics requires an informed sensitivity to the different personalities that fabrics possess, coupled with an instinctive creative approach. Consideration of the suitability of different fibre types for specific products underpins effective sourcing.

To work with the inherent nature and properties of the fabric, manipulate a large piece of cloth and drape it; observe how it relates to the body and consider how it feels next to the skin. It may be stiff, structured and hold pleats crisply, or it may be dense, fluffy and sculptural, or conversely have a tactile and supple drape that clings to the body. The structure and tightness of the weave is important as it will affect the handle and drape, the way the fabric behaves and its potential durability.

Purpose and market

Another important aspect is the suitability of the chosen fabric for its intended purpose. The lifestyle of the **target consumer** needs to be taken into consideration to identify how the products will be used, laundered and the expected level of wear and tear. Fabrics from reputable mills are usually pre-tested for an identified range of uses. Alternatively fabrics can be sent for independent testing to specialist laboratories. This is especially useful for high-performance clothing.

Useful fabric sampling vocabulary

Colour-ways Alternative fabric colour options

Drape The way the fabric hangs and moves

Dye lot Minimum meterage required to dye to a specific colour

Handle/Touch Describes the characteristics of a fabric eg soft, firm etc

Lead times The length of time it takes to receive the fabric (usually applies to bulk fabric)

Minimums Minimum meterage required to place an order to produce a fabric

Print runs Minimum meterage required to print a design or colour

Sample colour For sampling purposes; not all colour options may be available, sample colour implies the available colour

Sample lengths Small meterage required to make a prototype sample

Swatches Small fabric pieces used in pre-selecting a fabric range

It is also important that the selected fabrics reflect the brand image and the target consumer's perception of the brand. Certain consumers respond to specific types of fabrics positively. For example, natural fibres may give added value, or high-tech performance fibres may provide a unique selling point for certain categories of products.

Eco considerations

The geographic origin of the fibre and processing of the fabric may also be relevant considerations. The carbon footprint and ethical and fairtrade issues regarding manufacture may make certain choices inappropriate. How a fabric needs to be looked after throughout its life cycle and, ultimately, how it will be disposed of are growing concerns that are impacting on all levels of the market.

Cost, sizing and fabric direction

Pricing awareness is vital in today's competitive market, and the price per metre or yard needs to consider the width of the fabric in the costing.

The standard widths for different fabric types have until recently been 36, 45 or 60 in wide (90, 112 and 150 cm), with some specialist fabrics as narrow as 18 in or as wide as 150 in (45 or 375 cm). Today most fabrics are made to a standard 60 in (150 cm) wide, which is a more cost-effective width for a **lay planning** (economical arrangement of garment pattern pieces onto the fabric) and also best suited for general factory production.

Further cost considerations when selecting fabrics include **one-** and **two-way** directional fabrics and fabric matching.

A one-directional fabric implies that the design (printed or woven) needs to be cut in a single direction. Alternatively, a one-directional fabric may imply that it has a pile or raised surface and that the fabric must be cut with all garment pattern pieces following the same direction. One-directional fabrics are less cost effective than two-way fabrics. Fabric matching further increases fabric usage or costing.

Testing

Fabrics from reputable mills will have been pre-tested with all the relevant information available for the buyer, designer or merchandiser. Alternatively fabrics may be sent for testing to independent laboratories, which is particularly useful for performance clothing.

Seasonal cyclical industry process

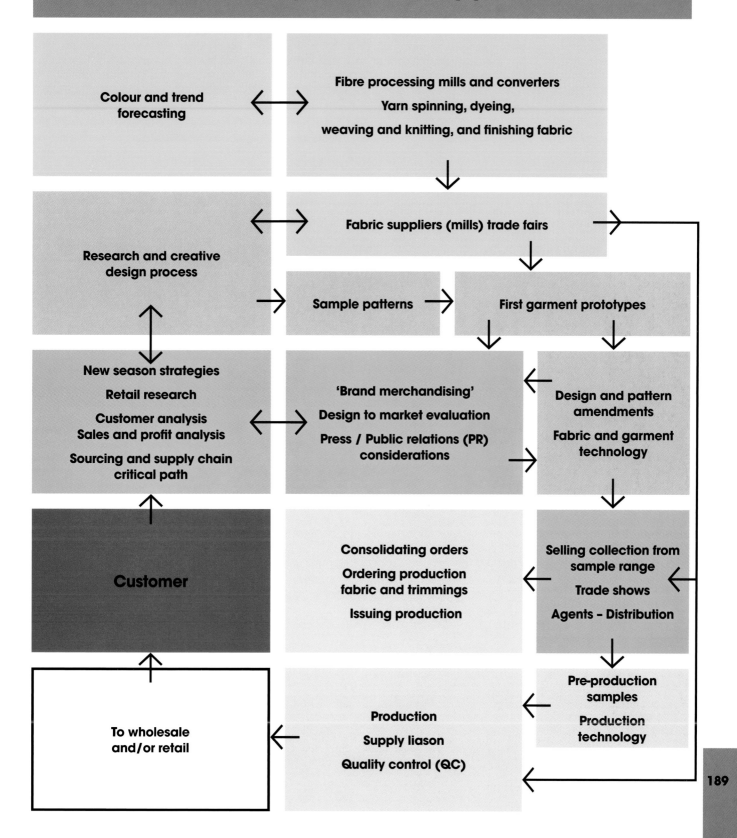

Colour and trend forecasting ↔ **Fibre processing mills and converters** Yarn spinning, dyeing, weaving and knitting, and finishing fabric

Research and creative design process ↔ **Fabric suppliers (mills) trade fairs**

Sample patterns → **First garment prototypes**

New season strategies Retail research Customer analysis Sales and profit analysis Sourcing and supply chain critical path ↔ **'Brand merchandising'** Design to market evaluation Press / Public relations (PR) considerations → **Design and pattern amendments** Fabric and garment technology

Customer

Consolidating orders Ordering production fabric and trimmings Issuing production

Selling collection from sample range Trade shows Agents – Distribution

To wholesale and/or retail

Production Supply liason Quality control (QC)

Pre-production samples Production technology

Manufacture and processing

The structure of the fabric industry has changed considerably in the last 30 years, although many of the disciplines within it have remained the same.

Design

In a competitive, consumer-savvy market good design is instrumental to a company's success. Today's designer needs a wide skill and knowledge base, from marketing knowledge to manufacturing skills. Design schools produce multi-talented graduates that are ripe for French, Italian and American design companies.

Design product management

This is a wide area, which has gone through radical changes and expansion in recent years. There is now a need for more graduates within merchandising, buying and product development departments, dealing with anything from sourcing to branding; range-building and line-planning to product distribution.

Liaising with **offshore** manufacturers creates problems with communication even if the accepted *lingua franca* is English. At retail, information technology has made information instant: once it took a few weeks to know a bestseller, now it's possible by return.

Pattern cutting

Pattern cutting for higher-end products and **tailoring** is still usually carried out domestically. However, for the greater majority of clothing the patterns are cut in the country of manufacture, the advantages being cost and proximity to the factory.

Garment technology

Technologists were historically linked to the factory, where they could be hands-on with issues as they arose. Today they deal with problems long-distance, requiring greater accuracy of information and better communication.

Sample making

Similarly to pattern cutting, where samples are made is dependent on the product level; an expensive dress manufacturer may have domestic sampling whereas a multiple brand will sample at its offshore factory. The advantage is twofold, in terms of cost and production manufacturing techniques. A factory will always produce a tailoring sample, irrespective of level.

Manufacturing

Today offshore manufacturing is not only the domain of inexpensive volume brands, but also many high-profile labels take advantage of the cheaper labour costs the developing world has to offer. The choice is between **manufacturing hub** and the quality level of the factory. Better brands will be more selective with their trimmings and may well have these transported from other global sources. For example, today around 60 per cent of men's tailoring is made from fabric sourced in a different country from where the production is based. Thirty per cent of T-shirt cotton is grown and knitted into fabric, then shipped to be manufactured in another country or even continent. While this travel increases a company's carbon footprint and questions its ethics, the lure of a better **margin** does nothing to dampen its resolve.

Quality control

Once this was only a component discipline of the manufacturing process; today, with the explosion in offshore manufacturing, it has become all-important. **QC** is now as much a part of buying or product development as it is a manufacturing component.

Fabric suppliers

The majority of Far East manufacturing takes advantage of its domestic fabric production, especially with cotton piece goods. Therefore, fabric sourcing would be part of the same exercise as sourcing the manufacturing production.

Sales

Once the collection is ready or launched, it is the task of the sales department to generate sales. Depending on the size of the company this could be handled in-house or by an agent/representative. Sales to foreign countries can be via a fashion trade fair or given over to an agency or **distributor** in the respective country that has a better understanding of national characteristics and particular requirements.

Trade fairs

Yarn trade fairs

The purpose of a yarn trade fair is to showcase a new season's yarn and colour direction.

Expofil Paris, France. Yarns, textile fibres and fashion services.

Indigo Paris, France. Prints. Same time as Première Vision.

Intercot Changing venue. Global approaches to organic yarns and textiles.

Pitti Imagine Filati Florence, Italy. Yarns and fibres.

Peru Moda Lima, Peru. Luxury yarns such as vicuña and alpaca.

Printsource New York, USA. Tri-annual international print design and finishing.

Yarn Expo Beijing, China. Centralized for the whole of China.

Fabric trade fairs

These showcase all new fabrics and colour directions for the next season. Trend directions tend to be six months ahead of the wholesale fashion trade fairs, although many companies also show stock or short lead-time fabrics.

Important European fairs now also take place in the USA, China and India.

Première Vision Paris, France. Very important bi-annual fair with forecasting, accessories and print halls. Also Moscow, Tokyo, Shanghai and New York.

Denim By Première Vision Paris, France. Smaller shows concentrating on denim and related materials.

Fabric at Magic New York, USA. Fabrics, trimmings and colour trends.

Idea Como Milan, Italy. The very best fabrics, predominance of silks.

Interstoff Frankfurt, Germany. Bi-annual fair showing international fabrics.

Interstoff Asia and Interstoff Russia Derivatives of the original, exhibiting in Hong Kong and Moscow.

Intertextile Beijing, Shenzhent and Shangai, China. Part of the Interstoff organization for the Chinese markets.

Japantex Tokyo, Japan. International fabrics.

Modatisimo Porto, Portugal. National and international fabrics.

Moda in Tessuto e Accesori Milan, Italy. Bi-annual, fabrics and accessories.

Prato Expo Florence, Italy. Important fair due to the sheer number of new ideas showcased

Texworld India and Texworld USA Part of the Interstoff organization exhibiting in Bombay and New York.

Texbridge/Turkish Fashion Fabrics: Bi-annual shows held in London, Milan and New York.

Useful organizations and publications

The following organizations, services and publications can provide useful information regarding a variety of different aspects of the fibres and fabrics discussed in this book, from the raw material to the finished product.

Fabric and colour publications

There are many textile and colour journals published worldwide. Some are more factual while others are more creative and inspirational, and of great use when starting a design collection.

Journal Du Textile, France, 42 issues.
Mood Textiles, Italy, 4 issues.
Noa Colour, Japan, 2 issues.
Provider (View On Colour), The Netherlands, 4 issues.
Selvedge, UK, 6 issues.
The Society of Dyers and Colourists, UK, 10 issues.
T Design Living Textile Tendence, Italy, 4 issues.
Texitura, Spain, 2 issues.
Textile Asia, Hong Kong, 12 issues.
Textile Forum, international, 4 issues.
Textile History, UK, 2 issues.
Textile Horizons, UK, 6 issues.
Textile Month, UK, 6 issues.
Textile Outlook International, UK, 6 issues.
Textile Report, France, 4 issues.
Textile Research Journal, US, 12 issues.
Textile View, Netherlands, 4 issues.
Textile Wirschaft, Germany, 52 issues.
Textiles Eastern Europe, UK, 1 issue.
Textiles, UK, 4 issues.
View Point, Netherlands, 2 issues.

Wool

Australian Wool Innovation Ltd:
www.wool.com.au; and
Australian Wool Services:
www.wool.com
Both are part of the Australian Woolmark Company, which is considered to be the world's leading wool fibre textile authority, with over 60 years of experience.

British Wool Marketing Board:
www.britishwool.org.uk
Central marketing system for UK fleece wool.

ENco: www.cbwt.co.uk/enco
ENco is the environmental textile division of the Confederation of British Wool Textiles Ltd. It concentrates on solving environmental problems in the wool supply chain.

International Wool Textile Organization: www.iwto.org
Representing the world's wool textile trade and industry, including spinners, weavers, garment manufacturers and weavers.

Izzy Lane: www.izzylane.com
Ethically sourced British woollen products from ethically farmed Shetland and Wensleydale sheep.

Merino Advanced Performance Programme MAPP:
www.mapp.co.nz
Performance-based fabric developments incorporating New Zealand merino wool.

Merino New Zealand:
www.nzmerino.co.nz
Represents the merino producers of New Zealand and promotes the merino characteristics of brightness/whiteness, strength, extra staple length and thus advanced manufacturing efficiency, and is associated with the highest quality manufacturers.

Testex®: www.testex.com
An international Swiss-based company that provides testing services to the textile industry at all levels, including analysis and quality assurance.

Tongue River Farm
www.icelandicsheep.com
Information on Icelandic sheep, yarn and spinning.

UK Agriculture:
www.ukagriculture.com
The livestock (sheep and wool) link contains information on the UK industry and further background information.

Uruguay: Wool Secretariat Secretariado Uruguayo De La Lana (SUL): www.wool.com.uy
Works to promote and develop all aspects of Uruguayan wool in a similar way to the larger Australian Woolmark Company.

Wool is Best: www.woolisbest.com
A factual guide to the Australian wool industry.

Wools of New Zealand:
www.fernmark.com
Works to promote and develop all aspects of New Zealand wool. It originally used to promote interior textiles and since 1996 now includes apparel textiles.

The Woolmark Company:
www.wool.com.au
The aim of the company and organization is to improve the profitability of wool growers by building and sustaining demand. It also aims to increase productivity through research development and marketing. It was formerly the IWS (International Wool Secretariat) and was formed in 1937 primarily by Australian wool growers who recognized the need to promote their product worldwide. In 1998 the IWS became The Woolmark Company and continues this work. It has offices in approximately 20 countries and representation in 60. It also has design and development centres in Biella, Italy and Ichinomiya, Japan. It also encourages industry partner projects. Central to the company is the Woolmark, which is an international trademark that promises high quality performance and fibre content. It also confirms that the products on which it is displayed are of pure new wool.

Zque™ Fibre: www.zque.co.nz
Ethically sourced New Zealand merino wool with an accreditation programme that ensures environmental, social and economic sustainability as well as animal welfare, with traceability back to the source.

Luxury animal fibres

Australian Alpaca Association:
www.alpaca.asn.au
Comprehensive information on the Australian alpaca industry.

Australian Cashmere Breed and Fleece Standard:
www.acga.org.au
Information on the Australian breed evolved from the bush goat.

British Alpaca Society:
www.bas-uk.com
Comprehensive information on the British alpaca industry.

Camdeboo Mohair:
www.camdeboo.com
Supplier of high quality certified South African angora fibre (mohair).

Canadian Llama and Alpaca Registry:
www.claacanada.com
Comprehensive information on the Canadian llama and alpaca industry.

Cape Mohair Wool:
www.cmw.co.za
A group of South African mohair textile production companies.

Cashmere and Camel Hair Manufacturers Institute:
www.cashmere.org
US-based international institute for research and promotion of camel hair and cashmere.

Coloured Angora Goat Breeders Association: www.cagba.org
Promotes the development and marketing of coloured angora goats and fibre.

Import and Export of Vicuña. (US Wildlife Services):
www.fws.gov
Information on legalities and restrictions on the trade in vicuña fibre.

Resources

International Alpaca Association (Peru): www.aia.org.pe
Peruvian-based association with extensive information on all South American camelids and their hybrids.

Pygora Breeders Association:
www.pygoragoats.org
US-based association dedicated to the 'advancement' and well-being of pygoras.

Roseland Llamas:
www.llamas.co.uk
Informative site regarding llama attributes.

South African Mohair Growers Association:
samga@xsinet.co.za
Representative association of mohair producers.

Yampa Valley Yaks:
www.yampayaks.com
Colorado-based site dealing with yaks.

Silk

Ahimsa Peace Silk:
www.abolitionist-online.com
Dedicated to animal rights.

Indian Silk Export Promotion Council: www.silkepc.org
Offers information on the silk industry of India, exporters, manufacturers and more.

Peace Silk suppliers:
www.ahimsapeacesilk.com
Suppliers of peace silk.

Silk Association of Nepal:
www.nepalsilk.org
European Union-funded trade organisation for silk producers and exporters.

Silk Mark Organization of India (SMOI): www.silkmarkindia.com
Silk quality mark organization sponsored by the Textiles Ministry.

Linen

Class Act Fabrics:
www.classactfabrics.com
Supplier of fabrics, including good-quality linen.

CELC: Confédération Européenne du Lin et du Chanvre (Linen and Hemp): www.belgianlinen.com
A non-profit-making trade organization for linen in Western Europe. Affiliated countries are Austria, Belgium, France, Germany, Italy, Holland, Switzerland and the UK.

The Irish Linen Centre and Lisburn Museum: www.lisburncity.gov.uk
Information and artefacts relating to the Irish linen industry. Lisburn, Northern Ireland.

The Irish Linen Guild:
www.irishlinen.co.uk
Founded in 1928, promotes and monitors quality Irish linen. Gives a seal of quality to fabrics or yarns that are made and finished in Ireland.

Maison du Lin: www.lin.asso.fr
Organization promoting French linen.

Masters of Linen:
www.mastersoflinen.com
Paris-based subsidiary of CELC. Provides information and promotes European linen.

Saneco: www.saneco.com
Statistics and information on the flax industry.

Cotton

Cotton Australia:
www.cottonaustralia.com.au
Organization servicing Australian cotton growers, dealing with environmentally conducive and sustainable production issues.

Cotton Foundation:
www.cotton.org
US cotton export and research foundation.

Cotton Incorporated:
www.cotton.inc
A company with offices worldwide that offers extensive information on all aspects of cotton from farming and green issues to design and manufacturing. It also offers extensive fabric resources.

The Seam: www.theseam.com
Online trading and interactive market place for cotton agriculture.

United States Cotton Board:
www.CottonBoard.org
Information for producers, buyers and importers.

International Cotton Advisory Committee: www.icac.org
Association of governments of cotton producing and consuming countries.

International Cotton Association:
www.ica-ltd.org
International trade association and arbitral body.

National Cotton Council News and Current Events:
www.cotton.org/news
Global news and information site.

100 Per Cent American Supima cotton: www.supimacotton.org
Information on American Pima cotton.

Plains Cotton Cooperative Association: www.pcca.com
Largest producers and suppliers of Texan-style cotton.

Spinning the Web:
www.spinningtheweb.org.uk
Comprehensive information on the history of the cotton industry.

Naturally coloured cottons (some organic) producers

Natural Cotton Colours Inc:
www.textileweb.com
Manufactures naturally coloured cotton.

Peru Naturtex Partners:
www.perunaturtex.com
Organic production with sustainable processing for textile products. The site has good information on the origins of cotton, organic and naturally coloured cotton. It also has several links to fashion companies using organic cotton.

Vreseis Ltd: www.vreseis.com
Retail and mail order for naturally coloured cotton.

Facts and figures on the cotton trade

www.pbs.org/now/shows/310/cotton-trade.html
www.cottonorg/econ/cropinfo/cropdata/rankings.cfm

Sustainability; ethical and fair trade issues

Ecological, Fairtrade and organic organizations

Biomat: www.biomatnet.org
Sustainable resources, bio-products from non-food crops.

Centre for Fashion Science and Centre for Sustainability:
www.fashion.arts.ac.uk
London College of Fashion, research centre for fashion products and sustainability.

The Clean Clothes Campaign:
www.cleanclothes.org
Aims to improve working conditions and to empower workers of the global clothing industry.

A Deeper Luxury:
www.wwf.org.uk/deeperluxury
A report on the findings of WWF-UK's analysis of the environmental and social performance of the luxury goods sector.

Environmental Justice Foundation:
www.ejfoundation.org
Information on empowering those affected by environmental abuse.

Ethical Fashion Forum:
www.ethicalfashionforum.com
Network of designers, businesses and organizations focusing on environmental and social sustainability in the fashion industry.

An Ethical Industry: www.fashioninganethicalindustry.org
A Labour Behind the Label project.

Ethical Trading Initiative:
www.ethicaltrade.org
Information on the promotion of ethical trade.

The Fairtrade Foundation:
www.fairtrade.org.uk/
www.fairtrade.net
Registered charity that licenses the FAIRTRADE mark to products that meet internationally recognized ethical standards.

International Fairtrade:
www.ifat.org
Information on members practising fair trade in business.

Labour Behind the Label: www.labourbehindthelabel.com
Resources and information on clothing labels.

No Sweat: www.nosweat.org.uk
Information on the global campaign against sweatshops and child labour.

Organic Trade Association:
www.ota.com
Organization listing members
using organic cotton.

World Fair Trade Organization:
www.wfto.com
Global authority on fair trade.

Oxfam: www.oxfam.org.uk
Charity with ethical and recycled
clothing shops.

Pesticide Action Network UK:
www.pan-uk.org
Working to eliminate pesticides
and to promote fair trade and
organic alternatives. Website
has many related liks.

SKAL: www.skal.com
Dutch-based international
organic inspection body.

Soil Association:
www.soilassociation.org
Information on organic farming
and sustainable forestry.

**The STING (Sustainable Technology
in Nettle Growing):**
www.dmu.ac.uk
The STING project consortium
comprises seven partners
representing academic and
industrial organizations and
is coordinated through
De Montfort University.

Textile Environmental Design (TED):
www.tedresearch.net
Chelsea College of Art
and Design
Collaborative projects looking at
creating textiles with a reduced
impact on the environment.

Vote Hemp: www.votehemp.com
US advocacy group which holds
comprehensive information on all
aspects of hemp, from legislative
and sustainable issues to
production and retail information.

Recycling organizations
**Ragtex, Textile Recycling
Association:**
www.textile-recycling.org.uk
The Recylatax Bonded scheme
helps local authorities, charities
and other organizations set up
recycling services for re-use of
clothing and shoes.

Waste online:
www.wasteonline.org.uk
An overview of recycling with
facts, figures and details of what
happens to the clothes we
recycle. Run by Waste Watch.

TRAID: www.traid.org.uk
Charity recycling organization.

Eco fabrics and yarns
All Things Green:
www.allthingsgreen.net
Alternative 'green' products.

Bamboo Clothes:
www.bambooclothes.ca
Supplier of bamboo products:
fabric, yarn, fibre, clothing.

Bambrotex: www.bambrotex.com
Bamboo fabrics and resources.

Green Fibres: www.greenfibres.com/
acatalog
Supplier of organic fabrics.

House of Hemp:
www.houseofhemp.co.uk
Supplier of craft yarns and fabrics.

Ingeo: www.ingeofibers.com
Man-made yarn made of corn,
100 per cent annually
renewable resource.

Litrax: www.litrax.com
Manufacturers of bamboo fibres,
yarns and fabrics using
100 per cent eco-friendly process
and no chemicals.

Hemp Fabrics UK:
www.hempfabric.co.uk
Online hemp textiles.

Swicofil: www.swicofil.com
Swiss raw material manufacture
and sourcing company.
Good links to sourcing and
ecology concerns.

Eco brands
Bamboo clothing:
www.bambooclothing.co.uk
Online brand selling bamboo
and organic clothing.

From Somewhere:
www.fromsomewhere.co.uk
Sustainable fashion from textile
waste and remnants.

Good One: www.goodone.co.uk
Sustainable fashion, one-off
pieces from recycled fabrics.

Linda Loudermilk:
www.lindaloudermilk.com
A luxury eco fashion brand.

naturevsfuture®:
www.naturevsfuture.com
Organic fashion brand.

Noir: www.noir-illuminati2.com
Ethical fashion brand.

Ciel: www.ciel.ltd.uk
Ethical fashion brand.

Enamore: www.enamore.co.uk
Fashion brand using organic,
sustainable and vintage fabrics.

Further reading
and exhibitions

The Book of Silk
Phillipa Scott
(Thames & Hudson, 1993)
Chinese Silk: A Cultural History
Shelagh Vainker (The British
Museum Press, 2004)
Colour
Edith Anderson Feisner
(Laurence King, 2006)
Colour
Helen Varley, ed.
(Marshall Editions, 1998)
*Colour: A Workshop for Artists
and Designers*
David Hornung
(Laurence King, 2005)
The Colour Eye
Robert Cumming and Tom Porter
(BBC Books, 1990)
*An Economic History of the Silk
Industry*
Giovanni Federico (Cambridge
University Press, 1997)
Fair Trade
A. Nicolls and C. Opal
(Sage Publications, 2005)
Fashion and Textiles
Colin Gale and Jasbir Kaur
(Berg, 2004)
Fashioning the Future
Suzanne Lees
(Thames & Hudson, 2005)
Fashion Zeitgeist
Barbara Vinken (Berg, 2005)
*Global Silk Industry: A Complete
Source Book*
R. Datta and M. Nanavaty
(Universal Publishers, 2005)
*Green Chemistry: Theory and
Practice*
Paul T. Anastas and
John D. Warner
(Oxford University Press, 2000)

The Green Imperative
Papanek, Victor
(Thames & Hudson, 1995)
Green is the New Black
Tamsin Blanchard
(Hodder & Stoughton, 2007)
*Hemp for Victory: History and
Qualities of the World's
Most Useful Plant*
Kenyon Gibson (Whitaker
Publishing, 2006)
Mantero 100 anni di storia e di seta
Guido Vergani (Fos Editoria e
Communicazione, 2002)
Seven Deadly Colours
Andrew Parker (Free Press, 2005)
Silk
Jaques Anquetil
(Flammarion, 1995)
Silk
Mary Schoeser
(Yale University Press, 2007)
*Small is Beautiful: Economics
as if People Mattered*
E. F. Schumacher (Vintage, 1973)
Sustainable Fashion and Textiles
Kate Fletcher (Earthscan
Publications, 2008)
Techno Textiles 2
Sarah E. Braddock Clarke
and Marie O'Mahony
(Thames & Hudson, 2005)

Wonderland
www.helenstoreyfoundation.org
Exhibition curated by Helen Storey
and Tony Ryan in collaboration
with London College of Fashion,
February 2008

Glossary

A

Abacá: The leaves of the abacá plant (*Musa textilis*) which produce **Manila hemp** fibres.

Acrylic: The generic name for a **synthetic polymer** fibre.

Acrylic monomers: Methacrylic amide is commonly used as part of the **weighting** process of silk production, and facilitates the absorption of dye.

Added value crop: A crop grown under a written contract with the intent of receiving a premium because of its particular attributes.

Additive colour: The process of mixing coloured light, as in theatrical or retail applications.

After-image: The reaction seen on a blank surface when the viewer's brain supplies the opposite colour after staring at a particular **hue** for a few seconds.

Agent: A representative showcasing and selling a brand or company's products either domestically or abroad.

Ahimsa peace silk: Made from the cocoons of several species of wild and semi-wild silk **moths** and promoted in parts of southern India as ethical silk.

Ahimsa philosophy: A rule of conduct not to harm any living thing. Ahimsa is a Sanskrit term meaning non-violence, and the philosophy – part of the 3,000-year-old Indian Jain philosophy, and important to Buddhism and Hinduism – supports the philosophy of karmic consequence.

Alpaca: *Vicugna pacos*, a domesticated species of the *Camelidae* family. It is the principal South American fibre-producing animal.

Alpaca fleece: The term for marketing fibre from **huacaya alpacas** (see also **alpaca suri**).

Alpaca suri: The term for marketing fibre from **suri alpacas** (see also **alpaca fleece**).

Ambari hemp: See **Kenaf**.

Ambary: See **Kenaf**.

Analogous hues: Colours that are adjacent to each other on the **colour wheel**.

Angora: A specific breed of goats, rabbits and cats that share a similar type of hair fibre.

The name is derived from the city of Angora (Ankara) in Turkey. The fibre of the angora goat is called **mohair**.

Appliqué: Decorative technique using pieces of fabric or other materials stitched or embroidered onto a base cloth to create designs.

Aran: A style of Gaelic fishermen's knitwear originating from the Aran Islands off the west coast of Ireland. Typically features raised **cable**-stitch patterns and uses **Aran wool**.

Aran wool: Undyed wool that still contains its natural lanolin.

Argyle (also Argyll): A Scottish knitwear pattern made up of diamond blocks of colour.

Artificial fibres: Made from **cellulose** and not to be confused with **synthetic** fibres, which are man-made.

Art silk: A textile term originally coined to describe artificial silk. See also **Rayon**.

Australian cashmere goat: A hybrid, and a different breed from the 'standard' **Himalayan mountain goats**, that produces **cashmere**.

Azo or azoic dye: Petroleum-based dye typically used on **cellulose** fibres.

B

Bactrian: *Camelus bactrianus*, a species of camel from which camel-hair fibre is produced.

Bamboo kun: Natural **cellulose** contained within bamboo, which is used in fibre processing. It also protects the plant from pests and biological pathogens, which can create disease in the host plant.

Barong Tagalog: A traditional embroidered shirt from the Philippines, made from **piña cloth** and worn for formal occasions and ceremonies.

Bast fibres: These are obtained from the **phloem** or inner skin of a plant, and are separated from the **xylem** or woody core.

Bat: A flat, orderly mass of fibres formed by machine **carding**.

Batik: Wax is applied to fabric prior to **dyeing** to produce a pattern that resists the dyeing process.

Batt: A large bundle of multiple strands of fibres partway through the **spinning process**, also known as a **web**.

Bergello: A form of **canvas-work** embroidery.

Bias: Fabric cut at 45 degrees to **warp** and **weft**. This cut exploits the natural stretch of the fabric so that it **drapes** well over the curves of the body.

Biella: An important textile-producing town – primarily woollens – near Milan, Italy.

Bimli: See **Kenaf**.

Bimlipatum jute: See **Kenaf**.

Biodegradable: The process by which organic substances are broken down by **enzymes** produced by living organisms.

Biopolymers: Naturally occurring polymers produced by living organisms such as starch and sugar.

Biotechnology: The term used for any technology that uses biological systems, living organisms and derivatives to make, modify or process products for specialist use.

Bleeding: A loss or transfer of colour in printed fabric.

Blend: A yarn mixed from two or more different fibres.

Block printing: Wooden blocks carved with a design in relief are used as a means of transferring **dye** onto fabric. Originated in China.

Blowing: A treatment that uses steam to remove creases from fabric.

Blue collar: Manual work.

Bobbin lace: A textile made by braiding and twisting threads, wound on bobbins and held in place by pins on a pillow.

Boll: The 'fruit' capsule of the cotton plant, containing the seeds covered in white hairs – the cotton fibres.

Bollgard ®: A registered trademark for a quality of **GM cotton**.

Bolt: A complete piece of fabric folded over a card. Cotton is rolled, so a bolt will usually be **woollen/worsted** fabric.

Bombay hemp: See **Sunn**.

Bombyx mandarina moore: Believed to be the wild ancestor of the cultivated *Bombyx mori*.

Bombyx mori: The cultivated **silk moth**, which feeds on the leaves of the mulberry tree. It is both blind and flightless.

Bonding: Attaching two or more layers of fabric together, often by an adhesive heat treatment.

Botany wool: **Merino** wool originating from Botany Bay, where the first merino sheep in Australia landed .

Bouclé: Yarn or fabric with a curled, looped surface.

Breaking: (1) The process of adding a soft **handle** and brilliance to the surface of silk fabric. (2) One of several processes in flax production, which converts the raw material into linen yarn.

Brightening agent: Increases whiteness or brightness of fabric.

British Colour Group (BCG): British colour consultancy.

Broadcloth: A term for fabric over 150 cm wide, cotton or woollen.

Brocade: Rich fabric with woven raised pattern.

Brushed: Fabric with a brushed, raised surface.

Brushing: Process that removes loose fibres and can raise the surface of the fabric for warmth.

Bt cotton: Naturally occurring soil bacterium *Bacillus thuringiensis*.

Burlap: American-English term for **jute** or **hessian**.

C

Cable knitting: Knitted three-dimensional twisting effects that mimic ropes.

Calendering: The process of adding sheen to fabric using heated steel rotary cylinders.

Canvas work: Form of **embroidery** that completely covers the under-fabric.

Carding: Process of brushing raw or washed fibres to ensure that they are thinned out and evenly distributed to facilitate **spinning**. Carding can also be used to create mixes of different fibres or of different colours.

Carding machine: A device featuring a series of rollers that straighten and align fibres into an orderly mass. See also **Carding**.

Cash crop: Crops grown for money as opposed to domestic subsistence.

Cashgora: A blend between **cashmere** and **mohair**, one of three types of fibre produced by **nigora** goats.

Cashmere: The fine, downy undercoat produced primarily, but not exclusively, from the **Himalayan mountain goat** (*Capra hircus laniger*), popularly known as the **cashmere** goat for its fine, downy undercoat.

Ccara: One of two 'light wool' types of llama. See also **Curaca**.

Cebu hemp: See **Manila hemp**.

Cellulose: This organic compound is the primary structure to all green plants, forming the primary cell wall and also part of the secondary wall.

Cellulose fibres: Natural and man-made fibres regenerated from plants, such as **viscose** and **modal**.

Chacu: An inca ritual involving the communal rounding up of **vicuña**, once every three to four years, for **shearing** and releasing back into the wild. This practice continues today as part of the Peruvian government's vicuña conservation policy.

Changeant: Different colours in the **warp** and **weft** threads produce a fabric that appears to change colour depending on the angle it is viewed at. Also referred to as two-tone or **shot** fabric.

Charkha (or churka): An Indian precursor to the **cotton gin**, used for long-**staple** cotton but not adequate for short-staple varieties.

Chenille: Yarn or fabric with a furry, velvety 'caterpillar' appearance.

Chemical finishes: Treatments applied to fabric to give a specialist finish.

Chrome dye: Type of **dye** typically used on wool.

China grass: One of two types of **ramie**, a **bast** vegetable fibre of the **nettle** family, also known as **white ramie**.

Chinoiserie: Eighteenth- and nineteenth-century trend influenced by **orientalism**.

Chintz: A finishing process on cotton fabric that produces a glazed surface.

Chroma: The **saturation** or brightness of a colour. The term also defines the purity and strength of a colour.

Chromatic: Having a **hue**.

Chromatics: The science of colour. Chromatics considers the human perception of colour, colour theory, and the eyes' and brain's perception of colour.

Chrysalis: **Pupa** case, the third of four life stages (embryo/larva/pupa/imago) of the **silk moth**.

Circular knitting: Knitted on a circular machine resulting in tubular fabric.

Clip: A generic term applied when clipping or **shearing** a herd of **angora** goats. Also refers to the amount of wool cut from a flock of sheep at one shearing.

CMYK system: The four-colour screen system used to reproduce colour photographs: cyan, magenta, yellow, black.

Cocoon: **Pupa** casing made by the **silk-moth** larvae.

Color Association of the United States (CAUS): Colour standards and forecasting organization, established in 1915. Its current title dates to 1955.

Colourant: **Dye** or **pigment** colouring substance.

Coloured angoras: Hybrid **angora** goats.

Colour fade: Loss of colour due to light, washing or other agencies.

Colourfast: Fabrics **dyed** in colours that resist fading.

Colour harmony: Colour relationships in proportion to each other.

Colour Marketing Group (CMG): A colour forecasting service.

Colour migration: Colour moves from one part of the fabric to another.

Colour value: See **Value (colour)**.

Colour-way: One of several alternative colour combinations.

Colour wheels: The colour spectrum organized into wheels to help rationalize and predict colour interactions.

Combing: Process of making fibres smooth prior to **spinning**.

Comfort stretch: Implies approximately a 2 or 3 per cent stretch in a fabric, provided by the knit or weave structure, or by the inclusion of an **elastane** yarn.

Commision Internationale de L'Eclairage (CIE): Founded in 1931 following the exploration of the need for a standardization of colour.

Como: Italian city and region famous for manufacturing silk, and still the centre of the Italian silk industry.

Complementary hues: Opposite colours on a **colour wheel**.

Composite materials: Engineered materials made from two or more constituent materials with significantly different physical or chemical properties, that remain separate and distinct on a macroscopic level within the finished structure.

Concession (retail): A dedicated retail space within a large department store that is rented or allocated to a specific brand. This gives the brand a retail presence it may not normally be able to obtain.

Condensers: Machines that separate the **web** or **batt** into predetermined weight strands as part of the **spinning process**.

Contrast: The visual difference between colours. For example black and white are high-contrast colours.

Converter: A company that buys **greige** fabric then **dyes**, prints or finishes it.

Cooking: A term in silk processing that refers to the **cocoons** being immersed in boiling water to soften the **sericin**, also referred to as maceration.

Cotton belt: Term used to describe the cotton-growing regions of the US.

Cotton count: Numerical expression for size of yarn, denoting a certain length of yarn for a fixed weight, in this case the number of 840-yard lengths or hanks per pound weight.

Cotton gin: An abbreviation of cotton engine, this machine separates the cotton fibres from the seedpods. The American inventor Eli Whitney (1765–1825) is credited with inventing the modern gin in 1792, patented in 1794.

Cottonizing: Method of processing linen or hemp fibres using cotton processing machinery.

Cottonopolis: A term used to describe Manchester, England, as the most important city for cotton manufacturing in the world in the nineteenth century.

Cotton picker: A machine used to remove the cotton from the **boll** without damaging the plant.

Cotton stripper: A machine that strips the entire **boll** from the cotton plant.

Counted-thread embroidery: The **warp** and **weft** threads of the base fabric are counted and bear a relation to how the surface is embroidered.

Course: In **knitting**, the row of loops that runs across the width of the fabric, equivalent to the **weft** in a woven fabric.

Crease-resistant: Fabric that has been treated to improve its recovery.

Creole cotton: *Gossypium barbadense*, a luxurious long-staple cotton.

Crêpe: Yarn or fabric with a high **twist** that has a granular texture.

Crewel-work: A form of **freehand** embroidery.

Crimp: A natural or artificial wave to the fibre or yarn.

Crocheting: Decorative technique that creates fabric by using a hooked needle to pull loops of yarn through other loops.

Crocking: A rubbing test for **colourfast**ness.

Cross-dyeing: The dyeing of a component in a mixture of fibres where at least one is coloured separately to produce a **mélange** effect.

Cross stitch: Style of **counted-thread** embroidery.

Curaca: One of two 'light wool' types of llama. See also **Ccaca**.

Cut-and-sewn knitwear: Knitted garments made by stitching together pre-knitted fabric, in much the same way as woven garments are made.

D

Damask: Figured fabric, with the **figure** (design) of a contrasting weave. Usually constructed with **satin-weave warps** and **wefts** in **sateen weave**. Named after Damascus in modern-day Syria.

Daveo: See **Manila hemp**.

Deccan hemp: See **Kenaf**.

De-cortication: The removal of the hard outer bark from plants such as **ramie**.

De-gumming: The removal of **sericin** as part of silk production. In the production of **ramie** it is the process of extracting the fibres prior to **spinning**.

De-hairing: The removal of coarse outer **guard hairs** from the soft under-down of animal fibres in preparation for **spinning**.

Denier: A unit of measurement used to measure the linear mass density of fibres. Several **filaments** together are referred to as 'total denier'. The system is used in Britain and the US for hosiery.

Denim: A cotton **twill-weave** fabric where the **wefts** pass under two or more **warps** producing a diagonal rib effect. The fabric was originally called *serge de Nîmes* from the French town where it was made.

Devoré: A partially sheer fabric containing two or more fibre types. One of the fibres is 'eaten' away to produce a pattern by screen printing with an acid that 'burns out' or 'devours' the natural fibre to reveal the sheer **synthetic** base **filaments**.

Dhoti: Traditional unstitched cloth garment worn wrapped around the lower body. Considered authentic formal attire for men in the Indian subcontinent.

Direct printing: Commonly used industrial printing method. **Dyes**, thickeners and **mordants** are printed directly onto the fabric.

Discharge printing: Colour is chemically removed from parts of the fabric to reveal the base colour. Alternatively, adding an additional colour that is unaffected by the discharging agent.

Distributor: A person or organization involved in making a product or service available for use by a consumer or other retailer.

Double-cloth weaving: Weaving technique that creates a fabric with two **face** or right sides and no wrong or reverse side.

Double face: Any fabric that has two **face** sides and no reverse side.

Double jersey: All needle rib-knitted fabric where both the **face** and reverse side are the same. See also **Jersey**.

Drape: The behaviour of the fabric, how it handles, falls and hangs.

Drawing and finisher drawing: Two processes that further improve the evenness and regularity of yarn, prior to final **spinning**. Each technique gives a uniquely different character, in both appearance and feel, to the fabric and end product.

Dromedary: *Camelus dromedarius*, the single-humped Arabian camel, not used in the production of camel-hair fibre. See also **Bactrian**.

Ductile strength: The mechanical property describing how much deformation a material can sustain before fracturing.

DuPont: American chemical company founded in 1802. In the twentieth century it led the **polymer** revolution by developing successful materials such as neoprene, **nylon**, **Lycra** and Teflon.

Dye: **Pigment** dissolved in a fluid for **dyeing**

Dyeing: The process of transferring **colourant** to fibres, **yarns**, fabrics or ready-made garments.

Dye lot: A batch of **yarn** that has been **dyed** together in the same **vat**.

E

Egyptian cotton: *Gossypium hirsutum* and *Gossypium barbadense*. All cotton grown in Egypt is called Egyptian cotton, however it is these two cotton species, with an extra-long **staple**, that produce the luxury fabric synonymous with the name.

Ells: English measuring system from the Tudor period, whereby 30–40 ells was equal to 35–50 yards (32–46m).

Embossing: A relief pattern is embossed onto the fabric, usually by a heated press.

Embroidery: Handicraft surface decoration. Designs are stitched onto fabrics using threads and yarns. Beads, sequins and other applied decorative **trimmings** can be embroidered onto the fabric.

Ends: **Warp** threads.

Enzymes: Proteins that catalyse/accelerate chemical reactions.

Eri silk: A type of **wild silk** gleaned from the **eri silk moth**.

Eri silk moth: *Philosamia ricini*, a type of wild **silk moth** found only in India, it feeds on the castor plant and producing silk yarn from its **cocoon** is considered to be ethical and equivalent to organic rearing.

F

Fabric dyeing: **Dyeing** process that occurs after **weaving** the fabric. Also known as **piece dyeing**.

Face: The correct side of the fabric.

Fair Isle: A traditional, complex hand-**knitting** technique featuring horizontal patterns using five to seven different colours, and originating in Fair Isle, north of Scotland.

Fairtrade: An independent labelling scheme, initiated in the Netherlands for food production, it has now been extended to textiles; particularly cotton. The label assures the consumer that the product has met the international Fairtrade standard for production and is eligible to carry the FAIRTRADE mark, which guarantees that the farmer has been paid a premium above the market value of their commodity.

Fashioned: In **knitting**, increasing or decreasing stitches forms the garment shape.

Fast (colour and light): Does not lose colour with exposure to light or after washing.

Felt: A non-woven fabric made by matting and condensing fibres together.

Felted: A matted appearance.

Felting: Process of making **felt**.

Fibre: A long, thin, flexible structure. Plant and animal fibres are spun to create yarn.

Fibrillation: A natural defect to which silk is prone, and which occurs if the outermost layer is roughened up off the filaments by harsh washing or abrasion. The resulting fibrils reflect light, giving a 'peach bloom' effect. This effect is also purposely reproduced over the whole surface of the fabric by 'scuffing' with an enzyme treatment or mechanical abrasion. The result is a desirable, tactile, 'sueded' or 'sand-washed' silk.

Fibrils: Nanometre fibres.

Figure/figured: A motif or raised part of the design that contrasts with the ground fabric.

Filament: A single, continuous strand of fibre. Any man-made yarn of one or more strands running the entire length of the yarn.

Fire-retardant: Able to delay or prevent combustion.

Fixing: Method of making a **dye colourfast** on a fabric by use of a **mordant**.

Flax: *Linum usitatissimum*, an annual herb of the *Linaceae* family used to make linen.

Float: A portion of yarn that extends under or over adjacent **warps** or **wefts**. The term is also used in **knitting** when the yarn 'floats' across several stitches.

Fulling: A finishing process that compresses fabric by means of heat, steam and pressure.

Fully fashioned: A term applied to knitwear when each piece is knitted to the exact shape required by increasing and decreasing stitches.

G

Gandhi, Mohandas Karamchand: (1869–1948) A major political and spiritual leader of India and its independence movement, commonly known as Mahatma (Great Soul). He exhorted Indians, both rich and poor, to spin **khadi** (homemade cloth) in support of the independence movement, which resulted in a boycott of British textiles.

Garment dyeing: **Dyeing** ready-made garments.

Gauge: Describes the fineness or chunkiness of a knitted garment achieved by needle size and spacing.

Geo textiles: Permeable fabrics that, when used in association with soil, have the ability to separate, filter, reinforce, protect or drain; usually made from polypropylene or **polyester**.

Gin: The building where cotton is processed. See also **Cotton gin**.

Ginning: Generically implies the complete process of preparing cotton.

Glazed: Smooth, glossy surface on fabric.

GM cotton: Genetically modified or transgenic cotton.

Grease-wool: The term used to describe wool before it has been cleaned and **scoured**, also known as wool-in-the-grease.

Green chemistry: Twelve principles that aim to help define the true ecological, ethical and sustainable credentials of a raw material or product.

Green ramie: One of two types of **ramie**, a **bast** vegetable fibre of the **nettle** family.

Greige: Fabric in its raw state, before it has been bleached, **dyed** or finished.

Ground colour: Usually a print term indicating the background or main colour of the fabric.

Guanaco: *Lama guanicoe*, a member of the South American *Camelidae* family.

Guard hairs: Coarser outer hairs that protect the finer under-hairs or down on many animals.

H

Hackling: Process by which the short, broken linen fibres, or **tows**, are combed out, leaving only the desirable long fibres, ready for **spinning**.

Hair sheep: A type of sheep that does not produce wool.

Halo effect: The effect created by the fine downy surface of **angora** yarn that, in pale colours, appears slightly luminous in the light.

Handle: The touch or feeling of the fabric.

Hank: Unsupported coil of yarn. The ends are tied together to maintain the shape. Also called a **skein.**

Hank dyed: Dyed as yarn.

Header cards: Also known as a fabric 'hanger', the header card is a large fabric swatch, or 'feeler', used for displaying and demonstrating the quality of a fabric. Information regarding fibre types, yarn count, width, weight and finish appear on the card that supports the swatch.

Hemp: The generic name for the entire *Cannabis* family of plants.

Henduan: A breed of yak from the alpine regions of Tibet, producing the best fibre yield. See also **Jiulong**

Hessian: See **Jute.**

High street: A generic marketing and retail term implying competitive mass-market fashion.

Himalayan mountain goat: *Capra hircus laniger*, popularly known as the **cashmere** goat.

Hollow fibre: A tube-like man-made fibre that provides good insulation.

Homespun: Cloth woven on a small domestic scale. The term can also suggest a desirable rustic craft appearance that implies a handmade authenticity.

Horsehair: Originally tail and mane hair, now a generic term for canvas **interlining** generally used in **tailoring**

Huacaya: Pronounced wua'ki'ya, one of two types of **alpaca**, producing a dense, soft, sheep-like fibre with a uniform crimp. See also **Suri.**

Huarizo: An **alpaca**-llama cross breed**.**

Hue*:* Colour. Pure hue has no other colour mixed in with it.

I

Icelandic wool (sheep): Wool from the fleece of Icelandic sheep, which is double layered, made up of fine **cashmere**-like inner fibres and coarser, medium outer fibres.

Ikat: A **weaving** technique where the **wefts** and/or **warps** are **dyed** different colours at predetermined intervals. The designs produced when using this technique appear to have a blurred effect.

Indigo: A naturally derived plant **dye** still in popular use for denim products to provide the distinctive shade of blue that fades desirably.

Industrial hemp: The term given to the variety of **hemp** (*Cannabis sativa* L. subsp. *sativa*) grown for fibre and other non-narcotic purposes.

Ingeo™: A high-performance trademarked **biopolymer** fibre made from corn.

Inkjet printing: Droplets of ink are transferred or propelled onto almost any medium. Common means of printing on home computer printers.

Inlaid yarn: Yarn that is held in place by the loops of the **knitting** rather than being knitted in.

Intarsia: A knitted fabric with several solid colours in one row of **knitting**. The pattern is formed by stopping one colour and twisting in a new colour over the needles each time there is a colour change.

Interlining: A firmer fabric that is applied to parts of the outer fabric of a garment to give a stronger **handle** or firmer shape, usually on collars and cuffs and chest panels in **tailoring**.

International Colour Authority (ICA): Colour prediction organization.

Isan: Northeastern area of Thailand where **ikat weaving** is traditionally a speciality.

Itten wheel: Colour wheel devised by Johannes Itten (1888–1967) to document a logical format for working with colour.

J

Jacquard: A type of **weaving** or **knitting** process and a type of fabric. In woven fabric the process allows for an unlimited variety of designs, in knitwear it implies that every colour of yarn used is knitted into the back of the fabric when not in use on the **face** side.

Jacquard loom: Developed by French inventor Joseph Jacquard (1752–1834), the loom features a string of punch cards that can be processed mechanically in the correct sequence.

Jamewar weave: An intricate Kashmir **weaving** technique producing expensive shawl fabrics worn, originally, by nobles.

Japonisme: Eighteenth- and nineteenth-century trend influenced by **orientalism**

Jersey: Generically used to describe many types of knitted fabric. **Single jersey** is **plain knit** on one side and **purl** on the reverse and is used for tops. **Double jersey** is plain on both sides and can be double in weight. It does not unravel when cut so is fine for cutting and sewing more complicated styles.

Jerseywear: Generic term for various garments, such as T-shirts and polo shirts, that are cut and made from fabric that has been previously knitted.

Jiulong: A breed of **yak** from the plateau regions of Tibet, producing the best fibre. See also **Henduan**.

Johnston's of Elgin: The oldest **cashmere mill** still in operation, located in Elgin, Scotland.

Jute: A coarse, strong, **bast** vegetable fibre.

K

Kapok: Vegetable seed fibre from the kapok tree.

Karakul: Also known as Persian lamb, this sheep has a tight glossy curl, often in black or grey.

Kasuri: Japanese type of **ikat** weave.

Kemps: Short, thick, coarse, stiff, hollow fibres on coarser wools, such as those of **angora** goats, usually unaffected by **dye**

Kenaf: A species of hibiscus with visual similarities to **jute**.

Keratin: Animal protein found in wool, hair, nails, feathers and horn.

Khadi: Indian hand-spun, hand-woven cloth made from cotton, silk or wool, traditionally spun on a domestic spinning wheel called a **charkha**.

Khadi hand-loom: Indian hand-spun, hand-woven cloth of either cotton, silk or wool.

Kimono: Traditional Japanese costume made from silk.

King Cotton: A term used to describe the financial importance of cotton production to the US economy in the nineteenth century.

Knitting: Method of constructing fabric from yarn by a series of interlinked loops. Refers to hand and machine techniques.

L

Lab dips: Small pieces of yarn windings or fabric swatches sample **dyed** for approval prior to larger **dye lots** and bulk production dyeing.

Lace: Fabric or trim made up of intertwined or embroidered threads.

Lanolin: Produced from wool grease. Medical-grade lanolin is hypoallergenic and bacteriostatic.

Lanuda: One of two 'heavy wool' types of llama. See also **tapada**.

Lay planning: The placement of garment pattern pieces onto the laid fabric in the most economical format prior to cutting. In mass production, this process is usually executed by computer.

LEA: A US measuring system for grading the fineness of linen – 1 LEA = 1 x 300 yards (yarn) to the pound weight.

Lead time: The amount of time it takes to manufacture fabric and or garments and the delivery transport time.

Lehnga: Long skirt and top traditionally worn by Muslim women in India and Pakistan.

Light wheel: Based on the **additive colour** system, this wheel shows information concerning light rays and transparent colour. Used for lighting and as the basis for video and computer graphics.

Lignin: A chemical compound commonly derived from wood and an integral part of the cell walls of plants.

Linen Board: Established in 1711, The Board of Trustees of the Linen Manufacturers of Ireland was set up to develop the Irish linen industry.

Linenopolis: A term used to describe Belfast in the nineteenth century.

Linen union: Fabric with a linen **weft** and a cotton **warp**.

Lint: Cleaned cotton. Also describes a fuzzy surface. Linen is lint-free.

Linters: Fuzzy down removed from cotton as part of the **ginning** process.

Living Linen Project: Records first-hand information about the linen industry in Northern Ireland in the twentieth century.

Llama fibre (or llama wool): Referred to as fibre because, technically, llama hair is not wool due to its particular structure.

Lofty (or loft): Descriptive of the appearance of woollen fibre or fabric, meaning voluminous, supple, soft and springy.

Long-line fibres: One of two categories of **flax** fibre, the short fibres are called **tow** fibres.

Loop-back fabric: Type of **pile**-woven fabric, with the loops left intact, such as towelling.

Luminosity: Refers to colour **value**. The lighter a colour the greater is the reflection of light back to the eye, lighter colours are therefore more luminous than darker colours.

Lurex: The brand name of a type of metallic yarn, usually a **synthetic** fibre, with a vaporized layer of aluminium. The term may also refer to fabric that contains **metallic yarn**.

Lycra: A trade name for an **elastane** fabric made by **DuPont**.

Lyon: French city and region famous for manufacturing silk, and still the centre of the French silk industry.

M

Maceration: See **Cooking**.

Machine embroidery: Automated **embroidery**.

Macramé: Fabric created by the interlinking of knots.

Manila hemp: Also known as **daveo** and **cebu hemp** and produced from the leaves of the **abacá** plant.

Manufacturing hub: Describes an important centre of manufacturing, and is often used in reference to the developing world.

Margin: A gross margin implies the difference between buying and selling a product before overheads have been deducted. Net margin is the profit after overheads have been deducted.

Marl yarns: Two different-coloured yarns twisted together.

Mashru: Meaning 'permitted', a fabric development using silk **warps** and cotton **wefts**, which allowed Muslim men to wear silk.

Mauvine: First **synthetic dye**, discovered in1856 by William Perkins.

Medulated fibres: Intermediate fibres on an **angora** goat, less coarse than the **kemp** fibres but coarser than the true **mohair** fibres.

Mélange: A mix of colours worked together in yarn or fabric form.

Mercerized cotton: See **Mercerizing**.

Mercerizing: A caustic soda solution is applied to cotton yarn and/or fabric to give it a more lustrous and smoother appearance. Named after John Mercer who invented the technique in the mid-nineteenth century.

Merino: A distinctive breed of sheep originating in Spain but now the source of the bulk of Australian wool production. A luxury wool.

Metallic yarns: Yarns containing metal threads or metallic elements.

Microfibre: Fine man-made fibre or **filament** that is under 1 **denier**. Ten kilometres should weigh less than one gram.

Micronaire: A system for assessing cotton fibre fineness and maturity. A poor count affects the value of the cotton.

Microns: Unit of measurement, one micron is one-millionth of a metre.

Mill: The place where yarn and fabric are manufactured.

Milled: Fabric that has been treated to age or soften its appearance, or to blend colours together.

Milling: A treatment that ages and softens the appearance of fabric by blending the colours, obscuring the weave and making the fabric more compact.

Modal: Generic name for regenerated natural **polymer cellulose fibre**.

Module builder: Machine that compresses cotton into large modular blocks.

Mohair: The fleece of the **angora** goat and fabric produced from it.

Mommes: System of weight measurement for silk, quantifying the density of silk as opposed to the thread count.

Monochromatic: Of one **hue** or colour. One hue harmony combines colours derived from a single hue, graduated shades of the same base colour.

Mordant: Chemical compound used as a **dye** fixative.

Mordant printing: A design pattern is printed using a **mordant** that resists colour when **dyed**, thus forming the pattern.

Moso bamboo: *Phyllostachys*, the species of bamboo cultivated for textile production.

Muga silk: A variety of **wild silk** gleaned from the **muga silk moth**.

Muga silk moth: *Antheraea assamensis*, a wild and semi-wild species of **silk moth** living in a restricted area in Assam, India.

Mulberry silkworm: See **Silkworm**.

Multivoltine: Term applied to **silk moths** that produce at least ten batches of eggs per year.

Munsell wheel: A partitive colour system based on five **primary hues** and **after-image** perceptions that are derived from hues we see in nature.

Muted colour: A subdued version of a **hue**.

N

Napa (or nappa): Sheep leather.

Narrow fabric: Fabric less than 45 cm (18 in.) wide (UK) or 30 cm (12 in.) wide (Europe/USA).

Naturally coloured cotton: Cotton that is naturally plant pigmented. Peruvian **Pima** and **Tangüis** cottons are naturally coloured.

Natural polymer: See **Polymer**.

Natural protein fibre: See **Protein fibre**.

Needle lace: Handmade **lace** using a needle where all the stitch work is based on **buttonhole** or **blanket** stitch.

Needlepoint: A form of **canvas-work embroidery**.

Neps: Entangled fibres or knots.

Nettle: A **bast fibre**.

New Zealand cotton: Fibre from the **bast** of the New Zealand ribbon tree. It has a strong fibre that resembles **flax**.

New Zealand flax: *Phormium tenax*, or *harakeke* in Maori, native of New Zealand and not related to linen **flax**, *Linum usitatissimum*.

Nigora: A cross between an **angora** goat and **cashmere**-producing Nigerian dwarf goat. The fibre it produces is known as **cashgora**.

Nm: Metric measuring system used for linen/**flax** – the number of 1,000-metre lengths per kilogram.

Noils: Short fibres left over from **combing** wool or **spinning** silk.

These fibres are weaker than normal fibres and considered inferior.

Nylon: The first **synthetic** fibre from the **DuPont** chemical company, used as a replacement for silk for stockings during the Second World War. It is also a generic term for synthetic **polymers** also known as polyamides.

O

Off-grain: The garment pattern pieces are not correctly placed on the straight **grain** of the fabric (unless **bias** cut).

Offshore: A term used to describe manufacturing in a foreign country; it usually implies production in the developing world.

Oiled wool: Undyed, unscoured wool containing natural **lanolin**.

Oiling (cloth): Water-repelling treatment applied to fabric.

One-way fabric: Implies the fabric has a single direction and that all the pattern pieces must be cut in the same direction to avoid noticeable **shading**.

Organic cotton: Cotton grown without pesticides from plants that are not genetically modified.

Organzine: Twisted threads used as **warps** in the silk **weaving** process.

Orientalism: A generic term applied to trends and fashions inspired by oriental art and culture.

Oshima: A Japanese type of **ikat** weave.

Over-dye: To apply the same or different **dye** colour as a second process over the initial dyeing. Can be used to produce a deeper intensity of colour, to correct or darken an unwanted colour instead of **stripping**, or be applied over an existing printed fabric.

Over-print: An additional design or motif printed over an existing all-over print.

P

Paco vicuña: A vicuña–alpaca cross breed.

Pantone Professional System: An international colour matching and referencing system.

Partitive colour: The process of placing colours next to each other in order to produce different reactions.

Pashmina: A Kashmiri word for shawls made of **cashmere**. The term is derived from the Persian word *pasham*, meaning 'goat wool'.

Pattern cutting: The art or science of interpreting a drawing or design into a two-dimensional pattern, which when translated into fabric and sewn together becomes a three-dimensional representation of the original design drawing.

Peace silk: Refers to silk that has been produced without harming the moth that has produced the silk **cocoon**. The moth is allowed to emerge naturally, before the cocoons are harvested. Also known as vegetarian silk.

Pectin: Light substance derived from the cell walls of plants (the non-woody parts). Pectin helps to bind cells together.

Percale: Denotes a close weave, high thread count, irrespective of yarn type.

Peruvian alpaca: Alpaca marketed with its own distinctive branding.

Petit point: A form of **canvas-work embroidery**.

Phloem: Living plant tissue that carries nutrients. See also **Bast fibres**

Photosynthesis: The process by which green plants use carbon dioxide, water and sunlight to produce sugars.

Picker: A machine that beats, loosens and mixes cotton fibres.

Picks: **Weft** threads.

Piece: A complete or full length of fabric, which may be in the form of a **bolt** or a **roll**.

Piece dyeing: See **Fabric dyeing**.

Pigment: Insoluble colour.

Pigment print: Printed with **pigment** and binder rather than **dyes**.

Pigment wheel: A 12-step **colour wheel** for working with **subtractive colour**, showing how colours react when used in combinations to create the other **hues**.

Pile fabric: Generic term for a raised surface fabric, such as velvet or corduroy.

Pile weaving: Weaving technique that uses rods to make loops on the surface of the resulting fabric. The loops can be cut to create **pile fabric**, or left intact to create **loop-back fabric**.

Pill or pilling: Entangled fibres after washing or wearing form little balls known as pills.

Pima cotton: Indigenous American long **staple** cotton (*Gossypium barbadense*) named after North American Pima Indians .

Piña: Fibres obtained from the leaves of the pineapple plant.

Piña cloth: Fabric woven from **piña** fibres.

Plain knit: The **face** side of basic **jersey**, the reverse side is known as **purl**.

Plain weave: A basic weave construction of **warps** and **wefts** criss-crossing each other at right angles.

Ply: Two or more single yarns twisted together.

Polyester: Generic name for **synthetic polymers**.

Polymer: A substance composed of molecules with a large molecular mass linked by repeated structural units or monomers. It can be naturally occurring or have a **synthetic** substance. DNA and plastics are well-known examples.

Prato: An important centre for the Italian wool industry, near Florence in Italy.

Première Vision: A bi-annual fabric **trade fair** in Paris, France, and also at other international venues.

Pre-shrunk: Fabric that has been shrunk at the **weaving mill** and should not shrink further.

Primary colours: Red, yellow and blue, the three colours that cannot be made from other colours.

Primary triad: The three **primary colours**.

Process wheel: A 12-step process for the three basic primaries that when mixed result in purer **hues**.

Production run: The total number of garments of a style that is manufactured at one time. The number of pieces given as an order to a factory.

Protein fibre: Animal hair/wool or silk.

Pupa: An insect between the usually passive stage of larva and adulthood.

Pure dye silk: Indicates that **weighting** was not added to silk at the **dyeing** stage.

Pure new wool: See **Virgin wool**.

Purl knit: The reverse side of basic **jersey**, the face side is known as **plain**.

Pygora: A cross between an **angora** goat and a **cashmere**-producing pygmy goat.

Q

QC: Quality control of fabric and clothing manufacturing.

Qiviut (or qivent): The under-wool of a musk ox, *Ovibos moschatus*, whose habitat is the Arctic regions of Canada, Alaska and Greenland.

Quilting: A method of stitching a layer of fabric to a layer of insulative **wadding**, commonly in diamond patterns, but often with decorative stitch patterns. This produces a light and warm material, often used for linings.

R

Raffia palms: Used to make raffia fabric.

Raker: A component design line in an **Argyle** design.

Rambouillet or French merino: A cross between a Spanish **merino** and an English long-wool sheep, originally bred at Rambouillet, near Paris, France.

Ramie: (*Boehmeria nivea*) a **bast** vegetable fibre of the **nettle** family. See also **China grass** and **Green ramie**.

Raw silk: The short fibres left over from **spinning** silk.

Rayon: A manufactured, regenerated **cellulose fibre**. The name was first used in the US in 1924, in Europe it was referred to as **viscose** or **art silk**, because it was an inexpensive alternative to real silk.

Reactive dyes: Dyes used primarily on **cellulose** and **protein fibres**.

Reeling: Process of extracting the silk **filament** from the **silkworm's cocoon**.

Repeat: One complete unit of a design, either printed or woven.

Resist dyeing: Generic term for the different methods of patterning fabric by preventing **dye** reaching certain parts of it.

Retting: Process used on all **bast** vegetable fibres to separate the fibre from the plant's stalk.

Reversible: Fabric that can be used either side up, or a style of garment that can be turned inside out.

Ribs: Usually on the waist and cuffs of a sweater for better elasticity and closer fit. May also be used as an all-over knit effect.

Rippling: A process in the production of **flax** fibres for making linen, entailing the removal of the seeds by a mechanical process.

Rolag: A loose roll of fibres produced by **carding**.

Roller printing: Commercial printing using engraved rollers to transfer colour and design onto fabric.

Roundup Ready®: A registered trademark for a quality of **GM cotton**.

Roves: Continuous lengths of fibre ready for **spinning**.

Roving: A long narrow bundle of fibres with a slight twist to hold it together.

Ruff: Item of clothing worn around the neck, usually of linen. Prominent in Europe from the mid-sixteenth to mid-seventeenth centuries.

Run (print): A complete, continuous length of printed fabric.

S

Sand-washed silk: Silk fabric washed with sand or other abrasive materials to 'scuff' the surface and produce a tactile, suede-like **handle** and peach-bloom appearance.

Sari: Traditional Indian women's costume.

Sateen: **Satin-weave** fabric with a polished sheen to the **face** side.

Sateen weave: A weave construction with the maximum amount of **wefts** on the face of the fabric, achieving a soft touch and a smooth finish.

Satin weave: A weave construction with the maximum amount of **warps** on the face of the fabric, achieving a flat, smooth and lustrous finish. Satin weave is not to be confused with satin, which, while of a satin weave construction, refers to the fabric itself.

Saturation: The purity or intensity of a specific colour.

SCOTDIC (Standard Color of Textile Dictionnaire Internationale de la Couleur): A worldwide colour codification system for fabric. The system is applicable to **polyester**, cotton and wool. The coding defines **hues**, **value** and **chroma** for thousands of colours. Head office in Kyoto, Japan.

Scouring: Removal of natural fats, oils and dirt from a yarn, giving fullness to the fibre and bulking up the fabric.

Scutchers: See **Scutching**.

Scutching: Process of separating fibrous stalks from the woody stems of **bast fibres** using metal rollers.

Sea Island cotton: *Gossypium barbadense*, a luxurious long-**staple** cotton.

Secondary colours: The colours that result from mixing two **primary colours**. The secondary colours are green, orange and violet.

Secondary triad: The three **secondary colours**.

Seed cotton: Pre-cleaned cotton. i.e. before the harvested cotton has gone through the **ginning** process.

Selvedge: The firm side edges of the fabric running parallel to the **warp**.

Sericin: A water-soluble protective gum produced from the glands of the **silkworm**.

Sericulture: The process of breeding and cultivating **silk moth**s.

Shalwar kameez: Traditional dress worn, principally, by Muslim women in Bangladesh, Sri Lanka, Pakistan and Afghanistan. *Shalwars* are loose pyjama-like trousers; a *kameez* is a long shirt or tunic.

Sharara: Traditional Muslim women's garment popularized in India since the time of the Mughal invasion.

Sharecropping: In agriculture, a landowner gives a share of the profits to a tenant who works the land. In particular applied to black farmers (ex-slaves) in the US working on white-owned cotton plantations after the American Civil War.

Shatoosh: A shawl made from the down of the chiru or Tibetan antelope, *Pantholopas hodgsonii*.

Shearing: The process of removing the fleece of a sheep or other fibre-producing animal in one piece.

Shetland sheep: Of Scandinavian origin, with a fleece featuring distinctive fine fibres.

Shoddy: Recycled or re-manufactured wool made by tearing apart existing wool fabric and re-**spinning** it.

Shot: Fabric that appears to change colour when viewed from different directions.

Shous: Woody stems prior to their separation from the fibrous part of the stalk in processing **bast fibres**.

Shuttle: A **weaving** tool designed to store and pass **weft** yarns back and forth through the shed (space between two **warps**) in order to weave in the wefts.

Silk moth: The cultivated silk moth, *Bombyx mori*, feeds on the leaves of the mulberry tree and is blind and flightless. Silk is harvested from the **cocoon** of the caterpillar.

Silk noil: See **Raw silk**.

Silk Road: Ancient trade routes connecting China with Asia Minor and the Mediterranean.

Silk-screen printing: Technique using a screen and ink to print a design, by hand or mechanized. **Synthetics** are now used for the screens.

Silkworm: The larva or caterpillar of *Bombyx mori*, the cultivated **silk moth** that feeds exclusively on mulberry leaves.

Single coat: Implies there are no **guard hairs** in the coat of the animal.

Single jersey: **Plain knit** on the face side and **purl** on the reverse. See also **Jersey**.

Skein: Coiled yarn with tied ends to keep the shape.

Skirted: Angora fibres when clean, with all stains removed.

Slivers: (Pronounced sly-vers) untwisted ropes of fibre**s**.

Smocking: Decorative stitch-work or embroidery technique used to gather and hold fabric together. See also **Hank**.

Space dyeing: **Dyeing** technique. Colours are applied at random or regular intervals along the yarn, creating a random multicolour effect when woven or knitted.

Spinnerets: Openings in the **silkworm**'s head that secrete the protective **sericin** gum.

Spinning: The singular specific process of applying **twist** to yarn.

Spinning frame: An eighteenth-century invention often credited to Richard Arkwright (1733–1792), however others developed the invention while under his employment. It was later developed into the water frame (patented 1769) increasing textile production and producing stronger threads than the earlier **spinning jenny**.

Spinning jenny: A multiple yarn-**spinning** machine invented by James Hargreaves (1720–1778) in Lancashire, England, in 1764

(patented 1770). It enabled the spinning of eight and later up to 80 yarns simultaneously. Considered a factor in starting the British Industrial Revolution. It was named after his daughter.

Spinning process: A generic term for several separate processes, including **carding**, **combing**, **drawing** and **spinning**.

Spiralling: Knitted fabric distortion.

Staple: Quantifies textile fibre characteristics of length, quality and grade.

Staple fibre: Fibre of finite length.

Stitches: Individual linked loops that form the fabric.

Stock houses: Wholesale companies that hold stock fabrics from a variety of sources, with the advantage of dealing in smaller quantities than placing an order directly with a **mill**.

Strike-off: Preliminary small-print sample for approval of colour and print.

Stripping: Removal of unwanted colour from printed fabric.

Subtractive colour: A method of creating colours based on **pigments** or **dyes** from natural or chemical sources. The colours mix by absorbing some wavelengths of light and reflecting others.

Sunn: A variety of **hemp** produced in India and also known as **Bombay hemp**.

Super 100s: An international system that identifies a range of fine **worsted** fabrics from Super 100s through to Super 210s, the higher the figure the finer the yarn. Ideal for good **tailoring**.

Supply chain: All the separate disciplines, services and people involved in processing a product from concept to retail.

Suri: Pronounced soo'ree, one of two types of **alpaca**. They have silky, pencil-fine, mop-like locks. See also **Huacaya**.

Synthetics: Man-made fibres derived from petrochemicals (which may be produced in **staple** or **filament** yarns). Not to be confused with artificial fibres (part natural and part synthetic), which are chemically treated **cellulose** derivatives.

T

Taffeta: A fine, plain, tightly woven silk cloth, with a dry **handle** and crispy 'rustle'.

Tailoring: The art or craft of cutting and sewing together a garment to a high standard and incorporating a high level of labour content.

Tamponing: An even film of oil is applied to silk fabric to smooth out irregularities.

Tangüis cotton: Variety of cotton grown primarily in Peru, often organically. Some species are **naturally coloured**.

Tapada: One of two 'heavy wool' types of llama. See also **lanuda**.

Tapestry weaving: Vertical loom **weaving** technique, sometimes called **weft**-faced weaving because all the **warps** are hidden.

Target consumer: Marketing term implying an ideal profile customer.

Tassah moths (also tassar): *Antheraea mylitta* and *Antheraea proylei*, wild and semi-wild **silk moth**s respectively.

Technical fabric: Manufactured to perform certain functions.

Technologist: An expert in all aspects of either garment or fabric construction, manufacturing and quality issues.

Tensile strength: Measures the stress required to pull something to its breaking point.

Tertiary colours: The colours that result when a **primary** and an adjacent **secondary colour** are mixed together.

Terylene: A trade name for a **polyester** fibre.

Tex: An international system of measurement used to measure the linear mass density of fibres.

Thorn proofs: Generic term for different types of strong, durable fabrics traditionally used for outdoor pursuits. Often produced from Cheviot wools or New Zealand cross-bred wools. A hard twisted yarn produces a firm-touch fabric that feels almost indestructible.

Thread count: A measure that determines the coarseness or fineness of fabric, achieved by counting the number of threads contained in one square inch of fabric, including **warps** and **wefts**.

Threader: A machine-feeding device used in the production of silk **filament**.

Throwing: Applying a **twist** to silk **filament**.

Thrown threads: The different types of thread produced by **throwing** silk.

Tie-dyeing: Process of tying, knotting or stitching a design on fabric prior to **dyeing**, then releasing after dyeing to reveal a pattern.

Tone: Variously describes a colour's lightness, **value**, brilliance, greyness and **luminosity**.

Top-stitching: Refers to the visible optional stitching on a garment as opposed to the functional stitching that holds the garment together.

Tow: Mass of man-made **filaments** without **twist**. In the production of linen, tow also describes one of two categories of **flax** fibre. Tow fibres are short, whereas the long fibres are called **long-line fibres**.

Trade fairs: Where manufacturers of yarn, fabric or clothing assemble together to showcase and sell new developments.

Trade name: A specific brand.

Triadic hues: Any three equidistant colours on the colour spectrum when configured as a circle of hues.

Tri-blended: Three different types of fibre blended together.

Trimmings: A generic term used to describe any number of functional components used on a garment, such as buttons and zips, as well as decorative accessories such as braids.

Tussah silk: The most common variety of **wild silk**, harvested from **tassah moths**.

Tuxing: The process of separating the outer and inner sheaths of leaves to reach the fibres that run through them.

Twill weave: A weave construction resulting in a visual diagonal line effect.

Twist: A spiral formation applied to fibres during the spinning proccess to give additional strength and which allows for different colours and fibres to be twisted together for visual and tactile effect. The term also describes the direction in which the yarn is spun ('S' or 'Z' twist).

Two-way fabric: Fabric that can be cut with the pattern pieces in either direction without compromising the end product

U

USP: Unique selling point, a marketing term.

V

Value (colour): A colour's **luminosity** and clarity.

Vat: A **dyeing** vessel.

Vat dyes: Common cotton **dyes**.

Vicuña: *Vicugna vicugna*, the smallest of the South American camelid family. Garments and fabrics made from vicuña fibres should be registered by the Peruvian government, which is the only international body recognized for the task, and assures the conservation of the animal.

Virgin Wool or **pure new wool:** The wool product has been produced from fibres that have not been previously processed.

Viscose: Generic name for regenerated natural **polymer cellulose fibre** (man-made). It cannot be dissolved naturally and therefore needs to be chemically processed, then regenerated by extrusion into a **filament** yarn. The first viscose yarn was produced from wood pulp in the early twentieth century .

Visual wheel: A 16-step **partitive** and **subtractive colour wheel** created by Leonardo da Vinci, whose understanding of **complementary** colours greatly influenced Renaissance painting.

W

Wadding: Usually non-woven padded fabric used to create added insulation.

Wales: (1) Columns of loops that run along the length of the fabric. (2) Raised ridges or ribs that run vertically down corduroy, parallel to the **selvedge**. The wider the wales, the lower the numerical expression, and vice versa. The number of wales that fit into one inch (2.5 cm) is the wale count. 21-wale corduroy implies there are 21 wales per inch.

Warp: The yarns that run the length of the fabric, top to bottom.

Waterproof: Completely resistant to water penetration.

Water-repellent: Partially water-resistant.

Water-resistant: Resists but does not entirely prevent the absorption of water.

Waxing: Impregnating fabric with wax to make it shower-proof

Weaving: The process of interweaving **warp** and **weft** threads to make fabric.

Web: Single or multiple sheets of fibres partway through the **spinning process**, also known as a **batt**.

Weft: The yarns that run across the fabric, **selvedge** to selvedge.

Weighting: The application of metallic salts to silk fabric prior to dyeing and finishing. During silk processing the fibres are **de-gummed** of their natural **sericin** gum that gives the fabric a stiff and papery feel. The loss of mass that occurs during this process is restored by the application of metallic salts to add back body, lustre and physical weight.

White collar: Office work.

White ramie: See **China grass**.

Wick: The process of evaporating away moisture and perspiration.

Wild silks: These are characterized by a rough, slubby appearance that differs in colour from farmed silk. The **cocoons** are 'damaged' by the emerging moth eating its way out.

Winnowing: A method of separating the grain from the chuff sometimes used in processing **flax**.

Wool blends: A mixture of different wools and/or other fibres.

Wool classes: Classifications that grade the quality of wool fibres. Diameter of fibre, finesse, crimp, fibre length, cleanliness, colour, breed of sheep and end purpose of the wool are taken into consideration

Woollen or **Wool count:** Refers to yarns spun on the woollen system – the number of 256-yard (512m) strands to 1 pound (454g).

Woollen spun yarn: Yarn that has been **carded** and **drawn** but not **combed**.

Woolmark: A registered mark used for branding different types of Australian wool, used as a means of guaranteeing a standard of quality.

Wool sheep: The type of sheep used for wool production

Worsted count: Yarns are bought and sold by weight rather than length. The relationship between the weight of yarn and its length is expressed in terms of numbers or count, which also indicates the diameter or thickness of the yarn. The count refers to the number of hanks each measuring 560 yards (512m) that weigh 1 pound (454g). To convert worsted count to a metric count, multiply the length by 1.129. For example, a 1/15 worsted count becomes a 1/17 metric (or Nm) count.

Worsted spun yarn: Yarn that has been **carded**, **drawn** and **combed**.

X

Y

Yak: *Bos grunniens*, a generally domesticated beast of burden living on the Tibetan plateaus that is also used for fibre.

Yamami silk moth: Believed to be an indigenous species to Japan.

Yarn: A continuous length of interlocked fibres with or without **twist**.

Yarn count: Numerical expression for size of yarn, denoting a certain length of yarn for a fixed weight. The higher the count, the finer the yarn.

Yarn dyeing: Yarn is **dyed** before being woven or knitted into a fabric.

Yolk: The grease on the fleece of an **angora** goat.

Z

Index

Photo credits

p.9 Advertising Archives; p.11 courtesy Helen Storey, photograph by Alex Maguire ©; p.12 © istockphoto/ImesCreative; p.13 all by myka baum; p.14 (top) © istockphoto/tankbmb, (centre) ©istockphoto/danishkhan, (bottom left and right) courtesy Doris and Walter Van Buskirk, Lightfoot Farms LLC, Kennebunk, Maine; p.15 courtesy Ioannis Dimitrousis (design and styling), photograph by Dimitris Theocharis; p.16 all by myka baum; p.17 (top left) courtesy Blow PR, design by Ashish, photograph by Ian Gillett, (top right) courtesy Derek Lam, photograph by Dan Lecca, (centre left) courtesy Linton Tweeds Ltd ©, (centre right) myka baum, (bottom) Robert Decelis courtesy GARYHARVEYCREATIVE; p.18 all by myka baum; p.19 (top) courtesy Ioannis Dimitrousis, photograph by catwalking.com, (centre) courtesy of Gloverall, (bottom) L.A. Litchfield, courtesy of Gloverall; p.20 (left) myka baum, (right) Chris Moore, courtesy Alexander McQueen, S/S 2007; p.21 Philip James, courtesy Tamerlane's Daughters; p.22 all by myka baum; p.23 (top left) Uli Holz courtesy SANS, (bottom left) myka baum, (top right) Paul Harness, design by Hildigunnur Sigurdardottir, (centre right) courtesy Blow PR, design by Ashish, photograph by Ian Gillett, (bottom right) Chris Moore, courtesy James Long; p.24 Chris Moore, courtesy Alexander McQueen, spring 2005; p.25 (top) © istockphoto/AlexKhrom, (centre and bottom) myka baum; p.26 (top and right) courtesy Ravensbourne College of Design and Communication, design by Su Pei Ho, (bottom) courtesy Anne Kyyrö Quinn ©, design: Block; p.27 (top) Olek and Miranda Lloyd, (bottom) Demetrious Noble, courtesy Ladene Clark Designs; p.28 (left) Mike Figgis, courtesy Marina Shlosberg, (top right) Jessica Cassar, courtesy Rachael Cassar, (bottom) myka baum; p.29 (right) © Georgina McNamara, (left top and bottom) courtesy Anne Wilson, Rhona Hoffman Gallery, Chicago and Paul Kotula Projects, Detroit, design by Anne Wilson ©

2008 Topologies; p.30 Chris Moore, courtesy James Long; p.31 Ugo Camera, courtesy Armand Basi One; p.32 (top) © istockphoto/DesignGeek-1, (centre) myka baum, (bottom left) © shutterstock/paul prescott, (bottom right) © istockphoto/mandygodbehear, p.33 (top) ©shutterstock/Imagemaker, (bottom) courtesy Isabella Whitworth; p.34 courtesy Isabella Whitworth; p.35 courtesy Lakme India Fashion Week, design by Anand Kabra; p.36 (top left and bottom left) courtesy Undercover – Jun Takahashi ©, (bottom) catwalking.com, courtesy Ioannis Dimitrousis; p.37 (top) courtesy Screencraft Speciality Printing, (centre and bottom) Aleta Reese, courtesy Print House Inc.; p.38 myka baum; p.39 (top) Ian Gillett, courtesy Blow PR, design by Bora Aksu, (left and bottom) courtesy Hayley Cheal; p.40 (left) Ian Gillett, courtesy Blow PR, design by Ashish, (right) Mo Saito, courtesy Tamerlane's Daughers; p.41 (top) courtesy Josep Font, Couture A/W 08/09, (left) Jessica Cassar, courtesy Rachael Cassar, (bottom) Max Botticelli, courtesy Carta e Costura; p.42 (top) courtesy Vivienne Westwood, S/S 09 'Do It Yourself', (bottom) Yannis Vlamos, courtesy Blow PR, design by Manish Arora (right) courtesy Maria Francesca Pepe Jewellery-Wear Design, www.mfpepe.com; p.44 courtesy Guerra de la Paz ©, collection of Richard Harris; p.45 Fernada Calfat, courtesy Blow PR, design by Basso & Brooke, S/S 2006; p.46 all by myka baum, p.49 courtesy Aiwa Yau; p.50 myka baum; p.52 courtesy Isabella Whitworth; p.53 myka baum; p.55 fashion shots clockwise from top left, courtesy Noir A/S ©, ©Marc Hom; courtesy Timothy Everest Bespoke Fitting; Georgina McNamara, courtesy Blow PR, design by Rui Leonardes; all others by myka baum; p.56 fashion shots clockwise from top left, Johan Hellsröm, courtesy Gudrun Sjödén; courtesy Noir A/S ©, © Marc Hom; Etienne Tordoir, courtesy Kris Van Assche; Gaetan Bernard, courtesy Kris Van Assche; catwalking.com, courtesy John Rocha S/S 2007; (bottom right) Paul Crossman, handwoven silk scarf by Sallie Temple; all others by

myka baum; p.57 fashion shots clockwise from top left, Ian Gillett, courtesy Blow PR, design by Bora Aksu; © Fagner Bibiano; © Georgina McNamara; all others by myka baum; p.58 fashion shots clockwise from top left, Ian Gillett, courtesy Blow PR, design by Ashish; Yannis Vlamos, courtesy Blow PR, design by Manish Arora; courtesy Pavel Ivancic; Sabahar Addis Ababa, courtesy Sabahar Ethiopia; all others by myka baum; p.59 fashion shots clockwise from top left, Fergus Padel, courtesy Kostas Murkudis, styling by Jodie Barnes; Jean-Louis Coulombel, courtesy Maurizio Galante; © Marc Hom, courtesy Noir A/S; all others by myka baum; p.62 Cheryl Benda, courtesy Wild Turkey Felt Woolworks; p.63 courtesy Angelika Werth; p.64 Advertising Archives; p.65 myka baum; p.66 (left top and bottom) myka baum, (right) catwalking.com, design by Natalie Jacobs; p.67 courtesy Australian Wool Innovation Limited; p.68 (top) courtesy Doris and Walter Van Buskirk, Lightfoot Farms LLC, Kennebunk, Maine, (bottom) myka baum; p.69 courtesy Linton Tweeds Ltd; p.70 (top) Ian Gillett, courtesy Blow PR, design by Ashish, (centre) Fergus Padel, courtesy Kostas Murkudis, styling by Jodie Barnes, (right) courtesy adidas Y3, © 2008 adidas AG, adidas, The Globe, The 3-Stripes Mark and Y-3 are registered trademarks of the adidas group. Yohji Yamamoto is a registered trademark of Yohji Yamamoto, Inc.; p.71 (top) Ian Gillett, courtesy Blow PR, design by Edward Sexton, (centre) V&A Images, Victoria and Albert Museum, (bottom) Gaetan Bernard, courtesy Kris Van Assche; p.72 (top) Kevin Davies, courtesy Timothy Everest, styling by James Sleaford, (bottom left and right) myka baum; p.73 (top left) David Richardson, courtesy Gabrielle Miller, (top right) courtesy Abyssinia Sollitt-Davis, (bottom right) courtesy Linton Tweeds Ltd, (bottom left) myka baum; p.74 courtesy Blow PR, design by Rui Leonardes; p.75 (left) Chris Moore, courtesy Alexander McQueen, A/W 2008, (right) courtesy Josep Font, Couture A/W 08/09; p.76 courtesy John Smedley; p.77 Ivo Corda, courtesy IVANAhelsinki; p.78 Matt Easton, courtesy Ria Thomas; p.79

Stelianour, courtesy Huwaida Ahmed; p.80 Mitsuaki Murata, courtesy Colenimo, (bottom) myka baum; p.81 Chris Moore, courtesy London College of Fashion, design by rani jones; p.83 (bottom right) courtesy International Wool Textile Organisation, all others courtesy Australian Wool Innovation Limited, The Woolmark logos are reproduced with the permission of Australian Wool Innovation Limited, owner of The Woolmark Company; p.84 myka baum; p.85 (left and right) myka baum, (centre) © shutterstock/Christian McCarty; p.86 myka baum; p.88 (left) courtesy Marsha Hobert at Suri Network, (top right) Mark Dodge, (bottom right) © istockphoto/NNehring; p.89 Chris Moore, courtesy Julia Neill (designer and creator); p.90 © istockphoto/aventurus; p.92 myka baum; p.93 (top) David Goldman, courtesy Timothy Everest, (bottom) myka baum; p.94 © shutterstock/yansherman; p.95 (top) Chris Blott, courtesy Johnstons of Elgin, (left) Ugo Camera, courtesy Armand Basi One, (bottom) © Georgina McNamara; p.96 © shutterstock/Kitch Bain; p.97 myka baum; p.98 catwalking.com; p.99 courtesy Timothy Everest Bespoke Fitting; p.100 © istockphoto/Tomo75; p.101 courtesy Large Animal Research Station, University of Alaska Fairbanks; p.102 (left) myka baum, (right) © shutterstock/Teresa Levite; p.103 (top) catwalking.com, (left) Ivo Corda, courtesy IVANAhelsinki, (bottom) myka baum; p.104 courtesy Karren K. Brito; p.105 Yannis Vlamos, courtesy Blow PR, design by Manish Arora; p.106 (left) courtesy Paul Smith, design Paul Smith for Gainsborough Silks, (right) Vivienne Westwood, S/S 'Do It Yourself'; p.108 courtesy Pavel Ivancic; p.109 catwalking.com; p.110 courtesy Lakme India Fashion Week, design by Anand Kabra; p.111 (left) courtesy Etro, (right) Hans Fonk, courtesy Jim Thompson; p.112 Michael Schoedel M.A., courtesy german-hosiery-museum.de; p.113 (left) courtesy Vivian Westwood, S/S 09 'Do It Yourself', (right) courtesy Narciso Rodriguez; p.114 (left) Peter Stigter, courtesy ANTOINE PETERS S/S 2009, (right) courtesy Etro; p.115 (top) Prabuddha Das Gupta, courtesy Rohit Khosla

Foundation, New Delhi; (left and bottom) myka baum; p.116 (top left) catwalking.com, (top right) myka baum, (bottom left) © istockphoto/roset (bottom right) © istockphoto/VickieSichau; p.117 (left) courtesy Isabella Whitworth, (right) courtesy The Gainsborough Silk Weaving Co. Ltd; p.120 (top) Peter Stigter, courtesy ANTOINE PETERS A/W 2008-2009, (left) © istockphoto/Fyletto; p.121 © Marc Hom, courtesy Noir A/S; p.122 (top and bottom left) Ugo Camera, courtesy Armand Basi One, (bottom centre) Fergus Padel, courtesy Kostas Murkudis, (bottom right) courtesy Roksanda Ilincic A/W 2008; p.123 (left) V&A Images, Victoria and Albert Museum, (right) Uli Holz, courtesy SANS; p.124 (top) Chris Moore, courtesy Alexander McQueen, S/S 2007, (left) Jean-Louis Coulombel, courtesy Maurizio Galante, (centre) Jessica Cassar, courtesy Rachael Cassar, (bottom right) courtesy Sallie Temple, photograph by Paul Crossman; p.125 (right) Ugo Camera, courtesy Armand Basi One (left) courtesy catwalking.com, design by Ada Zanditon, (centre) Jochem Sanders, courtesy ANTOINE PETERS; p.128 D. Sawyer, courtesy Donghia Inc.; p.129 Johan Hellsröm, courtesy Gudrun Sjödén; p.130 myka baum; p.131 (top) catwalking.com, design by Nabil El Nayal, (bottom) courtesy Blow PR, design by Rui Leonardes; p.133 (left and middle) catwalking.com, courtesy John Rocha S/S 2007, (right) courtesy Irish Linen Guild; p.134 courtesy CELC European Confederation of Flax and Hemp; p.135 Mike Figgis, courtesy Marina Shlosberg SS09; p.136 courtesy CELC European Confederation of Flax and Hemp; p.137 Christian Lartillot, courtesy Icona Vera; p.139 courtesy CELC European Confederation of Flax and Hemp; p.140 (top left) courtesy CELC European Confederation of Flax and Hemp, (top right) © istockphoto/dononeg, (bottom) courtesy Linda F Learn, Class Act Fabrics; p.141 (left and bottom right) myka baum, (top right) courtesy Yohji Yamamoto Homme S/S 2009 collection; © Monica Feudi; p.142 © shutterstock/ Georgy Markov; p.143 (left) © istockphoto/AM29, (right)

petrovsky & ramone, courtesy Kuyichi; p.144 (left) © istockphoto/ KarenMassier, (right) courtesy John Smedley; p.145 Time & Life Pictures/Getty Images; p.147 © istockphoto/tonda; p.148 courtesy ars.usda.gov, United States Department of Agriculture, National Agricultural Library; p.149 (left) shutterstock, (right) Dr. James M. Vreeland, Jr. of Peru Naturtex Partners; p.150 Matt Easton, courtesy Ria Thomas; p.151 (left) courtesy John Smedley, (right) myka baum; p.152 Fergus Padel, courtesy Kostas Murkudis; p.153 courtesy San Francsisco Fashion Week, design by oda; p.154 (left) © Marc Hom, courtesy Noir A/S, (right) Matthieu Granier, courtesy Celine Faizant; p.155 (left) Dr. James M. Vreeland, Jr. of Peru Naturtex Partners, (right) courtesy Stella James; p.156 courtesy Ecoyarns PTY Ltd; p.157 Prabuddha Das Gupta, courtesy Rohit Khosla Foundation, New Delhi; p.158 courtesy San Francsisco Fashion Week, design by oda; p.159 © Marc Hom, courtesy Noir A/S; p.160 (top) petrovsky & ramone, courtesy Kuyichi, (bottom) courtesy COMO NO www.como- no.fr, C&M Les Petits Bonheurs SARL, Candice Augereau, Boschat Emmanuelle, Arnaud Lafontaine; p.161 Peter Stigter, courtesy ANTOINE PETERS; p.162 (left) David Richardson, courtesy Gabrielle Miller, (right) courtesy Maria Francesca Pepe Jewellery-Wear Design; p.163 (top) catwalking. com, design by Nabil El Nayal, (left) Gaetan Bernard, courtesy Kris Van Assche, (bottom) Etienne Tordoir, courtesy Kris Van Assche; p.164 catwalking.com, design by Elaine Kinney; p.165 (top) Robert Decelis, courtesy GARYHARVEYCREATIVE, (bottom) Alexei Hay, courtesy Adam Kimmel; p.166 © shutterstock/kd2; p.167 Milomir Kovacevic, courtesy g=9.8; p.168 courtesy Linda Loudermilk, p.169 myka baum; p.170 Prabuddha Das Gupta, courtesy Rohit Khosla Foundation, New Delhi; p.172 Matthieu Granier, courtesy Celine Faizant; p.173 Matthieu Granier, courtesy Celine Faizant; p.174 myka baum; p.175 © istockphoto/clu; p.176 myka baum; p.177 Paul Morgan, design by Ada Zanditon; p.178 courtesy Creollus LCC, design by artisan

Analia Lino for Creollus LLC; p.179 (top) catwalking.com, design by Rachel Caulfield, (bottom) myka baum; p.180 myka baum; p.181 courtesy San Franscisco Fashion Week, design by oda; p.182 istockphoto/ AVTG; p.183 (left) Paul Morgan, design by Ada Zanditon, (top right) courtesy catwalking.com, design Ada Zanditon, (bottom right) Matthieu Granier, courtesy Celine Faizant; p.186 (top) courtesy Première Vision, (bottom) © JUPITERIMAGES/ GOODSHOOT/Alamy

Acknowledgements

We would like to thank the following people:

For their technical expertise and images:
Nigel and Christine Maitland of Maitland Designs,
Marie Demaegdt at Masters of Linen,
Dr. James M. Vreeland, Jr. at Peru Naturtex,
Linda F. Learn at Class Act Fabrics.

For their generosity with images and their contribution with information:
Cheryl Benda at Wild Turkey Felt Makers,
Nell Trotter at Blow PR,
Marsha Hobert at Suri Network,
Johnstons of Elgin,
Australian Wool Innovation Limited,
Ursula Hudson at London College of Fashion.

For their original images and artwork assistance:
Nicholas Vivian, Artist,
Georgina McNamara, Artist– photographer,
Fagner Bibiano, Artist– photographer.

For consultation and support:
Dilys Williams, Director of the Centre for Sustainable Fashion,
London College of Fashion

Myka Baum
Very special thanks are reserved for Myka Baum, whose original remit was to source the broad variety of images needed for this publication. Myka's tenacity, professionalism and organization deserve much credit, but it is her acute interpretative sense and proactive creative input that has exceeded our original expectations of her role. She has worked tirelessly to generate original imagery and produced many specially commissioned photographs, for which we are profoundly grateful.

Lastly, we would like to thank our publisher Laurence King and his team, especially Helen Evans, Susie May and Roger Fawcett-Tang.

This book is dedicated to Ron Johnston 1930–2008